5/22/87

21.20

# THE
# AMERICAN
# CONSERVATIVE
# MOVEMENT

## The Philosophical Founders

# JOHN P. EAST

 **REGNERY BOOKS**

Chicago                    Washington, DC

Regnery Books is a division of Regnery Gateway, Inc.
All inquiries concerning this book should be directed to Regnery Books,
950 North Shore Drive, Lake Bluff, IL 60044.

**Library of Congress Cataloging-in-Publication Data**

East, John P.
  The American Conservative movement.

  Bibliography: p.
  1. Conservatism—United States—History—20th century.  I. Title.
JA84.U5E18   1986      320.5'2'0973                    86-42793
ISBN: 0-89526-58206

TO
Dr. William Cullen Dennis,
President, Earlham College
1929-1946

Unpractised he to fawn, or seek for power,
By doctrines fashioned to the varying hour;
Far other aims his heart had learned to prize....

*—Oliver Goldsmith, "The Deserted Village"*

# Table of Contents

# Acknowledgments

To list acknowledgments in any major venture one undertakes would be a task of extreme difficulty, for the listing by the nature of things would be long and the potential for overlooking subtle yet significant influences would be unavoidable. Aware of my predicament, I hereby offer apologies for omissions and opt for conciseness.

I am deeply indebted to Dr. George W. Carey, Professor of Government and Politics at Georgetown University and editor of *The Political Science Reviewer,* for initially putting the idea in my head for such a book with his request that I write an article for his journal on the political thought of Willmoore Kendall. After completing that task, I continued with pieces on Russell Kirk, Richard M. Weaver, Frank S. Meyer, Leo Strauss, Eric Voegelin, and Ludwig von Mises, which were published in *Modern Age* with the incalculable enthusiasm and encouragement of its late editor Dr. David S. Collier.

Upon Collier's death in 1983, Dr. George A. Panichas, Professor of English at the University of Maryland, who became the new editor of *Modern Age,* continued with the same degree of enthusiasm and support as Collier had shown that I press on to completion of the book. Indeed, Dr. Panichas gave gratis and unstintingly of his formidable talents in the final stages of proofing and editing. In brief, Carey, Collier, and Panichas were the principal persons encouraging me to completion of this exciting intellectual venture. I acknowledge my enormous indebtedness to them.

In addition, I am exceedingly grateful to Dr. Samuel T. Francis for his great assistance in the final stages of proofing and editing and for his invaluable counsel on final editorial matters, and I offer my thanks to Mr. Steven R. Valentine for allowing me to submit the final manuscript to his keen eye for final examination. Finally, to Patricia Helms I extend my deep gratitude for her inexhaustible patience and skill in typing the manuscript.

These then were the key and indispensable players on the team. As is always the case, I must bear full responsibility for the completed work, and I exonerate the other players from any misdeeds of an intellectual or technical nature.

Senator John P. East died on June 29, 1986.

# Introduction

If there is a single philosophical premise that distinguishes recent American conservatism, it is the conviction that "ideas have consequences." We live in a decade in which, for the first time in generations, the ideas of self-identified conservatives seem ascendant —an era in which the arguments of "academic scribblers" of the Right are being translated, however imperfectly, into public policy.

Such a moment, like all transitional moments, is marked by both exhilaration and anxiety: exhilaration at the attainment of influence so long yearned for; anxiety lest the very possession of influence breed complacency and corruption of the intellect. How does one navigate from the realm of scholarship and "high thinking" to the world of political maneuver and compromise? How does one, in Whittaker Chambers' phrase, successfully "dance along the precipice" between principle and pragmatism, contemplation and activism, unyielding philosophic truth and flexible managerial expediency?

At such times of uncertainty, when the way forward seems so obscure, it is always useful to rediscover the intellectual perspective that impelled us to action in the first place. In the book before us Senator John East has done just that. He has written a series of essays not on "issues of the Eighties," prospects for the next election, or some other ephemeral topic, but on a subject he clearly deems more fundamental: the formative political theory of the "Founding Fathers" of modern American conservatism.

It is a book, first of all, about scholars: in particular, seven learned and dedicated men who laid the theoretical foundations for today's American Right. These were not the only architects of the conservative renascence, to be sure—a fact Mr. East would no doubt be the first to acknowledge. Other uncommon men and women—professors, journalists, politicians, builders of the infrastructure of conservative institutions—have played indispensable roles as well. But it is the seven individuals he has selected, Mr. East contends, who did the most to infuse American conservatism with intellectual substance and coherence—who made it, in short, a formidable movement of ideas.

At one level this book may be read as a straightforward exposition of the thought of conservatism's "philosophical founders." As such it has real value—and not just for those who may be curious to learn more about the intellectual origins of the Reagan Revolution. In these busy days few of us have the time or inclination to immerse ourselves systematically in the writings of those whose hard-won insights we perhaps too casually adopt as our own. Senator East's lucid essays are therefore especially welcome. By concisely reintroducing us to our heritage, he offers a timely refresher course on the philosophy that undergirds our strivings.

Mr. East's book, however, has more than a narrowly pedagogical purpose. What emerges from his meticulous *explications de texte* is a subtle but persistent emphasis on the underlying theoretical unity of modern conservatism. He observes that despite all the manifest variations in content and in style, the conservatism of these "Founding Fathers" does in fact have discernible "common denominators." This "philosophical core" is the Great Tradition of classical and Judeo-Christian thought, against which are arrayed the fanatic legions of heretical, secular modernity. Conservatism for Senator East is ultimately and essentially spiritual in character. The personal virtues it celebrates—such as piety, humility, and self-sacrifice—require an "openness to transcendence" and acceptance of the God-given nature of things. It is part of Mr. East's intention, one suspects, to recall American conservatives to their inescapably religious roots. Quietly he reminds us that conservatism properly understood is not only a philosophy of government but of self-government, that conservatism at its best is a meditation not simply on what to think but on how to live.

Mr. East does not conceal the unresolved tensions in contemporary conservative thought—particularly the problematic place of the libertarian perspective in the larger conservative firmament. Consider this sentence that he quotes from Ludwig von Mises: "The keystone of Western civilization is the sphere of spontaneous action it secures to the individual." For conservatives of all persuasions this is a brilliant perception; freedom for the individual is indeed at the center of Western experience. No one contemplating the totalitarianism of a Soviet Union or a Vietnam, the fates of a Solzhenitsyn or a Sakharov, the forced collectivization of an Ethiopia or Cambodia today, or Maoist China yesterday, will disdain the ineffable preciousness of individual liberty.

Yet as we simultaneously contemplate the accelerating nihilistic decadence around us—a phenomenon of which Mr. East takes frequent note—questions relentlessly intrude. Is all "spontaneous action" necessarily good? Are all individual choices equally valid and equally to be left alone? What is the proper response of conservatives (and of a conservative government) to those who "choose" drugs, pornography, and other forms of self-degrading behavior? What, in brief, should we *do* with our freedom? How *ought* we to live? As most of Senator East's conservative theorists teach us, the conservative mission is not coterminous with removing obstacles to individual initiative in the marketplace.

Another theme emerges from these essays. All of the scholars Mr. East examines were men of integrity who throughout their long careers stood resolutely against the times. Despite their often lonely status, and the costs—both pecuniary and professional—that it imposed, they did not become misanthropic pessimists. Instead they remained men of courage and even (Mr. East shows) men of hope. Hope and affirmation, the belief that virtuous men and women can make a difference, that error and evil can yet be held at bay: this, not despairing passivity, marked the seven whose intellectual labors are here analyzed. It is an example, Mr. East obviously believes, that can inspire and hearten us now.

It is said that the owl of Minerva takes its flight at twilight, that we can fully comprehend our heritage only when it is receding into the irrecoverable past. Thanks to books like Senator East's, the twilight need not become darkness. He has given us a study of the "first principles" of American conservatism as propounded by some of its most distinguished theorists. He has not only thereby rendered homage to famous men. He has illuminated (in Robert Frost's words) "the truths we keep coming back and back to."

George H. Nash
June 3, 1986

# Prefatory Note

My purpose in this book is to show that the seven thinkers analyzed are the seminal theorists of the American conservative movement in the post-World War II era, which produced a conscious and principled conservatism in American thought. These seven figures are the yeast that leavened the whole.

A listing of this sort is certain to be confronted with the charge that an element of arbitrariness, however small, in the selections made is inescapable. This charge may be true, but I would also suggest that the seven writers discussed would have to be included in any list of thinkers of major significance and impact. Frequently, in fact, one finds that even a possible addition, however distinguished, is a student of one or more of these theorists. In this category probably the premier example would be Friedrich von Hayek, who was a student of Ludwig von Mises.

The writers discussed are remarkably diverse in their backgrounds. Four are native-born Americans: Russell Kirk, Richard M. Weaver, Frank S. Meyer, and Willmoore Kendall. Kirk was a native of the Midwest (Michigan); Meyer of the industrial Northeast (New Jersey); Weaver of the South (North Carolina); and Kendall of the Southwest (Oklahoma). Meyer was a former Communist. Three of the group are of European extraction: Leo Strauss and Eric Voegelin were born in Germany, and Ludwig von Mises was a native of Austria. Concerning the designation "conservative," the four Americans accepted it; the three Europeans did not. Strauss and Voegelin denied all labeling, while von Mises considered himself a "classical liberal." These facts are merely suggestive of the great diversity in individual backgrounds.

These writers offer not only considerable variety concerning their personal biographies, they also vary extensively in their respective approaches and emphases. Still, one finds theoretical common denominators. These underlying and unifying premises form the philosophical core of the American conservative movement and are examined in the concluding chapter.

My method of analysis is that of presenting an intellectual portrait of each individual. As is the case with a portrait painter of physical features, the subject may or may not be content with the final product. In any case, I have tried to understand each individual as I felt he understood himself. Of course, I bear full responsibility for the results.


Know ye not that a little leaven leaveneth the whole lump?
*1 Corinthians 5:6*


West Branch, Iowa
May 9th, 1986

# The American Conservative Movement

# Russell Kirk

Born October 19, 1918, in Plymouth, Michigan, the son of Russell and Marjorie Kirk, Russell Amos Kirk was destined to become the principal intellectual founder of the American conservative movement in the post-World War II era. Graduating from Michigan State College (now University) in 1940, he received his master's degree from Duke University in 1941. A doctoral degree was conferred upon him by St. Andrews University, Scotland, in 1952. He married Annette Courtemanche in 1964, and they became the parents of four daughters. The Kirk ancestral residence, known as Piety Hill, is situated in Mecosta, Michigan.

Kirk was the founding editor of *Modern Age,* which he edited from 1957 until 1959. In 1960 he founded and has since edited *The University Bookman.* From 1955 to 1980 he wrote the column "From the Academy" for *National Review.* Kirk has been an extraordinarily prolific writer of articles and books.[1] His classic work, *The Conservative Mind* (1953), described by publisher Henry Regnery as "one of the most influential books of the postwar period," has emerged as the definitive work among the intellectual contributions to the American conservative movement.[2]

Concerning Kirk's pre-eminent role in the conservative movement, Edwin J. Feulner, Jr., wrote, "Dr. Kirk has watched the conservative intellectual revival develop around him...and as much as any other living American,...is responsible for the growth of that movement."[3] Kirk himself has written, "Somehow I found myself a leader of an intellectual movement, without having intended to be anything of the sort."[4] Among other things,

Russell Kirk has been a novelist, a historian, and a magazine and newspaper columnist.

This analysis treats Kirk as a political theorist. It seeks to identify the underlying theoretical premises of his political thought. The chief books to consult in this regard are *The Conservative Mind* (1953), *A Program for Conservatives* (1962), *Enemies of the Permanent Things* (1969), *Eliot and His Age* (1971), and *The Roots of American Order* (1974). Also of value are *Beyond the Dreams of Avarice* (1956), *Confessions of a Bohemian Tory* (1963), *John Randolph of Roanoke* (1978), and *Reclaiming a Patrimony* (1982). The task of a full listing is hazardous because Kirk's political theory undergirds and permeates all of his works. Kirk has explicitly acknowledged that he is a conservative: "From the hour I began to reason, and possibly from the hour I began to feel, I have been a conservative."[5] Then he added, "I am a conservative. Quite possibly I am on the losing side; often I think so. Yet out of a curious perversity I had rather lose with Socrates, let us say, than win with Lenin."[6]

## II

In Kirk's view the main roots of modern political theory are found in the spirit of the Renaissance and in the mind of the Enlightenment. He connects the former with "the theological and moral confusion from which our society has suffered since the sixteenth century."[7] More specifically, Kirk explained, "In some ages—the period we call the Renaissance conspicuous among these—the overweening ego claims too much."[8] The problem was essentially one of pride, the most ancient and cardinal of vices and evils: "Man was only a little lower than the angels...having it within his power to become godlike. How marvellous and splendid a creature is man!"[9]

The Renaissance was the great beginning surge of the spirit and the temper of the modern age. The earlier age of faith was viewed as primitive, confining, and inhibiting. Man was now free to expand fully his great creative potential in art, literature, and learning. Ushered in was a new era in which the "revival" and "rebirth" of man's creative genius would know no bounds, knowledge would build up, as the possibility for earthly New Jerusalems appeared on the intellectual horizon. Kirk observed: "In politics, the father of this modern denial of a higher will. . .is Machiavelli."[10] The subtle and ingenious mind of the Florentine divorced politics from traditional ethics and moral considerations, proclaimed that "all armed prophets have conquered and unarmed ones failed." Politics is exclusively a natural phenomenon; power is an end in and of itself; and the age of nationalism and ideology commences.

The hubris of the Renaissance was raised to higher levels of intensity with the coming of the Enlightenment and the ensuing modern age of the ideologue and ideology. By the Enlightenment, Kirk wrote, "is meant the strong intellectual tendency toward doctrines of progress, rationality, secularism, and political reform. The Enlightenment's center was France."[11] Noting "the strutting Rationalism of the Enlightenment," Kirk observed that its prime characteristic was its unyielding confidence that "man's private intellectual faculties. . .could. . .dissolve all mysteries and solve all problems."[12]

"The Goddess Reason whom the French revolutionaries would enthrone," Kirk claimed would lead to "the doctrine of the perfectibility of man and society [which] is derived from the Enlightenment of the eighteenth century."[13] He concluded: "The French Revolutionaries, hoping to transform utterly human society and even human nature, broke with the past, defied history, embraced theoretic dogmas, and so fell under the cruel domination of Giant Ideology."[14] The rise of modern ideology "was a kind of climax of the rationalism of the Enlightenment."[15]

What is ideology? Ideology and political theory are opposites. Political theory is rooted in understanding based upon experience and learning and is open to new knowledge; ideology is "the belief that this world of ours may be converted into the Terrestrial Paradise through the operation of positive law and positive planning."[16] In a word, it is utopian: "Ideology is meant to reconstruct and perfect society and human nature."[17] The mind of the ideologue is closed. As Karl Marx, the quintessential ideologue, proclaimed, the goal is to change the world, not to interpret it. The ideologue does not seek to attune himself to the givens of being as understood through experience and learning; rather, he seeks to impose upon mankind his view of what the perfected good life should be. Action, not reflection and thought, is required.

Ideology is scientistic in its method and egalitarian in its results. "Scientism," wrote Kirk, is the belief "that human nature and human society may be improved infinitely—nay, perfected—by the application of the techniques of the physical and biological sciences to the governance of men."[18] In short, "Science with a Roman S should supplant God."[19] Scientism, said Kirk, is "the employment of methods allegedly scientific to make society into one uniform, equalitarian tableland."[20] The ideologue is disdainful of diversity, variety, complexity, intricacy, subtlety, and nuance in human society; he seeks to treat men as things and to arrange and order them according to abstract patterns spun from the minds of radical innovators and visionaries.

Although the exponents of modern ideology are legion, Kirk laid heavy responsibility on Jeremy Bentham and Karl Marx. Bentham was "Burke's most powerful intellectual antagonist."[21] Commonly known as Utilitarianism, or Philosophical Radicalism, Benthamism broke sharply with the "great tradition" of the classical and biblical views. Benthamism was rooted in pride and in limitless confidence in human reason. Its arid rationalism was exclusively naturalistic and materialistic in perspective; it had no conception of the transcendent and spiritual. The Benthamite thirsted for progress, Kirk stressed, and ultimately succumbed to the allure of an egalitarian earthly utopia: "An omnipotent world state imposes an eternal compulsory uniformity upon the whole human race...Now I think that this is, indeed, the natural culmination of the Benthamite view of man and society."[22]

Regarding the relationship between Bentham and Marx, Kirk observed that "Marx's master was Bentham" and that "Utilitarianism was the ancestor of "scientific socialism."[23] Succinctly put, "Marxism was the bastard child of Benthamism."[24] Marx was the most prideful of the modern ideologues, for he unraveled the mystery of being; thanks to Marxist insights and understanding man can redeem himself within history. The foundation of Marxism is atheistic and materialistic; indeed, by its own proclamation it relies exclusively upon an economic interpretation of history. The sole variable is the economic class-conflict between the proletariat and the capitalists. After the proletariat has emerged by force and terror as dominant over the capitalists, there will ensue "the dictatorship of the proletariat," which will eliminate all vestiges of the capitalists. Then "the withering away of the state" will follow; and the final redemptive stage of an egalitarian utopia, with each person producing "according to his ability" and consuming "according to his need," will come.

The Marxist vision is simplistic and spun from whole cloth; it manifests the pride of the ideologue raised to the highest power. "Marx proposed to efface the whole extant social order and substitute a collectivistic life shaped upon a thorough materialism," Kirk stressed. For Marx the end of human endeavor was absolute equality of condition.[25] "That idea," Kirk concluded, "has been one of the chief causes of our modern upheaval and despair, throughout most of the world."[26] And he warned, "For outside the warm circle of the campfire, grim hostile powers always lie in wait."[27]

III

In Kirk's view, if ideology is one major component of modern thought, the other commanding element is cultural "decadence," which also is attributable to the pridefulness and self-centeredness of the modern age. In the preoccupation, indeed, the obsession, with the self, there are profound cultural consequences that Kirk delineates at great length in his writings.

What is culture? "Culture is that which makes life worth living," Kirk asserted; it is characterized by "such facets as urbanity, learning, philosophy, and the arts."[28] Ultimately culture is "the elevation of character which distinguishes the civilized man from the brute."[29] The quality of a culture is of vital importance since it determines "the tone of public life."[30] "Culture cannot really be planned by political authority," Kirk contended, "for much of culture is unconscious; and politics grows out of culture, not culture out of politics; and political planning itself is a product of culture."[31]

If, as Kirk stated, "the elevation of character" is the key to a high culture, the decay of culture, or "decadence," occurs when there "is the *loss of an object,* an end, an aim. Men and women become decadent when they forget or deny the objects of life, and so fritter away their years in trifles or debauchery."[32] Self-centered man is not interested in "the elevation of character"; he is concerned with pleasure-seeking, whether in the form of trifling amusements or of ingenious schemes for ever lower levels of debauchery. Modern man has become decadent and his culture reflects it.

In describing the trifling side of modern decadence, Kirk employed such words as "barrenness," "sterility," "thinness," "inanity," "shoddiness," "cheapness," "commonness," and "sensationalism," and he characterized the debauched dimension with such nouns as "ugliness," "hideousness," "vulgarity," and "deformity" and with such adjectives as "abnormal," "morbid," and "perverse." Two key symptoms of a decadent society are "boredom" and the mindless pursuit of "change" for its own sake. Decadence, boredom, and the lust for change are interrelated. Since decadence by definition means "the loss of an object" in life, Kirk reasoned that the inevitable result is "acedia, that sloth of spirit, that boredom with the universe."[33] Unfortunately, he observed, "Mankind can endure anything but boredom."[34] Concerning the cultural implications of this extreme boredom, he specified that "an age of social boredom is characterized by popular pursuit of material and sensual gratification to the exclusion of other ends"; that "sexual perversion and addiction to narcotics flourish in a bored age"; and that "out of boredom grow vice, crime, and the destructive compulsion of the mass-mind."[35]

Emerging out of decadence and boredom are "an infatuation with haste," an obsession with "vertiginous speed...unchecked motion."[36] In this "reign of King Whirl" arises an irresistible compulsion to flee the world of thought and reflection; indeed, there is "the negation of intelligence."[37] With the loss of a goal in life and with an ever-rising level of boredom, persons "hurry from one amusement to another, unable really to work or to contemplate."[38] Yet, Kirk lamented, "the Flight itself is a sham god" because with the unrelenting urge to escape boredom "the motion of our age has been centrifugal, not centripetal; the tendency has been eccentric, not centric," and the tragic result is that "the cement of society disintegrates."[39] The vital center will not hold in a decadent society. "Without judicious change we perish," Kirk concluded, "but change itself cannot be the end of existence."[40] A decadent society seeks change as an end in itself in order to flee the unbearable burden of social boredom.

Two philosophers frequently discussed in Kirk's writings illustrate those who contribute (perhaps unwittingly) to a decadent society: Jean-Jacques Rousseau and John Stuart Mill. Ostensibly these two figures are dissimilar, but ultimately they share the same trait of modern thought: pride. In Rousseau one discovers the pride of the man of passion; in Mill, the pride of the man of reason.

Regarding the significance of Rousseau, Kirk wrote, "Knowledge of the mind of Rousseau is as important as an apprehension of Burke's, for any man who would understand our present discontents."[41] But, Kirk added, "Rousseau and Burke stand at the antipodes."[42] What is the central and controlling premise of Rousseau's thinking? "Rousseau and his pupils exalt egoism as the essence of their new morality."[43] Pride is the founding concept in Rousseau's thought. Rousseau and his disciples have supreme confidence in the "Noble Savage," in natural man freed of all restraints. It was Rousseau who wrote in *The Social Contract,* "Man is born free; and everywhere he is in chains." Kirk further observed:

> Rousseau and his disciples were resolved to force men to be free; in most of the world, they triumphed; men are set free from family, church, town, class, guild; yet they wear, instead, the chains of the state, and they expire of ennui or stifling loneliness.[44]

Rousseau, according to Kirk, leads either to "the chains of the state" of modern ideology or to the "ennui" or boredom of a decadent society. "The disciples of Rousseau fall into the foolish notion that somehow primitive man was happier and better, because more natural," than civilized man. That way lies madness.[45] To escape the boredom of a decadent society, Rousseau's natural man resorts first to the "idyllic imagination." This is the trifling world of fantasy where glitter and pleasure are offered as palliatives. When these cease to satisfy, there arises "the diabolic imagination" that reflects the perverse and the sordid: "This 'diabolic imagination' dominates most popular fiction—and on television and in the theaters, too, the diabolic imagination struts and postures."[46] Kirk concluded, "Today the Savage God lays down his new commandments. The gods of . . . fire and slaughter return."[47] The pride of Rousseau's man of passion is a key contributor to a decadent society.

Not necessarily by design, John Stuart Mill, the apostle of reason and the "Age of Discussion," also contributed extensively to the decadence of the modern age. Mill was in the intellectual tradition of Bentham. His father, James, was an admirer of Bentham and the utilitarian doctrine. John Stuart Mill was a third-generation Benthamite and the author of *On Liberty.* Regarding the significance of Mill in modern thought, Kirk said, "Mill, rather than St. Augustine, is the authority of post-Christian man."[48]

The final weakness of Mill, from Kirk's perspective, is that basic flaw found in so much of modern thought: pride. In Mill's "Age of Discussion," Kirk explained, "an enlightened democracy would extend its benevolent empire of reason over all the world."[49] He added, "The Mills think that their convictions are the product of their private rationality."[50] Mill had little regard for history, tradition, continuity, and, in general, the wisdom and experience of the ages. While asserting full confidence in each generation to rely solely on its own intellectual talent, Mill also proposed that, unassisted, each person decides which intellectual direction to chart. Indeed, in *On Liberty* Mill went to the extent of urging "eccentricity" as an appropriate philosophical posture: "In this age, the mere example of nonconformity, the mere refusal to bend the knee to custom, is itself a service. . . . That so few now dare to be eccentric, marks the chief danger of the time."

Inescapably this call to the individual to pursue a course of nonconformity and eccentricity is rooted in pride. No respect is discernible for past learning, wisdom, or knowledge. A premium is placed on mere individual "opinion," not on genuine, substantive truth about the nature of things, implicit in such classical and biblical words as "wisdom" and "knowledge." A philosophy based primarily, if not exclusively, upon individual opinion soon gives way to simple license, a major symptom of decadent culture. There ensues a loss of object in life; there is no pursuit of "the elevation of character"; social boredom intrudes and the fascination with change and petty amusements for the sole purpose of escaping boredom emerges. Debauchery, the last refuge of a bored and decadent people, lies ominously ahead.

## IV

If the controlling themes of modern thought are ideology and decadence, both outgrowths of the pride of the Renaissance, the roots of the great tradition, which Kirk offered as the alternative, are found in awe, humility, and reverence for classical and biblical views. These latter qualities led to the quest for "the well-ordered commonwealth" of Plato, to be pursued through "the moral imagination" of Edmund Burke.

Regarding awe, Kirk mused, "The conservative finds himself . . . a pilgrim in a realm of mystery and wonder."[51] Specifically, we need a sense "of awe for the great intelligence, transcending human frailties, which governs this earth and all the stars."[52] And he concluded, "All things begin and end in mystery. Out of tales of wonder come awe and the beginning of philosophy."[53] Philosophy commences with a sense of awe because a philosopher is a "lover of wisdom" (as opposed to Mill's "opinion") and "aspires to teach wisdom."[54] Awe helps the philosopher in the pursuit and acquisition of wisdom, for it sensitizes him to an appreciation that man is not the originator of being nor of his own existence. Man is creature, not Creator; hence the need to discover the true nature of being so as to determine man's relationship to the whole of being and to attune himself accordingly. "We are part of an eternal order which holds all things in their places," Kirk wrote, and "the reflective conservative, far from denying the existence of this eternal order, endeavors to ascertain its nature, and to find his place in it."[55]

Among the great classical philosophers Plato understood the crucial need "to teach men how to bring their souls into harmony with divine order."[56] *"The Republic,"* Kirk explained, "is an inquiry into the real nature of spirit and social harmony. It is an... allegory of personal order, not a model constitution."[57] The Platonic notion of justice embodies the idea of attunement. Concerning *The Republic* and its definitive explanation of justice, Kirk observed, "Plato's *Republic*...is a noble beginning. In some respects we never got beyond it.... And what is a just state? It is that society in which every man does his own work, fulfilling the capacities toward which his nature inclines him."[58] The task of the individual is to know himself and to pursue goals to which his talents and interest impel him. Man must accept the givens of his being; he is not self-produced. In turn, the just state results when individuals are allowed and encouraged to follow their natural being.

For Plato the just state is the antithesis of the state offered by modern ideology. In the latter, justice is perverted into egalitarianism, whereby self-produced man is molded indiscriminately into a mass to be manipulated and controlled by centrally posi-

26

tioned, self-appointed elites. The Platonic just state is rooted in awe, humility, and reverence; the state of the modern ideologue is based on omniscience, pride, and disdain for the work of the Creator. The Platonic just state understands attunement and the ultimate reward of harmony; the state of the ideologue includes pursuing the ever-elusive goal of remaking created being and thus the resulting perpetual condition of conflict and disharmony. In Kirk's view the distinctions were fundamental and enduring.

The goal of political theory is "the well-ordered commonwealth," and the conspicuous characteristic of this commonwealth is harmony, which is a product of justice, attunement, wisdom, and philosophy, commencing with awe, that is, piety, the antipode of pride. *The Republic,* Kirk believed, is "meant to teach men how to bring their souls into harmony with divine order."[59] And what is the final goal? "Plato's whole endeavor was the recovery of order: order in the soul, order in the *polis.*"[60] In fact, Kirk urged, "The recovery of order in the soul and order in society is the first necessity of this century."[61] As to the significance of order, he explained, " 'Order' means a systematic and harmonious arrangement whether in one's own character or in the commonwealth."[62] Again, we are back to the goal of "the well-ordered commonwealth," and its most striking feature is harmony—harmony in the individual and harmony in society as a whole. "Conservatives," Kirk advised, "confront the tremendous dual task of restoring the harmony of the person and the harmony of the republic."[63]

## V

To Kirk it is Edmund Burke's "moral imagination" that is the key to the recovery of order and harmony in the individual soul and ultimately in the whole of society. The point of departure in a properly understood political theory is the "individual goodness of heart."[64] The moral imagination instructs and nourishes the individual and leads to the goodness and harmony of the whole of society. "The moral imagination," Kirk stressed, "aspires to the apprehending of right order in the soul and right order in the commonwealth."[65]

What precisely is moral imagination? "It is the moral imagination which informs us concerning the dignity of human nature; which instructs us that we are more than naked apes."[66] Kirk elaborated:

> It is man's power to perceive ethical truth, abiding law, in the seeming chaos of many events. Without the moral imagination, man would live merely from day to day, or rather moment to moment, as dogs do. It is the strange faculty...of discerning greatness, justice, and order, beyond the bars of appetite and self-interest.[67]

For example, Kirk wrote, "The Hebrew prophets were men endowed with moral imagination."[68] The moral imagination is similar to Cardinal Newman's "the Illative Sense...a source deeper than our conscious and formal reason.... It is the combined product of intuition, instinct, imagination, and long and intricate experience."[69]

The moral imagination is not related to the Benthamite or Marxist world of ideology, to that perspective of materialism, naturalism, and utopianism. It is at odds with "the idyllic imagination" of Rousseau and ultimately with "the diabolic imagination" of a decadent society. The moral imagination does not seek to entertain or placate; it seeks to inform, instruct, ennoble, and elevate. It cares little for the modern theoretical emphasis upon rights, demands, and entitlements; rather, it is connected with the classical and biblical emphasis upon duty, service, obligation. The concept of the moral imagination is pre-eminent and critical in understanding the political mind of Russell Kirk. "We must nurture the moral imagination, which draws upon theology and history and poetic images," Kirk warned, as he also offers hope that "the moral imagination...may lead us back from the fleshpots of abnormality to the altar of the permanent things."[70] It is the "keenest" of our "weapons."[71]

Burke originated the concept of the "moral imagination," and that more than any other single reason is why Kirk looked upon him as perhaps the definitive and authoritative political philosopher. Certainly, among conservative theorists, Kirk considers him pre-eminent. Kirk spoke of Burke as "the greatest of modern conservative thinkers," indeed, as "the founder of our conservatism."[72] Lest there be any question of Burke's pre-eminence, Kirk wrote, "He was the first conservative of our time of troubles" and concluded "If conservatives would know what they defend, Burke is their touchstone."[73] Concerning Burke's *Reflections on the Revolution in France,* Kirk believed it "the most brilliant work of English political philosophy" and "must be read by anyone who wishes to understand the great controversies of modern politics."[74]

By the moral imagination, according to Kirk, "Burke meant that power of ethical perception which strides beyond the barriers of private experience and events of the moment."[75] Burke offered a whole range of concepts as instruments in "his determination. . .to refurbish 'the wardrobe of a moral imagination.' "[76] There are the classical and biblical concepts of piety, awe, reverence, and veneration resulting in the notions of duty, service, and obligation; a respect for tradition, history, and prescription, as well as an appreciation of the individual's need for roots and community, "the little platoon," that is, "the humane scale." Whereas egalitarianism and leveling are at war with the nature of things, pluralism, hierarchy, and diversity are natural and are to be encouraged; innovation, mindless change, and unfettered "will and appetite" must be prudently checked by discipline, restraint, and the "unbought grace of life." Finally there is the insight that "first principles" are to be desired because they are rooted in wisdom, knowledge, and experience, while abstractions are to be avoided because they are spun in the a priori, sterile, and opinionated world of the ideologue. Ultimately, Burke's opening up of infinite vistas of "the life of the mind" to refurbish the moral imagination substantiates the critical premise that "he knew religion to be man's greatest good." As Kirk emphasized, "In examining Burke's conservative system, therefore, it is well to commence on the lofty plane of religious belief."[77] Kirk further observed: "He believed in a Christian universe, to which a just God has given moral order to permit of man's salvation."[78] Not surprisingly, Kirk also observed that Bentham was "Burke's most powerful intellectual antagonist"; that "Rousseau and Burke stand at the antipodes"; and that Burke "was not a man of the Enlightenment."[79]

Of twentieth-century figures, T.S. Eliot had the greatest influence on Kirk. In Eliot, noted Kirk, Burke had an "intellectual heir" Significantly the subtitle of *The Conservative Mind* in later editions is *From Burke to Eliot.*[80] Concerning his relationship to Eliot, Kirk explained, "He was thirty years older than I, but we had read the same books, knew the same places, were almost as one in literary and social convictions." He added, "My own progress from doubt to acceptance had resembled Eliot's."[81] And Kirk concluded, "I confess to writing in the spirit of Eliot."[82]

Kirk was unstinting in his praise of Eliot as "the most influential poet and critic of our century," "the great man of letters of our time." "The greater part of the twentieth century will be known, in letters, as the Age of Eliot,"[83] Kirk claimed. Regarding Eliot's influence on conservative thought, he speculated, "If there has been a principal conservative thinker in the twentieth century, it is T.S. Eliot, whose age this is in humane letters."[84] Kirk's admiration for Eliot is understandable, when one considers that "Eliot's whole endeavor was to point a way out of the Waste Land toward order in the soul and in society."[85]

Perhaps Kirk was also drawn particularly to Eliot as a literary figure whose "attention turned increasingly to political theory."[86] Eliot, too, had come to appreciate that "a nation must have a political philosophy...something more than the programs of parties."[87] In developing a political philosophy, Eliot, like Kirk, had come to the conclusion that the ultimate goal of political philosophy could best be accomplished by employing the theoretical tools of "the well-ordered commonwealth" and "the moral imagination." The former was to be accomplished by revitalizing and restoring the latter. Eliot had come to understand that "the order of the soul could not be parted from the order of the commonwealth."[88] To achieve the harmony characteristic of a well-ordered society, one had to commence with restoring order in the individual soul. After all, as Plato had taught, society was merely the individual writ large. To restore order in the individual soul meant a revitalizing and a quickening of the moral imagination. Thus, T.S. Eliot became "the principal champion of the moral imagination in the twentieth century."[89] Kirk added that Eliot, "more than any other poet of his age, had reinvigorated the moral imagination, and had expressed in poetry an experience of transcendence."[90]

In fashioning his vision of the moral imagination, Kirk stated, "He [Eliot] had striven to renew modern man's understanding of the norms or order...in the person and in the commonwealth. He had not offered the opiate of ideology: he had pleaded for a return to enduring principle."[91] To borrow Eliot's own terminology, he "showed the way back to the permanent things." Why the notion of "the permanent things?"[92] "Is everything ephemeral?" Kirk inquired. "Does not a permanent reality exist?"[93] "The poet senses that he is born to set the time right—not, however, by leading a march to some New Jerusalem but by rallying in his art to the permanent things."[94] What are the permanent things? They are the "norms," Kirk explained, "those principles of morals and politics and taste which abide from age to age, which create the truly human person, and which cement the civil social order."[95] In fact, Kirk argued, "the conservative is a champion of norms, of what Mr. T. S. Eliot calls "the permanent things.' "[96]

Ultimately in Eliot it is religion in general and Christianity in particular that make for the most enduring contribution to the permanent things and thus the vitality of the moral imagination and the harmony of the well-ordered society. Concerning religion, Kirk observed, "Eliot found it necessary to pass beyond ethics into theology."[97] Eliot had come to believe that "unless faith is regained ...we end barren."[98] In sum, Kirk wrote, "Eliot was saying, the world stood in need of religious and moral principle upon which to renew the civil social order."[99]

In connection with Eliot's commitment to Christianity, Kirk quoted from Eliot's own words in "Thoughts after Lambeth":

> The world is trying the experiment of attempting to form a civilized but non-Christian mentality. The experiment will fail; but we must be very patient in awaiting its collapse; meanwhile redeeming the time: so that the Faith may be preserved alive through the dark ages before us; to renew and rebuild civilization, and save the world from suicide.[100]

After the German invasion of Poland in 1939, Eliot believed "the world must choose either Christianity or Paganism."[101] It was then a matter of Eliot's "having decided from reflection and experience that there is truth in Christian teaching."[102] Stated concisely, "Eliot came to believe that only through Annunciation and Incarnation was the tyranny of time undone."[103] "Eliot's remedy was the recovery of Christian community," for "he had seen how the ignoring or denial of Christian teaching had been followed by private and public disorder."[104] With this commitment Eliot became "the most admired Christian poet of his age."[105] For Kirk, as for Burke and Eliot, religion, and particularly Christianity, was the key to restoring the harmony of a properly ordered society, since religion is indispensable to a revitalized and restored moral imagination. "At heart, all social questions are exercises in ethics; and ethics, in turn, depend upon religious faith."[106] In short, "Political problems, at bottom, are religious and moral problems."[107] Kirk went on to explain:

> Politics moves upward into ethics, and ethics ascends to theology. The true conservative, in the tradition of Burke...is a theist, for he sees this world as a place of trial, governed by a power beyond human ability to comprehend adequately; he is convinced that earthly perfection is a delusion and in our time, quite possibly, a notion employed by the power of Evil to crush Good by the instrument of a pseudo-good [108]

And here Kirk especially underlined "the power of religious

understanding—lacking which, there can exist no order in the soul and no order in the state."[109]

With regard to the pertinence of Christianity, Kirk wrote: "The foundation of our civil social order, like that of Burke's Britain, is not an ideology, some 'armed doctrine': rather, it is the Christian religion."[110] Why is Christianity the indispensable component? The answer lies in the symbol of the Incarnation: "Incarnation, the Logos made flesh, gives us the possibility of conquering past and future. If we do not know the divine, we are driven by the diabolical impulses of the underworld."[111] Elsewhere Kirk contended, "What Platonism could not provide, Christian belief did: an incarnate model of the way that man should live, and a mode of participating in the life eternal."[112] "The Incarnation has made it possible for us to enter into an abiding order of the soul, and so not to perish as beasts perish."[113] "Christian teaching. . . did enable many people to order their souls, and so to improve the order of the commonwealth."[114] Kirk reflected, "I trust that none of us shall become political Christians; but I hope that we shall not be afraid to infuse Christian faith into politics."[115]

As opposed to the pridefulness of the Renaissance, the biblical view offers an alternative grounded in awe and reverence for the profound mystery of being. This perspective seeks genuine wisdom, knowledge, and truth concerning the nature of being; that is, its intellectual character is philosophical and not ideological in tone. It does not seek to restructure the world according to utopian schemes concocted by the spirit of such passing historical eras as the Enlightenment. Rather it purports to learn of the reality of created being and to attune individual man and society thereto. Nor does the biblical view seek solace or escape in the other dimension of modern thought: the frenetic pursuit of pleasure so as to escape boredom and the inevitable loss of an object in life and the resulting decadence. The biblical view consciously seeks "the elevation of character," not its deliberate neglect and destruction.

In Kirk's thinking the biblical view offered the authoritative and definitive alternative to modern thought:

Conservatives...hold that "in Adam's fall we sinned all": human nature, though compounded of both good and evil, is irremediably flawed; so the perfection of society is impossible, all human beings being imperfect.[116]

Finiteness, frailty, sin, evil, tragedy, and sorrow inhere in the very nature and fabric of the human predicament. Yet rather than yielding to alienation, estrangement, and despair, which has been a fatal error of modern thought, Kirk found a powerful and unrelenting thrust for reclaiming and restoring individual dignity and the harmonious commonwealth through the Pauline doctrine of faith, hope, and love. What is the significance of faith? "Faith does not abolish sorrow: it makes sorrow endurable."[117] And what is the value of hope? "Men who cannot hope for salvation or dread damnation will make a Roman candle of their world."[118] Thus, with hope, "happiness is found in imaginative affirmation, not in sullen negation."[119]

Saint Paul had written, "So faith, hope, love abide; these three; but the greatest of these is love."[120] Without equivocation Kirk embraced Saint Paul's position:

What is the object of life? The enlightened conservative does not believe that the end or aim of life is competition; or success; or enjoyment; or longevity; or power; or possessions. He believes, instead, that the object of life is Love.[121]

Furthermore, Kirk argued

The "enlightened conservative" knows that the just and ordered society is that in which Love governs us, so far as Love ever can reign in this world of sorrows: and he knows that the anarchical or the tyrannical society is that in which Love lies corrupt [122]

Christian love is the key to a rekindled and vibrant moral imagination capable of restoring order in the individual and in the commonwealth. Kirk wrote, "As Dante knew, it is love that moves this world and all the stars."[123] Finally, lest there be any doubt concerning the supreme importance he attaches to the concept of love, Kirk insisted " 'Thou shalt love the Lord thy God with all thy heart and soul, and thy neighbor as thy self': upon this commandment is true community founded."[124]

Biblical love is the complete antidote to the pride of the Renaissance that is the primary theoretical weakness of modern thought. "Christian love, rather than ego," Kirk concluded, "should be the moral foundation of learning."[125] The ultimate Christian, the saint, reveals this trait: "The saint is a human being who has put down his vanity: one who really does love his God with all his heart and soul, and his neighbor as himself."[126] In place of ego and vanity there are the notions of duty, discipline, sacrifice, and the resulting role of servant. In Kirk's words, "The conservative finds himself...a pilgrim in a realm of mystery and wonder, where duty, discipline, and sacrifice are required—and where the reward is that love which passeth all understanding."[127]

With the absence of pride and with the resulting role played by biblical love, there is a reaching out beyond the self, and, in turn, there is the enormously enhanced potential for forming the harmony of genuine community. There is the "knitting" and "binding" effect among individuals, within the family and within the community. For example, Saint Paul, in speaking of being "knit together in love," advised, "And above all these put on love, which binds everything togetner in perfect harmony."[128] Stressing his agreement, Kirk declared, "Now the enlightened conservative stood for true community, the union of men, through love and common interest, for the common welfare."[129] In contrast, modern men "have lost their community; they are atoms in a loveless desolation; they are desperately bored."[130] Love is powerfully centripetal in effect and is the foundation for building first the harmony of self and then the well-ordered society, whereas modern thought, based on ego and pride, is centrifugal in effect and leads to disharmony within the individual and the disintegration of the modern family and community. For Kirk, biblical love was the critical and decisive element in rekindling the moral imagination and leading to the ultimate goal of political theory: moral harmony within the individual and a well-ordered society and commonwealth.

## VII

Kirk sharply distinguished between conservative and libertarian philosophy:

> These two bodies of opinion share a detestation of collectivism. They set their faces against the totalist state and the heavy hand of bureaucracy. That much is obvious enough. What else do conservatives and libertarians profess in common? The answer to that question is simple: nothing. Nor will they ever. To talk of forming a league or coalition between these two is like advocating a union of ice and fire.[131]

He believed that there are profound and irreconcilable theoretical differences between these two schools of thought. For example, Kirk maintained that "nineteenth-century liberalism," from which contemporary libertarianism emerged, is "in large part the creation of Jeremy Bentham."[132] Elsewhere Kirk referred to "doctrinaire libertarians," with Jean-Jacques Rousseau as their prophet, as carrying "to absurdity the doctrines of John Stuart Mill."[133] In contrast to these founding thinkers of libertarianism, Kirk offered as philosophical antagonists Eliot and Burke:

> I mean that the libertarians make up what T.S. Eliot called a "chirping sect," an ideological clique forever splitting into sects still smaller and odder, but rarely conjugating. Such petty political sectaries Edmund Burke pictured as "the insects of the hour," as noisy as they are ineffectual against the conservative power of the browsing cattle in an English pasture. If one has chirping sectaries for friends, one doesn't need any enemies.[134]

Not surprisingly, Kirk, in finding libertarianism indebted to the philosophical heritage of Bentham, Rousseau, and Mill, and conservatism as an outgrowth of the intellectual tradition represented in Burke and Eliot, found little theoretical compatibility between the two.

Ultimately in Kirk's thinking one is confronted with the fundamental differences between the pridefulness of secularism and the transcendent, enduring, and sacrificial love of the biblical view. This accounts for his powerful dissent on any proposition that conservatism and libertarianism are theoretically compatible, the latter constituting a "dreary secular dogma of individualism... the belief that we exist solely in ourselves, and for ourselves, so many loveless specks in infinite time and space...to whom Satan reveals that nothing exists except the boy and empty space."[135] Contending that libertarianism was "founded upon doctrinaire selfishness," he reserved special criticism for Ayn Rand: "She would supplant the Cross—the symbol of sacrifice—by the Dollar-Sign—the symbol of self-aggrandizement."[136] In short, Kirk believed, libertarianism was founded upon the notion of "a cosmic selfishness."[137]

In contrast Kirk contended that "Conservatism is something more than mere solicitude for tidy incomes."[138] Being rooted in biblical love, it looks beyond the self to the transcendent, enduring, and permanent. Notions of duty, service, and sacrifice are integral elements of its philosophical conceptions. In perceiving the mystery of being with a sense of awe and reverence, conservatism seeks for "the elevation of character" and the attunement of the individual to the moral order ordained by the Creator. Not only is this ineffably rewarding to the individual for its joy, peace, and promise in believing, it also contributes incalculably to the ultimate goal of political theory: the moral imagination sufficient to sustain the harmony of the well-ordered commonwealth.

# Richard M. Weaver

Born in Weaverville, North Carolina, in 1910, Richard Malcolm Weaver was raised in Lexington, Kentucky. Elected to *Phi Beta Kappa,* Weaver graduated from the University of Kentucky in 1932. In that year he joined the American Socialist Party; however, from the outset Weaver was disenchanted with that association, and his flirtation with socialism was brief: "I could not like the members of the movement as *persons.* They seemed dry, insistent people, of shallow objectives."[1] He attended graduate school at Vanderbilt University where he obtained his M.A. degree in 1934. At Vanderbilt, Weaver was influenced by the Fugitive-Agrarians who were assembled there. In particular, he was deeply moved by one of the most eminent of that group, John Crowe Ransom. Weaver contended that Ransom's *God Without Thunder,* published in 1930, was "the profoundest of books to come out of the Agrarian movement."[2] The subtitle of Ransom's work was "An Unorthodox Defense of Orthodoxy," and in his analysis Ransom warned against "the watered theology of the advanced moderns"; he proposed that we "do what we can to recover the excellences of the ancient faith." Weaver wrote his M.A. thesis, "The Revolt Against Humanism," under the direction of Ransom.

Weaver obtained his doctorate in English from Louisiana State Univeristy in 1943. His dissertation, "The Confederate South, 1865-1910: A Study in the Survival of a Mind and Culture," was directed by Cleanth Brooks, who was assisted by, among others, Robert Penn Warren. Having joined the faculty at the University of Chicago in 1944, Weaver was a professor of English at that institution at the time of his death in 1963. At his death, one admiring colleague wrote, "His success was extraordinary: he was, I think, the most distinguished teacher of writing this institution has had in the last twenty years."[3]

Weaver became a powerful intellectual force in the American conservative movement of the post-World War II period. His best-known work, *Ideas Have Consequences,* was published in 1948. Frank S. Meyer described this book as "the informing principle of the contemporary American conservative movement."[4] Subsequently, Weaver wrote *The Ethics of Rhetoric,* probably his most scholarly work, and *Visions of Order,* which Willmoore Kendall characterized as deserving "the political equivalent of biblical status" out of all American conservative books.[5] Weaver's dissertation was published in 1968 under the title *The Southern Tradition at Bay,* and he dedicated the book to "John Crowe Ransom, subtle doctor."

Aside from these key works, Weaver published numerous reviews and articles. An anthology of among the best of the latter is found in *Life Without Prejudice and Other Essays.* Included among the selections is Weaver's "Life Without Prejudice," originally published as the lead article for the first issue of *Modern Age* in 1957. *Language Is Sermonic,* appearing in 1970, is an anthology dealing exclusively with Weaver's works on rhetoric. Unquestionably, Weaver's work has had a profound impact upon the intellectual development of the American conservative movement; indeed, in keeping with Meyer's and Kendall's observations, it can be argued that intellectually he is the founding father. In the words of Russell Kirk, "Richard Weaver sowed deep his intellectual seed; and though there are no heirs of his body, the heirs of his mind may be many and stalwart."[6]

Weaver accepted the label "conservative" as descriptive of his philosophical position:

> The modifier which has been most frequently applied to my own writings is "conservative." I have not exactly courted this but I certainly have not resented it, and if I had to make

a choice among the various appellations that are available, this is very likely the one that I would wind up with. I must say that I do not see any harm in it, and in this I am unlike some of my friends, unlike some people with whom I agree on principles, but who appear to think that the term is loaded with unfavorable meanings or at least connotations.[7]

The principal components of Weaver's conservatism are the Platonic and religious strains of Western thought. Weaver succinctly explained: "The way for any writer to show responsibility is to make perfectly clear the premises from which he starts.... I maintain...that form is prior to substance, and that ideas are determinants. I am quite willing to be identified with the not inconsiderable number of thinkers in the Platonic-Christian tradition who have taken the same stand."[8] As Weaver viewed it, the "fearful descent" of the modern age had been precipitated by "nominalism," which was a rejection of the Platonic-Christian heritage, and the formidable task of restoration rested upon the capacity of the West to rediscover the verities inherent in that heritage. In the American setting, Weaver looked upon the Southern legacy as uniquely valuable in providing the philosophical base needed for the imposing work of revitalization. To understand the conservative mind of Richard Weaver, it is essential then to analyze his positions on Platonism, religion, nominalism, and the significance of the Southern experience.

## I

Throughout Weaver's work is found a profound appreciation for Plato and his contribution to the Western heritage. Indeed, Weaver's best-known and probably most influential work, *Ideas Have Consequences,* is a book-long lament that Western modernism has departed from the Platonic tradition. Plato, Weaver wrote, "possessed the deepest divining rod among the ancients."[9] In Plato, Weaver found the personification of that philosophical bent which pursued an understanding of "the structure of reality":

> From the time of the Greeks there have existed in most periods "wise men," philosophers, or scholars who make it their work to seek out the structure of reality, and to proclaim it by one means and another to the less initiated. The first Greeks began looking for the structure of reality in the constitution of matter: What was the prime element out of which all other things were made?[10]

Weaver reasoned that a mature conservatism would follow in that tradition:

> It is my contention that a conservative is a realist, who believes that there is a structure of reality independent of his own will and desire. He believes that there is a creation which was here before him, which exists now not by just his sufferance, and which will be here after he's gone.... Though this reality is independent of the individual, it is not hostile to him. It is in fact amenable by him in many ways, but it cannot be changed radically and arbitrarily. This is the cardinal point. The conservative holds that man in this world cannot make his will his law without any regard to limits and fixed nature of things.[11]

In keeping with the Platonic view, Weaver argued this "structure of reality" was composed of things which have "essential natures" and that these natures were "knowable." Moreover, we have an "intuitive feeling that existence is not meaningless."[12] It is, then, the function of the philosopher to discern the realities—the essential natures of things—and hopefully to perceive, even though dimly and imperfectly, the meaning and purpose of existence. As it was with Plato, so it was with Weaver, that philosophy was the highest of callings whereby through "right reasoning" knowledge, understanding, wisdom, and ultimately truth were to be pursued.

Consistent with the Platonic view, Weaver contended that basic and inherent in the "nature of things" was a dualism:

> The first positive step must be a driving afresh of the wedge

between the material and the transcendental. This is fundamental: without a dualism we should never find purchase
for the pull upward, and all idealistic designs might as well
be scuttled.... To bring dualism back into the world and to
rebuke the moral impotence fathered by empiricism is then
the broad character of our objective.[13]

The material side of this dualism related to specifics and concretes, to the impermanent and transitory. The transcendental
facet pertained to first principles, essences, universals, forms, and
finally to unchanging Ideals: Truth, Beauty, Justice, and Goodness. In Weaver's words: "Plato reminded us that at any stage of
an inquiry it is important to realize whether we are moving toward, or away from, first principles."[14] Similarly, Weaver wrote,
"Belief in universals and principles is inseparable from the life of
reason," and he noted, "[We] invariably find in the man of true
culture a deep respect for forms."[15] In this regard, probably Weaver's best-known observation was:

The true conservative is one who sees the universe as a paradigm of essences, of which the phenomenology of the world
is a sort of continuing approximation. Or, to put this in another way, he sees it as a set of definitions which are struggling to get themselves defined in the real world.[16]

Weaver's embrace of the Platonic concept of the transcendent led
to his observation that "the conservative image of history arises
out of primal affection and a desire to follow transcendental
ideals of justice. And it is this that gives content to the philosophy
of conservatism."[17] In the final analysis, the pursuit of ideals is
the Platonic quest for standards and values:

Standard means, first of all, something of general application and validity. A standard is something that is set up as a
measure for all. It is not contingent upon this man's preference, or whim, or that man's location in space and time....
A standard is, therefore, something of uniform and universal determination. This is one of the aspects of the meaning.

But in addition to this, the term standard in its more general usage has the imperative sense of an ideal.[18]

We must, Weaver argued, have ideals, standards, and values in order that we can distinguish and evaluate:

> Before we can have the idea of relative evaluation at all, we must have a *tertium quid,* a third essence, an ideal ideal, as it were. This is why a humanism which is merely historical-minded can be learned, but cannot in the true sense be critical.[19]

"Evaluation"—this is the ultimate objective of our pursuit, and through this quest we are seeking to reassert "the ancient affirmation that there is a center of things": "The reason for this is that every culture polarizes around some animating idea, figment, or value, toward which everything that it produces bears some discoverable relation."[20]

The most significant thing about a society is its conception of value; this conception "imparts tone to the whole of society by keeping before its members a standard of right and not right."[21] In brief, according to Weaver, this conception of value is "the centripetal image of an ideal of perfection and goodness," and "[t]he task in our time of the conservative is to defend this concentration and to expose as erroneous attempts to break down the discriminations of a culture."[22] Clearly, a key "conservative principle" is a "belief in the primacy of ideas and values," and to the extent that anyone "tries to pull back toward a position of value, he becomes a conservative."[23]

In his concern for values and evaluation, Weaver, in the tradition of Plato, admonished, "There must be a source of clarification, or arrangement and hierarchy...."[24] Or to state the matter otherwise: "in the final reach of analysis our problem is how to recover that intellectual integrity which enables men to perceive the order of goods."[25] And what is the position of conservatism on these matters of "hierarchy" and "the order of goods?" "The word is *order.* Order, or harmony as an expression of order, ...is the goal which most if not all conservative thinking has in view."[26] Undeniably, as Weaver perceived it, conservatism had "its passion for an order reflecting a meaningful hierarchy of the goods."[27] This is in keeping with that ultimate of the Platonic ideal which conceives of Justice as the proper ordering of things which in turn is productive of balance, proportion, and harmony—all contributing immeasurably to the health and stability of the well-ordered society. In fact, Weaver concluded, "Civilization is measured by its power to create and enforce distinctions.... The man of a civilized tradition, therefore, will find nothing strange in the idea of hierarchy."[28]

With this Platonic emphasis upon the importance of a hierarchy of values, Weaver warned, "[C]onservatives should treat as enemies all those who wish to abolish the sacred and secular grounds for distinctions among men."[29] Egalitarianism and leveling were insidious ideas; in a statement that is the quintessence of Platonism, Weaver elaborated:

A just man finds satisfaction in the knowledge that society has various roles for various kinds of people and that they in the performance of these roles create a kind of symphony of labor, play, and social life. There arises in fact a distinct pleasure from knowing that society is structured, diversified, balanced, and complex. Blind levelers do not realize that people can enjoy seeing things above them as well as on a plane with them.[30]

In sum, "It is an historic truth...that culture has developed from the liberty of the superior individual to love superior things."[31] Certainly the founder of the Academy would not have dissented from these observations.

## II

In addition to its roots in Platonism, Weaver's conservatism is firmly based upon the religious heritage of Western thought. Reflecting this religious perspective, Weaver wrote, "Man has an irresistible desire to relate himself somehow to the totality, to ask what is the meaning of his presence here amid the great empirical fact of the universe," and "[t]hrough religion [man] reveals his profoundest intuition regarding his origin, his mission on earth, and his future state."[32] Nor could there be any doubt that a religious bent of mind is found in Weaver's rhetorical question: "How could simple environmental influence have called forth the giraffe, the centipede, the butterfly, the orchid, the sunflower?" Likewise, Weaver said, "I found myself [over the years] in decreasing sympathy with those social and political doctrines erected upon the concept of a man-dominated universe and more and more inclined to believe with Walt Whitman that 'a mouse is miracle enough to stagger sextillions of infidels.' "[33] And could there be any question as to the religious character of this observation: "The final solution must accommodate the ideas lying behind our feeling that the appearance of man on earth was a destined miracle."[34] Moreover, with affection, Weaver wrote, "No one can study Greek philosophy or medieval Christianity or the other great religions of the world without realizing that these saw man as a creature fearfully and wonderfully made, and that each tried to lead him with appropriate imagination and subtlety."[35] If any doubt lingers as to the religious base of Weaver's thinking, it should be removed by Weaver's unequivocal and moving instruction: "But the road away from idolatry remains the same as before; it lies in respect for the struggling dignity of man for his orientation toward something higher than himself which he has not created."[36]

This religious character of Weaver's mind perhaps could be explained as merely another manifestation of his Platonism, for after all Plato too yearned for glimpsing and understanding the mysteries of the transcendent and eternal; he above all the ancients had sought to escape beyond the material confines of his earthly existence. The more fundamental question is: was Weaver a Christian? Weaver never concretely stated, "I am a Christian," but then Weaver was too subtle in his thinking to resolve the ultimate question in such a simple declaratory form. In Weaver's own words: "Literalism is the materialism of religion...."[37] To Weaver, the truth of Christianity was not something resolved by dialectic; human reason and language were inadequate to that formidable task. Christianity is a matter of "rhetoric"; that is, it is a matter of the perceived, the felt, and the intuited. More particularly, the matter of faith is not resolved through the abstract dialectic of debate; rather, it is established by the mind's grasp and reverence for the ineffable miracle of creation.

A careful reading of Weaver's works yields up a position that is markedly, if not openly, Christian. For example, Weaver's esteem for Christianity is reflected in his observation that there are "reasons for believing that Christianity made a cultural and ethical contribution surpassing even the high-water mark of the Greeks."[38] Similarly, with eloquence he maintained:

> The Greeks could out-argue the Christians and the Romans could subject them to their government, but there was in Christianity an ethical respect for the person which triumphed over these formalizations. Neither the beauty of Greek culture nor the grandeur of the Roman state system was the complete answer to what the people wanted in their lives as a whole.[39]

Elsewhere Weaver asserted, "[B]ut being a great writer does entail having the Christian-like view of man, which sees him as a dual creature, possessing the capacity for glory and damnation."[40] Even more revealing was this sweeping observation:

> It was inevitable that, lacking one vital element, the ancient governments should have collapsed into despotism. That vital element was introduced by Christianity. This was belief in the sacredness of the person and thus in a center of power distinct from the state. What the pagan philosophers in all their brilliance had not been able to do, that is, set effective barriers to the power of the state, was done in response to that injunction: "Render unto Caesar the things that are Caesar's and unto God the things that are God's." This insti-

tuted a basis of freedom upon which the world since that time has been able to build.[41]

Concerning a personal commitment to Christianity, perhaps most revealing was Weaver's review of Bertrand Russell's *The Impact of Science on Society*. In this work Russell reluctantly acknowledged the indispensability of Christianity in dealing with the "wide diffusion of malevolence" in the world. Regarding Russell's grudging admission, Weaver remarked:.

> It seems a long way around to find something which might have been discovered on the threshold. But sometimes we are firmer in our convictions for having surveyed the possible alternatives. Let us hope that this is true of all who like Lord Russell in this book make the long circuit to learn that society is not saved by bread alone.[42]

There is evidence Weaver considered Christianity the logical fulfillment of Platonism. Weaver had agreed that "Plato built the cathedrals of England," and, even more pointedly, he stated:

> It is generally admitted that there is a strong element of Platonism in Christianity. But if Plato provided the reasoning, Paul and Augustine supplied the persuasion. What emerged from this could not be withstood even by the power of Rome.[43]

This reference to Saint Augustine as the fulfillment of Plato is dramatically suggestive of Saint Augustine's own reasoning in *The City of God:* "For none of the other philosophers has come so close to us as the Platonists have, and, therefore we may neglect the others.... Some of our fellow Christians are astonished to learn that Plato had such ideas about God and to realize how close they are to the truths of our faith." This striking similarity between Saint Augustine's and Weaver's views does not end here. More specifically, the orthodox Christian concepts of original sin, evil, and "the tragic sense" go to the core of Weaver's conservatism.

48

In his classic autobiographical essay, "Up From Liberalism," Weaver wrote:

> It has been said that disillusionment with human nature most often turns the mind toward Christianity. I know that in my period of jejune optimism the concept of original sin seemed something archaically funny. Now, twenty years later [1958], and after the experience of a world war, there is no concept that I regard as expressing a deeper insight into the enigma that is man.[44]

What is original sin?

> Original sin is the parabolical statement that man is somehow originally flawed. He has the temptation, known allegorically as the curse visited upon the descendants of Adam, to do what he knows he ought not do. This flaw is no respecter of person or place or station.[45]

Sin leads to evil in the world, and it is great error to believe "that man is by nature good, and therefore not responsible for evil"; in addition, it is an error to assume "that man is merely the creature of circumstances, and again not responsible for evil.... The denial of evil is a very great heresy."[46]

Weaver contended that evil and "the tragic sense" were inseparable: "Hysterical optimism will prevail until the world again admits the existence of tragedy, and it cannot admit the existence of tragedy until it again distinguishes between good and evil."[47] Weaver was deeply religious and conservative in dealing with the problem of tragedy. Unequalled in this regard is the following assessment:

> The herd man never grows reconciled to the fact that life is a defeat, and that this defeat is its real story.... It does finally require some discipline of mind to accept the fact that life is not a triumphal progress, but a sadly mixed affair with many a disenchantment.[48]

Similarly, he wrote, "[M]an is born to suffer, to endure his passion, and to find redemption, if he finds it, through effort and struggle."[49] He summarized:

> Perhaps there is nothing in the world as truly educative as tragedy. When you have known it, you've known the worst, and probably also you have had a glimpse of the mystery of things. And if this is so, we may infer that there is nothing which educates or matures a man or a people in the way that the experience of tragedy does. Its lessons, though usually indescribable, are poignant and long remembered.[50]

In fact, "education in tragedy" is a lesson "with which other educations are not to be compared, if you are talking about realities."[51] To Weaver tragedy was the fundamental datum of the human experience. However, out of tragedy did not emerge anguish or despair; rather, Weaver's position was remarkably similar to that articulated by Saint Paul in his letter to the Romans: "[W]e rejoice in our suffering, knowing that suffering produces endurance, and endurance produces character, and character produces hope, and hope does not disappoint us...." In Weaver's words: "The noble view of life...tends always to be pessimistic.... It could not be otherwise, for...the...very plot of tragedy depends upon the 'good' man struggling in a net of evil."[52] The Pauline "hope" lies in the "good man" overcoming "the net of evil" by directing his vision to the transcendent and thereby ennobling and redeeming himself; thus out of evil and tragedy comes Good. As Weaver explained in the final paragraph of *Ideas Have Consequences:* "It may be that we are awaiting a great change, that the sins of the fathers are going to be visited upon the generations until the reality of evil is again brought home and there comes some passionate reaction, like that which flowered in the chivalry and spirituality of the Middle Ages."[53]

Together the Christian ideal and Platonism produced in Weaver's conservatism the final key concept of piety, which Weaver described as "one of the oldest and deepest human attitudes."[54] "I would define piety," he wrote, "as an attitude of reverence or acceptance toward some overruling order or some deeply founded institution which the mere individual is not to tamper with."[55] Or to put the proposition somewhat differently: "Piety comes to us as a warning voice that we must think as mortals, that it is not for us either to know all or to control all. It is a recognition of our own limitations and a cheerful acceptance of the contingency of nature, which gives us the protective virtue of humility."[56] A thinker imbued with a sense of piety will realize "[i]n the figure once used by a philosopher, we are inhabitants of a fruitful and well-ordered island surrounded by an ocean of ontological mystery. It does not behoove us to presume very far in this situation .... Therefore, make haste slowly. It is very easy to rush into conceit in thinking about man's relationship to the created universe."[57] Weaver warned, "[Man] must not, like the child, expect all delights freely; he must not...expect all paradoxes to be resolved for him. He must be ready to say at times with Thomas Hooker: "The point is difficult and the mystery great.' "[58]

Concerning Plato's contribution to the "ancient virtue of *pietas,*" as a quotation introductory to "Piety and Justice," the final chapter of *Ideas Have Consequences,* Weaver quoted from Plato's *Laws:* "Let parents, then, bequeath to their children not riches, but the spirit of reverence."[59] In this chapter Weaver discussed Plato's dialogue *Euthyphro*, which was devoted to the theme of "piety and impiety":

> It is highly significant to learn that when Plato undertakes a discussion of the nature of piety and impiety, he chooses as interlocutor a young man who is actually bent upon parricide. Euthyphro, a youth filled with arrogant knowledge and certain that he understands "what is dear to the gods," has come to Athens to prosecute his father for murder. Struck by the originality of this proceeding, Socrates questions him in the usual fashion. His conclusion is that *piety, which consists of co-operation with the gods in the kind of order they have instituted, is part of the larger concept of justice.* It can be added that the outcome of the dialectic does not encourage the prosecution. The implication is that Euthyphro has

no right, out of his partial and immature knowledge, to proceed contemptuously against an ancient relationship.[60]

Elsewhere Weaver wrote that in understanding the meaning of piety it had "proved impossible to dispense with appeal to religion"; he emphasized:

Every legend of man's fall is a caution against presuming to know everything, and an indirect exhortation to piety; and the disappearance of belief in original sin has done more than anything else to prepare the way for sophistical theories of human nature and society. Man has lost piety toward nature in proportion as he left her and shut himself up in cities with rationalism for his philosophy.[61]

The concept of piety permeates Weaver's works, and it is the key to his philosophy. As Weaver explained, "The recovery [of a sense of piety] has brought a satisfaction which cannot be matched, as far as my experience goes, by anything that liberalism and scientism have to offer."[62] Weaver contended there was a "structure of reality" called creation. Man was not the Creator; he was not self-produced. Man is a creature limited in his potential. Confronted with choices between evil and good, man frequently chooses evil with its accompanying anguish, and this condition is compounded by that ever-present matter of tragedy. In view of these imposing realities, would not wisdom and prudence dictate that man ought to be modest, restrained, and humble—in a word, pious? Should he not stand in reverence and awe before this miracle called life? Without equivocation, according to Weaver, the philosopher and theologian will answer that question in the affirmative, and the result is that "ancient virtue of *pietas*."

### III

Weaver reasoned it was the emergence of nominalism, the departure from Platonism and Christianity, which produced the intellectual heresies leading to the trauma and anguish of the modern era. "It was," he elaborated, "William of Occam who propounded the fateful doctrine of nominalism, which denies that universals have a real existence," and as a result, "For four centuries every man has been not only his own priest but his own professor of ethics, and the consequence is an anarchy which threatens even that minimum consensus of value necessary to the political state."[63] Weaver concluded, "Whether we describe this as decay of religion or loss of interest in metaphysics, the result is the same; for both are centers with power to integrate, and, if they give way, there begins a dispersion which never ends until the culture lies in fragments."[64]

Platonism and Christianity acknowledged there was "a center of things." This center suggested transcendent Ideals: Truth, Beauty, Justice, and the Good. Life had meaning and purpose, and the Platonic-Christian view allowed man to relate, to discern his position in the scheme of things; and it facilitated humaneness in the human condition, for man knew his nature and could be himself. But the spirit of modernity, rooted in nominalism, undercut that view. It rejected the notion that there was "a center of things," and it turned in "flight toward the periphery."[65] There was no longer an integrating Ideal; the pull of intellectual forces was "centrifugal" rather than "centripetal." Conceptually the life of the mind became "fragmented," and the press to the "periphery" became a powerful "obsession." There emerged a preoccupation with the factual and concrete—positivism manifested that trait. There was no desire to synthesize, to relate, to conceptualize, or to project notions of meaning and purpose. In fact, there emerged a profound hostility to the contention that essences—Truth, Beauty, Justice, Good—even existed, let alone could be defined. As Weaver explained, "The modernistic searcher after meaning may be likened to a man furiously beating the earth and imagining that the finer he pulverizes it, the nearer he will get to the riddle of existence." And to what end?[66]

It is a politics of infinite dispersion. Everything goes flying off in its own direction; liberalism becomes ever more liberal; hierarchies are toppled so that there is no longer any means of judging one thing as better or worse than another. Moral order is collapsed into something like the universe of modern astrophysics, with everything moving away centrifugally, nobody knows where or why. And this goes on forever....[67]

"It is," Weaver summarized, "just as if Plato's philosopher had left the city to look at the trees and then had abandoned speculative wisdom for dendrology."[68] This intellectual flight of the modern mind from the Platonic-Christian perspective is lamentable, for "[w]isdom does not lie on the periphery."[69]

Nominalism infected the American political character through its agent of relativism. Denying the notion that there were ultimate essences and absolutes by which judgments and evaluations were to be made, nominalism led inexorably to the premise that all values were relative:

Relativism denies outright that there are any absolute truths, any fixed principles, or any standards beyond what one may consider his convenience. A theory is true only relative to the point of view of the individual, or to the circumstances which prevail at the moment. Truth is forever contingent and evolving, which means, of course, that you can never lay hands on it. Relativism is actually the abdication of truth.[70]

And as to the political implications of relativism, Weaver observed:

The greatest injury that the idea of relativism had done to political thinking...lies in the encouragement it gives to middle-of-the-roadism.... Middle-of-the roadism is the departure of intellect from political thinking.... A political philosophy takes a stand in favor of certain values and the arrangements that follow from them.... Now the truth about the middle-of-the road position is that it has no such character. ...It doesn't see with its own eyes. It tries to get along by borrowing a little from those who have done the hard work of seeing the principles through.[71]

Weaver had no quarrel with the need to compromise "at the level where concrete facts [were] encountered." However, he added, "But I do deny strenuously that compromise itself is a political philosophy. After all, one has to have something to compromise *from*."[72] Relativism had produced the "Whig theory of history" which taught "that the most advanced point in time is the most advanced in development," and the demanding mistress Progress emerged as the new Goddess.[73] More pointedly, relativism had produced contemporary American liberalism. Concerning the latter, Weaver wrote, "[T]he essence of the liberal's position is that he has no position."[74] Moreover "[w]here no conception of a moral absolute exists, authority has no real basis" and this has ominous implications for the ideal of "human freedom and dignity"; Weaver asserted, "I am entirely convinced that relativism as a doctrine must eventually lead to a regime of force. The relativist has no outside authority, no constraining transcendent idea to appeal to or to be deterred by. For him 'all things flow.' "[75]

In addition to spawning the "Whig theory of history," nominalism had other devastating effects upon cultural life in the West and in America in particular. First, contrary to the Platonic-Christian patrimony, by "denying that universals [had] a real existence," nominalism destroyed the traditional conception of education. "Traditional education," Weaver wrote, "has always been based on the assumption that there is a world of data, a fixed reality, which is worth knowing and even worth reverencing."[76] Furthermore, in keeping with the Platonic-Christian view, traditional education felt "the upward pull of definite religious and cultural ideals," and, as a consequence, "Its content and method have been designed to develop the mind and the character in making choices between truth and error, between right and wrong."[77] Nominalism substituted "progressive education" for the traditional form. In promoting the "flight toward the periphery," nominalism reduced education to a formless, unstructured ritual void of substance. "The new education," Weaver explained, "is rather something dreamed up by romantic enthusiasts, political fanatics, and unreflective acolytes of positive science."[78] As there were no principles, no essences, no universals, no objective structure of reality, education, under the guidance of John Dewey and his disciples, became a fragmented and purely subjective personal experience: "In brief, learning is to be foregone in favor of the child's spontaneous desires and unreflective thoughts."[79] Weaver further noted:

> The boast of the innovating "progressive" schools is that they prepare the youth for a changing world. *Would it not be incomparably more sensible to prepare the youth to understand why the world is changing?* This is what the humanities do. There is little appeal here to the exponents of progressive education because they have no desire to rise above the confusion.[80]

Progressive education, Weaver lamented, "[N]either encourages reflection nor inspires a reverence for the good," and he concluded, "The conflict between [it] and the principal teachings of the Judeo-Christian-classical heritage of the West will be immediately apparent."[81] As the educational system was a key bearer of culture, the ravages of nominalism had been carried into the vital center of the American experience.

Beyond education, nominalism had taken a heavy cultural toll in journalism, painting, music, and rhetoric. The world of journalism, including that of the newspaper, radio, and television, projects a "sickly metaphysical dream. The ultimate source of evaluation ceases to be the dream of beauty and truth and becomes that of psychopathia, of fragmentation, of disharmony and nonbeing."[82]

In turning from any notion of an integrating ideal or center, modern journalism had sought refuge in a preoccupation with the specific and fleeting. Weaver compared the world of journalism with that of the Platonic cave.[83] In the cave the multitude sits with eyes fixed upon the wall where shadows rise and fall. The wall of shadows is the world of the ephemeral and trivial. As Plato instructed, it was the philosopher who sought to turn from the wall and to go out of the cave into the sun, into the world of the true and enduring. In contrast, the function of the modern journalist is to keep the focus of the multitude upon the wall. To accomplish this end, the journalist employs that giant machine, The Great Stereopticon.[84] As Weaver observed, "It is the function of this machine to project selected pictures of life in the hope that what is seen will be imitated.... We are told the time to laugh and the time to cry...."[85] To keep all eyes fixed upon the wall, the journalists—the operators of The Great Stereopticon—must war upon memory, form, and the reflective. The need was to gain and keep attention through "titillation"; all reserve was sacrificed, and "[p]roud of its shamelessness, the new journalism served up in swaggering style matter which heretofore had been veiled in decent taciturnity."[86] In making a "virtue of desecration," license is taken whereby "a certain recklessness of diction, with vivid verbs and fortissimo adjectives, creeps into the very language," and "substance itself is changed to appeal to appetites for the lurid, the prurient, and the sadistic."[87] Weaver concluded:

> What humane spirit, after [exposure to some form of contemporary journalism] has not found relief in fixing his gaze upon some characteristic bit of nature? It is escape from the sickly metaphysical dream. Out of the surfeit of falsity born of technology and commercialism we rejoice in returning to primary data and to assurance that the world is a world of enduring forms which in themselves are neither brutal nor sentimental.[88]

Likewise, modern painting had suffered extensively under the imprint of nominalism: "For when we plumb the deepest springs of the artistic impulse, we find a source much akin to that of philosophy. All philosophy, Aristotle declared, begins with wonder, and it appears equally true that the artist is a wonder-struck being."[89] However, modern art, in following contemporary philosophy, retreated from the notion of a transcendent ideal at the

57

center and opted for an obsession with fragments. Painting no longer had an integrating ideal, and there commenced a shift of emphasis to technique and to the subjective world of sensation. The ultimate in the decline of art is "[t]he movement of Impressionism, which is the revolutionary event of modern painting.... This meant the acceptance of life as good and satisfying in itself, with a consequent resolution to revel in the here and now. The world of pure sensation thus became the world of art."[90] Weaver asserted, "My interpretation is that Impressionism brings nominalism into painting. One of the cardinal tenets [of nominalism] is that outline does not exist in nature.... If form does not exist prior to things, naturally it is realism to paint things."[91] In giving birth to relativism and hence egotism, nominalism produced a decline in art where the goal was no longer the depiction of transcendent and integrating ideals; rather, the concern was with the subjective and sensate, with the expression of ego through technique—and all perpetrated in the name of "realism."

"The degenerative influences" of nominalism in music commenced with the departure from "the traditional forms ... of freedom and restraint, of balance and resiliency" furnished by Mozart.[92] "The portents of change came with Beethoven," Weaver wrote, whose emphasis upon "dynamism and of strains of individualism pointed the way which the succeeding century was to take."[93] Ultimately, Weaver observed, "Music had its Impressionist movement. With Liszt and Debussy, especially, it turned to the exploitation of color and atmosphere.... This phase was technically a flight from the construction and balance of classical form, in effect it was a concentration upon "emotive fragments'...."[94] As the ego was driven ever inward in search of meaning and solace, it turned to jazz (and later "rock") which was "the clearest of all signs of our age's deep-seated predilection for barbarism."[95] Jazz, Weaver argued, "[Was] a triumph of grotesque, even hysterical, emotion over propriety and reasonableness." Indeed, he wondered, "Jazz often sounds as if in a rage to divest itself of anything that suggests structure or confinement."[96] Jazz reflects a mood "impatient for titillation," and it reflects the desire of the performer for "fullest liberty to express himself as an egotist."[97] Weaver contended, "By dissolving forms, it [jazz] has left man free to move without reference, expressing dithyrambically whatever surges up from below. It is a music not of dreams—certainly not of our metaphysical dream—but of drunkenness."[98] In short, jazz "shows how the soul of modern man craves orgiastic disorder."[99] Even more tragically, "[o]ne can detect signs of suicidal impulse; one feels at times that the modern world is calling for madder music and for stronger wine, is craving some delirium which will take it completely away from reality."[100]

Finally, and most critically, rhetoric had succumbed to nominalism. What is rhetoric? "Rhetoric is anciently and properly defined as the art of persuasion."[101] Weaver wrote, "[Man is] born into history, with an endowment of passion and a sense of the ought.... His life is therefore characterized by movement toward goals. It is largely the power of rhetoric which influences and governs that movement."[102] More simply, rhetoric is "the attempt through language to make one's point of view."[103] Rhetoric then is concerned with words, written and spoken, and their use in the pursuit of values and goals. Depending upon the values served, rhetoric is good or bad. As the Platonic-Christian tradition had taught since antiquity, it was imperative to discern the "nature of things," to perceive the transcendent ideals, to comprehend the proper hierarchy of values, to eschew relativism, and to construct and preserve that language which rendered service to the ultimate good: "So rhetoric at its truest seeks to perfect men by showing them better versions of themselves, links in that chain, extending up toward the ideal, which only the intellect can apprehend and only the soul have affection for."[104]

Rhetoric is the key to a culture; it is the tie that binds and affords cohesion; it expresses the soul and essence of a people—it tells of their "being." If rhetoric is corrupt, this is a symptom that society is corrupt; conversely, a society of integrity will have a rhetoric of integrity. By denying that ultimate essences and values were knowable, nominalism had greviously afflicted rhetoric.

In erecting the new idol of relativism, nominalism had left us with "exactly the same atomization which we have deplored in other fields."[105] At best, language had become banal and frivolous—note the world of journalism and advertising; too often, even in supposedly serious literary forms, language reflected an ethic with an insatiable appetite for titillation through descriptions of the brutal, obscene, and debased. Indeed, it was a measure of the scandal of the new ethic of relativism that it could not even define "brutality," "obscenity," and kindred debasements— after all, "all is relative," and evaluations are dependent solely upon the subjective eye of the individual beholder.

By inducing the modern mind to repudiate the notion of integrating ideals at the center, nominalism had undercut the entire Platonic-Christian position. The effect was to set in motion a theoretical and cultural unraveling of far-reaching consequences: not only was there rejection of the concept of enduring essences at the center, there followed logically a denial of any discernible "structure of reality"; a denial that things had essential natures which were knowable; a denial of the dualism of the transcendent and material and the superiority of the transcendent; and a denial that hierarchy was inherent in the nature of being and that the development of standards and values consistent with this hierarchy was of the highest priority in a purportedly civilized culture. In addition, there was a complete turning away from certain theoretical essentials of the biblical view: namely, original sin, evil, and tragedy. Sin and evil were beyond the comprehension of the modern mind, for out of the relativism generated by nominalism there was no conception of right versus wrong, there were no standards by which to evaluate and judge. The position of the modern mind was either to ignore tragedy, as there were no philosophical resources to cope with it, or to pretend that, as man had only a material dimension, a perfected science would eventually eradicate it. Science then would redeem mankind—this was the final effrontery of the modern mind: there was an absence of piety, an absence of that "protective virtue of humility." Unrestrained and shameless egotism was the basic symbol of the modern age, and it stood as the stark antithesis to the Platonic-Christian heritage.

## IV

In the American experience, the heritage of the Old South, Weaver contended, offered the intellectual base for overcoming the debilitating effects of nominalism: "The South, which has spent so many years as America's stepchild, is proving to have the gift which may save the household from destruction."[106] Lest the shallow romanticists should misunderstand, Weaver cautioned that he was not speaking of the South of "the moonlight and magnolia tradition," nor of "the old rebel yell." Likewise, he noted that the South was a land of "anomalies" and "contradictions," and there was "the danger of taking hold of the South by a simple handle." Weaver admonished against accepting uncritically the ways of the Old South. He warned that things had to be looked at "in the round" and that the Old South had its deficiencies: on occasion it had worshiped status at the expense of warranted change; it had too frequently contributed to the "depreciation of the intellectual"; and thus it "needed a Burke or a Hegel," but "it produced lawyers and journalists."[107] Yet, in spite of these limitations, when compared with the New South model, which was merely a call for the contemporary South to conform to the national standard of nominalism, "The Old South may indeed be a hall hung with splendid tapestries in which no one would care to live; but from them we can learn something of how to live."[108] More than any other section of the country, the Old South afforded the philosophical material essential for reversing the momentum of nominalism and rekindling the Platonic Christian heritage. Although he was not prone to dwell extensively upon the particulars of the influence, clearly Southern Agrarianism in general, and that "subtle doctor" John Crowe Ransom in particular, had made an indelible mark on Weaver's thinking.

It appears paradoxical that Weaver should turn to that section of the country which is by conventional wisdom the most provincial in order to direct society from the fragmented world of nominalism to a restoration of faith in universals. But upon reflection there is no contradiction: the South is provincial in the American context precisely because it is that section with roots most deeply in the Platonic-Christian heritage. "Even in the South today," Weaver observed, "one can find surviving large segments of the classical Christian-medieval synthesis."[109] In contrast to the nation as a whole, the South had over the years nurtured its European roots, and this gave its thinking and way of life a degree of maturity not found in the more secular, optimistic, pragmatic, and progress oriented ethic of the broader national experience.

In keeping with the Platonic tradition, Weaver noted that the South was "based upon a paradigmatic ideal," meaning that Southern culture showed "a degree of centripetalism, or orientation toward a center, which was characteristic of all high cultures."[110] As evidence of this "orientation toward a center," one could speak of "the South" or "Southernness" and be understood as indicating a way of life; there was no other region of the country where that was so, for the other regions, under the fragmenting impact of nominalism, lacked "a center." Concerning this pull to the center as uniquely characteristic of the South, Weaver wrote, "An American reared as a Southerner is in a sense like a man born into the Church of Rome; it is questionable whether he ever finds it possible to repudiate the South entirely."[111]

Consistent with the Platonic view, the traditional Southern mind had accepted the notion that there was a "structure of reality," that things had essential natures. More particularly, the South had kept "at the heart of its faith and belief in the dual nature of man."[112] The components of this dualism are the material and transcendent, and "the basis of [Southern] culture, like that of all true cultures, is transcendental."[113] Indeed, it was in the Old South that one found *"the last non-materialist civilization in the Western World."*[114] Finally, the traditional South reflected the

Platonic interest in standards, evaluation, hierarchy, and antiega-
litarianism:

> [T]he South has never lost sight of the fact that society
> means structuring and differentiation, and that "society"
> and ''mass" are antithetical terms. It has never fallen for a
> simple equalitarianism, nor has it embraced the sentimen-
> talism that anyone on the bottom *ipso facto* belongs on
> top.[115]

In addition, Weaver reasoned, the South was best equipped to
serve as the "flywheel" of the American nation and to lead the
forces of restoration because of its traditional religious fundamentalism: "[M]ore conservative than America as a whole, [the
South] shows an almost unanimous opposition to those tendencies which would destroy the poetic-religious myths and create the
mass state."[116] Weaver added, "[T]he South remains the strong-
hold of religious and perhaps also of ethical fundamentalism":

> The typical Southerner is an authentically religious being if
> one means by religion not a neat set of moralities but a deep
> and even frightening intuition of man's radical dependence
> in this world.... I suggest that the Southerner's practice of
> viewing the world in this way is the postulate of all his think-
> ing.[117]

Historically, the Old South had put its confidence—its faith—
in "the older religiousness" rather than in "psychiatry and socialism." The Southerner implicitly understood the wisdom of
former North Carolina Governor Charles Aycock's statement:
"Nowhere within [North Carolina's] borders [is there] a man ignorant enough to join the fool in saying 'There is no God.' "[118]
The traditional Southerner was religious in the deepest sense, for
he comprehended the crucial meanings of the words "inscrutable" and "mystery": the Southerner has "a sense of the inscrutable, which leaves man convinced of the existence of supernatural
intelligence and power, and leads him to the acceptance of life as

mystery."[119] The South's religious patrimony was decidedly Christian and orthodox: the concepts of original sin, evil, and tragedy had unquestioned meaning to the Southerner. Concerning original sin and evil, the Southerner was "opposed to the chimerical notion that man is by nature good. He argued that on the contrary no government can hope to survive which does not proceed on the assumption that man is a fallen being."[120] To the orthodox religious mind of the South it was cardinal error and heresy "[t]o substitute a sentimental optimism and humanitarianism for the old and proved doctrine of man's natural depravity."[121] Above all else, the Southerner understood the reality of tragedy. As had no other section of the country, the South had tasted the bitter "cup of defeat." Yet out of this defeat did not emerge despair or bitterness; as one Southerner observed shortly after the close of the Civil War, "It is only the atheist who adopts success as a *criterion* of right. It is not a new thing in the history of men that God appoints to the brave and the true the stern task of contending, and falling, in a righteous quarrel."[122] As the Southern mind viewed it, Weaver explained:

> God had foreseen all, and our suffering and our defeats in this world were part of a discipline whose final fruit it was not given to mortal minds to perceive.... [G]reat calamities had to be regarded as part of the design of inscrutable Providence.[123]

Defeat and suffering were looked upon not as evidence of repudiation; rather, they were considered as parts of God's mysterious plan—the book of Job had artfully instructed men in this most fundamental of lessons. In Southern religious thought, there was no basis for questioning or despair in defeat, for even defeat was God's will and therefore good, and out of God's plan ultimately came hope and affirmation. In orthodox Southern religiousness it was "God who wielded the thunder," and there was no such thing as "the lost cause."

As a result of the Platonic-Christian heritage, the "ancient virtue of pietas" dominated the thinking of the older South. There existed veneration for the transcendent and the order of things;

there was reverence for nature, tradition, history, and status. Man was the creature, not the Creator, and it was that most ancient vice, hubris, that contended man was self-produced and thus entitled to war on creation and the nature of things; there was, then, a spirit of restraint and sensitivity, of chivalry and humaneness. Although man was finite and existed as a "mist" or "shadow," the ultimate forms and essences endured. In view of man's position in this scheme of things, the traditional Southern mind, in keeping with the Platonic-Christian tradition, had understood the meaning of piety. It was Robert E. Lee, the quintessence of Southernness, whom Weaver quoted to show the deep sense of piety present in the Old South. Lee wrote:

> [N]or ... do I despair of the future. The march of Providence is so slow, and our desires so impatient, the work of progress is so immense, and our means of aiding it so feeble, the life of humanity is so long, and that of the individual so brief, that we often see only the ebb of the advancing wave, and are thus discouraged. It is history that teaches us to hope.[124]

Weaver was profoundly moved by this assessment. He exclaimed:

> It is a rare distillation. If Lee had been a member of that archetypal republic which a great philosopher imagined, with its orders of valor and wisdom, is it not likely that he would have been promoted a grade? I think that he would have risen from warrior to philosopher king.[125]

"I see no way," Weaver concluded, "to sum up the offense of modern man except to say that he is impious."[126] As piety had historically existed in the South, more than in any other area of the country, it was understandable why Weaver looked to this region to commence the search for the philosophical resources to reverse "the fearful descent" of the modern age.

## V

Weaver accepted the label "conservative" as accurately describing his philosophical position; nevertheless he was sympathetic to the libertarian spirit: "My instincts are libertarian, and I am sure that I would never have joined effort with the conservatives if I had not been convinced that they are the defenders of freedom today."[127] In fact, Weaver observed, "I think conservatives and libertarians stand together.... Both of them believe that there is an order of things, which will largely take care of itself if you leave it alone."[128] A crucial question emerges: was Weaver saying libertarianism and conservatism are identical perspectives? Weaver never expressly elaborated on this question; however, a reading of his works does suggest he saw an important difference and that he preferred the conservative view.

From Weaver's perspective, libertarianism was eminently correct in its concern for individual liberty; yet it unduly limited itself by offering only "freedom from" and not confronting the deeper question, "freedom for what?" In fact, a narrowly conceived philosophy emphasizing only freedom for the individual to do as he chooses, depending upon the whim of the subjective inner self, is perilously close to the crude and unreserved egotism of nominalism—impiety lies close at hand. The concept of freedom alone is not sufficient to sustain that undeniable and irrepressible longing of man, reflected in philosophers and theologians, to know of the nature and order of things, to know of the meaning and purpose of man's being— in a word, to know of Truth. Libertarianism does not purport to answer those questions; still they persist, they do not melt away. In Weaver's thinking, it is American conservatism which, although sharing the libertarian's concern for human freedom, develops a more mature philosophy dealing with the ultimate questions, a philosophy which does seek to pursue and discern, however dimly and imperfectly, meaning, purpose, and truth in the human experience. More specifically, conservatism is a philosophy of affirmation:

> The conservative I therefore see as standing on *terra firma* of antecedent reality; having accepted some things as given, lasting and good, he is in a position to use his effort where

effort will produce solid results...The conservative wants to conserve the great structural reality which has been given us and which is on the whole beneficial.[129]

"There is," argued Weaver, "iron in our nature sufficient to withstand any fact that is present in a context of affirmation...."[130] Poignantly reflecting his conservatism of affirmation, Weaver concluded:

> [W]e are eager to know whether, on the broad issues of this life, [a man stands] with the pessimists or the optimists. This is putting the matter in simple terms, of course; but humanity has a clear mind on this issue; it will not have for its great teachers those who despair of the condition of man. It will read them for excitement; it will utilize them as a corrective, but it will not cherish them as its final oracles. It prefers Aristotle to Diogenes and Augustine to Schopenhauer. It does not wish to hear said, however brilliantly, that life is a tale told by an idiot; it wants an unmistakable, if chastened, recommendation of life.[131]

In seeking a philosophy sustaining a recommendation of life," Weaver turned to those venerable traditions of Western thought that spoke in terms of meaning, purpose, and truth— in terms of affirmation: He turned to the Platonic-Christian heritage and its manifestation in the American South. In response to this modern age that had denied categorically—and often perversely and gleefully—notions of meaning, purpose, truth, and that had succumbed to nominalism and its progeny of fanaticism and nihilism, Weaver declined to posit a conservatism of despair and negation. He responded by articulating a conservatism of hope and affirmation—a firm foundation for a founding father to have laid.

# Frank S. Meyer

Frank Straus Meyer generally is recognized as one of the key figures in the American conservative movement of the post-World War II period. Born in New Jersey, in 1909, he attended Princeton University and received B.A. and M.A. degrees from Balliol College of Oxford University. In addition, his formal education included graduate study at the London School of Economics and the University of Chicago. After over a decade of membership in the Communist Party, at the close of World War II Meyer broke intellectually and politically with communism and devoted the balance of his life to the American conservative movement. He played an active role in the founding and development of the American Conservative Union. Moreover, he served as an editorial advisor to *Modern Age*, where many of his most seminal works originally appeared, and he was well known as one of the senior editors of *National Review*, where his regular column, "Principles and Heresies," became an institution. At the time of his death in 1972, Meyer converted to Roman Catholicism. He was survived by his wife, Elsie, herself an active participant in the conservative movement, and two sons, John and Eugene.

## I

In the political philosophy of Frank S. Meyer the core concept is that of *the individual*. Throughout his works, one finds Meyer returning inevitably to the theory that it is the individual who lies at the center of a mature and developed political philosophy. In his major and definitive work, *In Defense of Freedom*, Meyer wrote,

"My central endeavor is to validate the individual person as the decisive concern of political action and political theory."[1] Similarly, in one of his most probing treatises, Meyer stated that "the individual person" is "the ultimate repository of meaning and value."[2] Finally, as one of the leading exponents of American conservative thought, Meyer contended, "[T]he primary reference of conservative political and social thought is to the individual person.... [C]onservative thought is shot through and through with concern for the person."[3]

In Meyer's view, the struggle in the West to place the individual at the center of political thought had been long and arduous. In the ancient Middle East, men were conceived as minute cellular parts of an organic whole. The cosmos was directed by hidden forces and the rhythms of nature; the individual was locked into circumstances beyond his comprehension and control; and fatalism and determinism were the keys to explanation. The Hellenic spirit moved understanding beyond this inscrutable fatalism of oriental despotism; however, it too had to be content with leaving man in a collectivity—the polis—whose principal virtue was to be a collectivism less brutal and total than that of earlier despotism. The Judaic experience was an improvement over the Hellenic, for the God of the Jews did often explain and define in terms of the individual person; yet even here, the emphasis was upon the collectivity of the Chosen People. Meyer explained:

> The potentialities for full individuation inherent in the concept of a God of Righteousness were collectivized. The concept of the *b'rith*, the compact between God and the Chosen People, placed the collectivity of the Judaic people, rather than the individuals who made up that collectivity, as the receptor of the interchange with transcedence. The Prophets strove mightily with these circumstances, as the Greek philosophers struggled with the circumstances of the *polis*. Future events have taken from them both an inspiration and an understanding that are derived from the thrust of their struggle towards individuation, but neither the philosophy of Hellas nor the prophecy of Israel ever completely

threw off the conditioning influence of their social and intellectual heritage.[4]

In the Western tradition, the symbol of the Incarnation establishes the individual permanently and irrevocably "as the ordering principle, the fount and end of social being."[5] According to Meyer, this is the irrefutable and primal fact of "the constitution of being": "The Great Commandment, which is the cornerstone of the structure of Western moral thought, reflects this hierarchy of values, ignoring utterly everything but God and individual persons: 'Thou shalt love the Lord thy God with all thy heart, and with all thy soul, and with all thy strength, and with all thy mind; and thy neighbour as thyself.' "[6] Regarding the central symbol of the Incarnation, Meyer concluded, "For no community, no state, no association–only persons, individual human beings—can receive the beatific vision or be redeemed by the divine sacrifice of love."[7]

The key to understanding Frank Meyer is to appreciate fully that the Christian faith is the *summum bonum* of his thinking, and all other ideas flow from that fact and are corollaries to it. It is the Christian view which elevates the individual person to the central position of Western political thought, for it is this view which goes beyond the collectivist limitations of earlier Middle Eastern, Hellenic, and Judaic thinking, and categorically asserts the moral reality of individual being and the existence of the transcendent. Moreover, the chasm between individual and the transcendent can be overcome only by accepting the reality and the power of the Incarnation. It is the Christian perception, Meyer argued, which gives the individual life worth and dignity: a worth and dignity decreed and guaranteed by the Creator. In sum, God creates and loves the individual, not abstract collectivities, and it is this primal fact which drives us to the profoundest level of understanding wherein the individual person is considered "the central moral entity, and society as but a set of relations between persons, not as an organism morally superior to persons."[8]

In addition to this core principle of the individual, Meyer embraces corollary principles of "virtue" and "freedom." From his perspective, the achievement of Christian virtue is the ultimate end to be pursued by the individual. This Christian virtue, rooted in faith, can be partially discerned through reason, and, of course, lest man become too prideful in reflecting on his own capacities, it is to be remembered that this virtue is ultimately dependent on "the sustenance of God's grace."[9]

In Meyer's thinking, the pursuit of Christian virtue is an individual moral question of the highest order; however, it is not a *political question*, and it is not a matter of concern to the state because "virtue" is only virtue when it is freely chosen. Virtue cannot be forced or coerced. To facilitate its achievement, the fundamental political problem is the establishment and maintenance of freedom.[10] Freedom means *choice*, and in Meyer's words, "[O]nly if there exists a real choice between right and wrong, truth and error, a choice which can be made irrespective of the direction in which history and impersonal Fate move, do men possess true freedom.... [T]he glory of man's being is that he is free to choose good or evil, truth or error...."[11] On another occasion Meyer reasoned, "I assert the right of individual freedom not on the grounds of utility but on the grounds of the very nature of man and the nature of the drama of his existence. He lives between good and evil, beauty and ugliness, truth and error, and he fulfills his destiny in the choices he makes."[12] If, as noted, "the primary reference of conservative political and social thought is to the individual person," Meyer concluded of his two corollary concepts, "[T]his double allegiance to virtue and to freedom is the over-all consensus of contemporary American conservatism...," and "[t]he love of liberty and the love of truth are not the hostile standards of irreconcilable parties; rather, they form together the twin sign of any viable conservatism."[13]

In view of his first principle of the free man pursuing Christian virtue, it follows that Meyer assigned to the state the fundamental responsibility to maintain conditions essential for political freedom. Christian virtue is the ultimate end; individuals (not collectivities) pursue virtue; virtue cannot be externally coerced, but must be freely chosen by individuals; therefore, it is the responsibility of the state to preserve the conditions of freedom.

What are these essential conditions of freedom? More particularly, what are the legitimate functions of the state? Meyer explained, "[T]he protection of the nation from foreign enemies; the preservation of internal physical order; and the concomitant existence of a system of justice to judge the disputes of man with man. These are the necessary functions of the state."[14] Concerning the American experience, Meyer wrote, "[A] government limited in its power to the maintenance of internal and external order [is] the concept upon which our Republic was founded," and he emphatically asserted the responsibility of American conservatism "to achieve the protection of individual liberty in an ordered society by limiting the power of government."[15] He elaborated:

> Conservatives support the preservation of the elements of the structure thereby created; restriction of government to its proper functions; within government, tension and balance between local and central power; within the Federal Government, tension and balance between the coordinate branches. They strive to reestablish a federal system of strictly divided powers, as far as government itself is concerned, and to repulse the encroachment of government, federal or state, upon the economy and the individual lives of citizens.[16]

It was Meyer's thesis that government grievously erred when it went beyond these "natural bonds" and attempted to coerce virtue and to promote the collective good:

> A 'law of parity' would seem to be operating whereby, as the State enlarges its claims and directs its power towards the total domination of society, it fails more and more to be able to do that for which we must depend upon the State: to preserve our order internally and against external enemies.[17]

In this connection, Meyer contended that as the United States had become increasingly welfare-state oriented, it had demonstrated a diminished capacity to preserve internal order. "Our great cities are becoming jungles where no man can go about his business or stroll in the public park in safety. . . ."[18] Similarly, with the rise of the welfare-state ethic, the courts, whose natural and proper function is to adjudicate disputes between individuals, have displayed increasingly less inclination to dispense "justice based on principle":

> In place of the immemorial counsels of jurisprudential and legal principle, expediency and climate of fashionable opinion (always, of course, unconscious factors bearing upon judges, but now consciously and unashamedly invoked) become the bases of judicial decision. With the sanction of positivist philosophy, enforcement of the prejudices of the Establishment becomes the norm, while the idea of even-handed and impartial administration of justice is scorned by the enlightened as a fairy tale from the Dark Ages.

> Thus the valid functions of the State decay with the growth of its tyrannical power over areas which should not be its concern.[19]

Finally, even in the vital area of affording protection from external enemies—the minimal responsibility of any state—the burgeoning American welfare state, although backed by a large military budget, had revealed an alarmingly reduced capacity to protect against foreign enemies:

> At the end of World War II and for a half a decade after, we possessed overwhelming military and material strength— and our enemies advanced one-third of a world closer to our jugular. In the years since, we have possessed, and we possess today, superior strength, and the enemy comes closer and closer without serious let or hindrance.[20]

Unquestionably, a careful analysis of Meyer's works yields up a political philosophy grounded in first principles: individualism, Christian virtue, freedom, and limited government. It is on this foundation that he builds; only by mastering this foundation can his political thinking be understood. In determining his theoretical position, Meyer did not choose on the basis of what appeared to be "the best" of currently available options; he rooted his position in those theoretical premises which he viewed as inherent in the order of being. Meyer came to his final philosophical position not as a matter of prudence or utility; he came to his ultimate conclusions because he perceived them as being the Truth: the Incarnation was a reality, and it required that we pursue a form of virtue; in order to pursue this virtue, reality demanded political freedom whereby individual choice could be made. These were the unyielding realities, and all sound human construction must be attuned to them. From Meyer's perspective, if the Incarnation is not ontologically the primal fact, then his entire theoretical structure collapses. He happily accepted that risk, for his depth of faith and his capacity for reason convinced him of the correctness of his position. One is reminded of Saint Paul's comment: "Christ Jesus himself being the chief cornerstone in whom the whole structure is joined together...."[21] As one commentator observed, "[Meyer] was, perhaps, more concerned with principle than almost any other leading conservative...."[22]

## II

The essential Meyer is missed if a discussion of his ideas is preoccupied with determining whether he was a "libertarian," a "traditionalist," or a "fusionist." Brent Bozell employed the term "fusionism" in describing Meyer's efforts to reconcile traditionalism and libertarianism.[23] Meyer's fundamental theoretical position is rooted in first principle, namely, the principle of the free man pursuing Christian virtue with a framework of limited government. To the extent that a theoretical position contributed to the achievement of that principled end, Meyer made it an integral part of his political philosophy; to the extent that political theories were obstacles to the attainment of that goal, Meyer rejected them.

In particular, Meyer utilized libertarian and traditionalist strains of thought to the degree that each strain contributed to the realization of his ultimate political ideal. Meyer himself used the term "fused" in describing his position: "That fused position recognized at one and the same time the transcendent goal of human existence and the primacy of the freedom of the person in the political order."[24] By "fusion" Meyer was not proposing a casual splitting of the difference between doctrinal libertarianism and traditionalism; nor was he talking about a forced amalgam of these two positions in order to placate their respective proponents. Rather, Meyer was unalterably wedded to his first principle of the politically free man pursuing Christian virtue. He accepted those facets of libertarianism and traditionalism that served this end, and rejected those that did not.

From Meyer's vantage point, libertarianism or classical liberalism (not to be confused, Meyer invariably warned, with contemporary statist liberalism) had made a substantial contribution to his theoretical ideal. In particular, it contributed to an understanding of political freedom, which is an indispensable element in Meyer's thinking. Classical liberalism, Meyer wrote, "[S]tood firmly for the freedom of the individual person, and in defense of that freedom developed the doctrine and practice of limited state power and the free economy."[25]

On the other hand, Meyer rejected those features of libertarian theory based on secularism, relativism, and utilitarianism. Concerning secularism, Meyer warned there is frightful danger in substituting "man for God and whim for value," and he cautioned, "[F]ree individualism uninformed by moral value rots at its core and soon surrenders to tyranny."[26] Secularism was the cardinal philosophical defect of the classical liberals: "Their error lay largely in the confusion of the temporal with the transcendent. They could not distinguish between the *authoritarianism* with which men and institutions suppress the freedom of men, and the *authority* of God and truth."[27] Without "the foundation of belief in an organic moral order," classical liberalism has left us adrift without rudder and compass; we are left with the moral aridity of relativism and utilitarianism. Relativism, Meyer explained, is

[T]he doctrine that no truth in reality exists; that whatever a culture believes is as good as what any other culture believes (cannibalism or human sacrifice are not wrong, only "culturally relative" modes of human action); that therefore the West has nothing of which to be proud, nothing for which to fight, nothing worth dying for.[28]

By virtue of relativist doctrine, "there is no good or evil, no high or low, no noble or ignoble."[29] Regarding relativists, Meyer admonished:

They are neither hot nor cold. And they cannot be responsible because no one has ever taught them to see the difference between good and evil, to define and to differentiate, to know a hawk from a handsaw. It is not possible to be responsible without the ability to define and separate good and duty from interest and passion.[30]

Classical liberalism, a progeny of secularism and relativism, leaves us ultimately with only utilitarianism as our operating norm, and that Meyer concluded is "a position not only philosophically unsound, but historically disastrous in its effects...."[31] In brief, without some conception of a transcendent moral order, it is impossible to develop an ethical and durable political theory, and the lack of that conception was the fundamental philosophical error of libertarianism. Hence, to the degree that libertarianism instructs us in the grammar of individual freedom, Meyer readily incorporated it into his political theory; to the extent it denies us any notion of an objective moral order, he repudiated it, for in the latter case it departs from an accurate understanding of the nature of being—its ontology is defective. Meyer summed up his position on the role of classical liberalism as follows:

The place of freedom in the spiritual economy of men is a high one indeed, but it is specific and not absolute. By its very nature, it cannot be an end of men's existence. Its meaning is essentially freedom from coercion, but that, important as it is, cannot be an end. It is empty of goal or norm. Its function is to relieve men of external coercion so that they may freely seek their good.[32]

As much as he respected and utilized its contributions, Meyer was critical of classical liberalism's making freedom an end in itself rather than a means to the end of the virtuous good life. Meyer's observation concerning Friedrich Hayek is revealing:

> I agree so strongly with almost all of Professor Hayek's analysis of contemporary social and economic problems, that it may seem somewhat churlish to note my disagreements with his theoretical position. I do so with the more diffidence—indeed with something approaching a sense of impiety—because I owe so much personally to his *Road to Serfdom*, which I read at a crucial moment in my life and which played a decisive part in helping me free myself from Marxist ideology. But I do not think that the utilitarian foundation upon which Professor Hayek bases his defense of freedom is either philosophically valid, or a bulwark strong enough to withstand the assaults of collectivist ideology.

> [Hayek] is a Whig, with all the moral and intellectual power of eighteenth-century Whiggism, infinitely superior to its French Revolutionary and Liberal successors. But he is a Whig with the flaw of Whiggism, its fear of acknowledging the absolute transcendent values upon which its strength is founded.[33]

Meyer's position on traditionalism's basic tenets depended, as was with classical liberalism, upon whether they served his first principle of the free man pursuing Christian virtue. As Meyer perceived it, European traditionalism was correct in its realization that the basic philosophical questions are those dealing with value, virtue, and the search for the Good Life; to that extent traditionalism was sound, and Meyer integrated it into his own philosophy. He found the weakness of traditionalism in its belief that virtue could be coerced by the state, by the rigid imposition of order. Here traditionalism was unwittingly borrowing from Rousseau; however, instead of man forced to be free, he was forced to be virtuous. To Meyer this was a perversion; it was at odds with the nature of things, for it misunderstood that virtue can only exist where it is *freely* chosen. Meyer explained:

> [European] conservatism, with all its understanding of the pre-eminence of virtue and value, for all its piety towards the continuing tradition of mankind, was far too cavalier to the claims of freedom, far too ready to subordinate the individual person to the authority of state or society.

> Sound though [European conservatives] were on the essentials of man's being, on his destiny to virtue and his responsibility to seek it, on his duty in the moral order, they failed too often to realize that the political condition of moral fulfillment is freedom from coercion.[34]

In warning of the excesses and defects of European traditionalism, Meyer observed that "truth withers when freedom dies, however righteous the authority that kills it . . ."; moreover, "the denial of the claims of freedom leads not to conservatism, but to authoritarianism and theocracy."[35] In sum: "*Virtue in freedom—* this is the goal of our endeavor."[36]

In concluding his critique of traditionalism, Meyer proposed: "The alternative to a Robespierre . . . is not a Bismarck but a Washington, not the agent of a Wilhelmine order, but the agent of a free constitutional order."[37] In his reference to George Washington and the American experience, we encounter a key tenet in Meyer's political philosophy; namely, that the American political philosophy, as conceived by its founders, is the best earthly expression we find of that ultimate political first principle: virtue growing in the soil of political freedom. Meyer contended that commitment to that principle is the great American consensus; it is *the* American political tradition.

Meyer reasoned that the American experience transformed European liberalism and conservatism. Classical European liberalism, he found, had been modified in the American thinking of the late eighteenth century from an excessive reliance upon the abstract, the amoral, the utilitarian, and the antireligious, to a more moderate, simple, and undogmatic emphasis upon individual freedom as the ultimate *political* good. Likewise, as Meyer viewed it, the founders of the American republic transformed European conservatism, in its obsession with authority, order, coercion, and control, into a moderate traditionalism that considered individual virtue the ultimate good. The genius of the American consensus, as envisioned by the Founders, Meyer contended, was to take the two incompatibles of classical European liberalism and conservatism, strip them of their excesses and rigidities, and in the process mold them together to form the bedrock of the American political tradition:

As Americans, indeed, we have a great tradition to draw upon, in which the division, the bifurcation, of European thought between the emphasis on virtue and value and order and the emphasis on freedom and the integrity of the individual person was overcome, and a harmonious unity of the tensed poles of Western thought was achieved in political theory and practice as never before or since. The men who created the Republic, who framed the Constitution and produced that monument of political wisdom *The Federalist Papers*, comprised among them as great a conflict of emphasis as any in contemporary American conservatism. Washington, Franklin, Jefferson, Hamilton, Adams, Jay, Mason, Madison—among them there existed immense differences on the claims of the individual person and the claims of order, on the relation of virtue to freedom. But their dialectic was conducted within a continuing awareness of their joint heritage. Out of that dialectic they created a political theory and a political structure based upon the understanding that, while truth and virtue are metaphysical and moral ends, the freedom to seek them is the political condition of those ends. . . ."[38]   This "joint heritage" was the essence of the American political tradition, and it was the vital center of contemporary American conservatism:

> The traditionalist and the libertarian within the contemporary American conservative movement are not heirs of European conservatism and European liberalism because they draw from a common source in the American constitutional consensus.

> In a sense, we American conservatives are at the same time both Tory and Whig, both traditionalist and libertarian.[39]

Meyer charged contemporary American conservatism with the responsibility of restoring and defending that "consensus" which was, as he saw it, under heavy siege from secular collectivism. In coming to his conclusions regarding libertarianism and traditionalism and their respective relationships to the American tradition and contemporary American conservatism, Meyer acknowledged his substantial debt to Richard Weaver's *Ideas Have Consequences*, which contains, according to Meyer, "the informing principle of the contemporary American conservative movement . . ."[40]

## III

As Meyer saw it, the utopian impulse was the fatal flaw in modern, secular collectivism. Where Reinhold Niebuhr spoke of "redemptive history," Thomas Molnar of "the perennial heresy," and Eric Voegelin of "gnosticism," Frank Meyer defined utopianism as an ideological bent of the modern mind that believes "human beings can be manipulated and 'structured' like beams of steel to satisfy an engineer's blueprint. . . ."[41] The utopian was at war with the nature of man, with "the constitution of being," and with "the ontological order laid up in Heaven."[42] The utopian becomes a hardened ideologue railing against God for the inadequacy of His work. Decreeing the death of God because of

81

His failure, the utopian proceeds to construct his own perfected, earthly New Jerusalem. Meyer explained: "Utopias—constructions which ignore the limitations of reality—have always been the creations of ardent souls who dream of a world free of imperfection and contradiction."[43] And what would the utopians' substitute for God's imperfect handiwork? They would, Meyer wrote, "[R]eplace God's creation of this multifarious, complex world in which we live, and substitute for it their own creation, simple, neat and inhuman—as inhuman as the blueprints of the bulldozing engineer."[44]

By rejecting God and the meaning of the Incarnation, the utopian commits egregious error, for he rejects the very order of being: Man is made the Creator—he is no longer merely creature—and he becomes "the center and measure of all things"; man becomes God. Human reason takes on the aura of the divine and the eternal. This new god, 'human reason', would reorder creation to conform to the mind's eye view of the utopian, the power of the state the instrument by which that end is to be attained:

> Utopians... seeing in political power the engine for the creation of a world in their own image of perfection, have glorified and divinized the state... The state, which is the sole universally accepted respository of force, need only be captured, and that force extended beyond its natural purposes. The state, therefore, becomes the great engine of social transformation. Every revolutionary movement of the last two centuries... ends by deifying the state it has captured and theologizing the concept of the state. Jacobinism, Marxism, Fascism, collectivist liberalism, each in its own way has joined intellectually and emotionally in the deification of the state...[45]

With American conservatism committed to that first principle of the free man seeking Christian virtue in a community of limited government, Meyer came naturally and inexorably to this conclusion:

The cast of American conservative thought is profoundly antiutopian. While it recognizes the continuing historical certainty of change and the necessity of basic principle being expressed under different circumstances in different ways, and while it strives always for the improvement of human institutions and the human condition, it rejects absolutely the idea that society or men generally are perfectible. In particular, it is perennially suspicious of the utopian approach that attempts to *design* society and the lives of human beings, whether in the light of abstract rationalist ideas or operational engineering concepts.[46]

From this explanation, it is clear that Meyer is not articulating an unreasoned, organic, evolutionary conservatism (a "natural conservatism" as he called it); he is acknowledging the limitations of reason and expressing confidence in it:

But to stress the impossibility of constructing a Utopia, to insist upon the inherent limitations in the nature of things that inhibit logical perfection in society, is not to resign the function of reason in political thought. Although social and political institutions can never reflect with the perfection of a geometrical image the ideal that a theory based upon the nature of man demands of them, it nevertheless remains true that it is only possible to think and act at the same time morally and intelligently in the political sphere if an ideal standard is constantly kept in view.

That the ideal can never be realized in an imperfect world is no more reason for giving up the effort to move towards it than—to use an analogy from mechanics—the impossibility of ever achieving the perfect frictionless machine is reason to give up the effort to reduce friction to a minimum.[47]

In essence, the difference between Meyer and the utopian is the difference between philosophy and ideology. The philosopher, conceding his mortal limitations, seeks knowledge and virtue; the ideologue, convinced of his omniscience, lusts after power and control, and he marshals ideas in service to the attainment of those ends. The man of philosophical bent pursues discourse and improvement; the follower of ideology resorts to propaganda (no need to discourse, for he knows the Secular Truth) to spread the dogma, and he seeks—nay, demands—not merely improvement, but immediate, earthly perfection. Where the philosopher is tolerant and relishes diversity and pluralism, the ideologist is bigoted and intensely hostile to spontaneity and to the contradictions and paradoxes of the human condition. In short, the philosopher is intellectually comfortable with the complexity wrought by human individuality, while the utopian—the practitioner of ideology—is impulsively driven to the realization of the collectivist whole.

As Meyer viewed it, collectivism in its variety of forms is the principal affliction of modern political thought. Moreover, the origins of modern collectivism are European, not American; in particular, in Meyer's analysis, Rousseau was the major theoretician of the collectivist mind and "became the presiding genius of the 200-year crisis of the West...."[48] Severing all ties from the biblical view of man, Rousseau and his disciples declared the innate goodness of man as a collectivity. To the extent that man fell short of perfection, the blame lay with institutions, with "priest" and "king." Because of the inherent goodness of man, remove the institutional restraints "imposed" by cloth and crown—in a word, by society—and man would flower into fulfillment. If the General Will could be "freed," the potential for achievement was limitless.

The abstraction of the General Will "was identified neither with the particular will of individuals nor of groups nor even of a majority, but with an assumed underlying real will of the totality...."[49] And who determines the "real will of the totality"? Is it a matter of individual choices or of group preferences or of majority will, as determined by an actual participating majority—or of any combination thereof? These are the crucial questions, and

Rousseau and his intellectual descendants answer that none of these—neither individuals nor groups nor majorities—will determine the "real will of the totality"; instead, a select body—elites—will make the ultimate determination. Modern collectivism, in the tradition of Rousseau, is then dependent on elites for direction, guidance, and control; the elites know what is best for the collective whole; they discern more keenly than the collectivist mass what should be the ends of society. A dichotomy arises between the elite and the masses. Individual choice, group differences, even majority and minority conflicts, are submerged into the collectivist whole which is under the control of the elites. In the collectivist mass, differentiation is destroyed; hierarchy, diversity, spontaneity, and individuality are viewed as the implacable enemies: egalitarianism is the new idol and it is the state to which the elites turn in search of the power needed to manipulate, control, and direct the inert mass. In brief, through control by the elites, we arrive at "[T]he primacy of society and the state over the individual, which is the essence of collectivism...."[50]

## IV

Contemporary American liberalism is the principal manifestation of the collectivist mind in the United States. In the American experience, as Meyer saw it, Andrew Jackson, Abraham Lincoln, and Franklin D. Roosevelt were the major architects of emerging liberal collectivism. Jackson, the least offensive of the three in Meyer's judgment, introduced the concept of "mass democratism." It was Jackson who promoted the theory of the activist, elitist President who would mobilize the masses (called "the people" in the American context) for the journey into the worldly promised land. It was Lincoln who destroyed, at the expense of the states, that vital balance of American federalism, and tipped the balance of the federal system in favor of the power of the central national government. Meyer is uncompromising in his strong condemnation of Lincoln's political role:

Sometimes there are judgments at which one hesitates to

state publicly, out of respect for deeply held beliefs and prejudices. I have over a number of years come to think that the general admiration for Abraham Lincoln is ill founded.... Particularly...it has been borne in upon me more and more that his pivotal role in our history was essentially negative to the genius and freedom of our country.

The issue is not really...whether Lincoln was or was not a humanitarian. So far as this is concerned, suffice it to say that against Lincoln's magnificent language and his personal acts of individual kindness there must be placed in the balance the harshness of his repressive policies and his responsibility for methods of waging war approaching the horror of total war.[51]

Nor does Meyer excuse "the incalculable damage for which Lincoln is responsible" on the premise that he was abolishing the evil of slavery (and Meyer agreed it was an evil institution) "because both Lincoln himself and most of his defenders...deny that the abolition of slavery was ever Lincoln's intent."[52] Instead, argued Meyer, "[U]nder the spurious slogan of Union, he moved at every point (no matter that he would have preferred to achieve his ends without war; so would every ideologue) to consolidate central power and render nugatory the autonomy of the states."[53] Thus Lincoln's goal, by his own admission, was maintenance of the Union through the creation of a powerful centralized government and through reliance upon total war:

Total war is war conducted to achieve victory neglecting every other moral end. It is least excusable, moreover, in a war between brothers. Nevertheless this was Lincoln's pattern of war leadership: in the North, a repressive dictatorship; against the South, the brutal meat-grinder tactics of "Unconditional Surrender" Grant and the brigand campaigns waged against civilians by Sherman; in war aims, no effort at reconciliation, only the complete triumph of central government.[54]

Continuing his indictment, Meyer wrote:

Nor, once battle was engaged, did Lincoln wage the war in a manner calculated to bring about the conditions of reconciliation. He waged it to win *at any cost*—and by winning he meant the permanent destruction of the autonomy of the states. We all know his gentle words, "with malice toward none, with charity for all," but his actions belie this rhetoric.[55]

In Meyer's judgment, it was Lincoln's responsibility to pursue a course of action consistent with the American political tradition of individualism and limited government. Lincoln violated both political tenets: he sacrificed the concept of individualism to that of some chimerical notion of an egalitarian, collectivist whole, and he enhanced the power of the central national government to such unprecedented proportions that the foundation of American federalism was dramatically and permanently altered. Under the historical circumstances, what alternative did Lincoln have?

Had he been less the ideologue, he could have let the seven states which seceded before Sumter go, and thus hold Virginia (the key to future unity) and the others in the Union, relying upon the passage of time, the congruity of natural interest, and the exercise of statesmanship to reunite the federal structure.[56]

In concluding his assessment of Lincoln, Meyer explained:

Were it not for the wounds that Lincoln inflicted upon the Constitution, it would have been infinitely more difficult for Franklin Roosevelt to carry through his revolution, for the coercive welfare state to come into being and bring about the conditions against which we are fighting today. Lincoln, I would maintain, undermined the constitutional safeguards of freedom as he opened the way to centralized government with all its attendant political evils.[57]

The "fateful election of 1932," and the ensuing New Deal, were "decisive in the triumph of liberal collectivism in the United States...."[58] Franklin Roosevelt build upon the foundations laid by Andrew Jackson and Abraham Lincoln and thereby brought about "the naturalization in the United States of 20th-century collectivist principles and methods..."[59] Nourished and developed by the theoreticians of the "Roosevelt revolution," American "liberal-collectivist dogma" took on its most defined and pronounced form:

> Socially, it assumes the existence of an organism, "society," as the being to which, and to the good of which, all moral (and by the same token, political) problems finally refer. Sometimes this principle is modified, but never by intrinsic reference to the individual person, only (when the totalitarian implications of total reference to "society" loom too large) by reference to collectivist images of specialized groups of individuals: "minorities," "the underprivileged," "the elite," "scientists," "gifted children," "backward children," "labor." Concern is never for, there is no moral reference to, a man who is a Negro, a poor man, a rich man, a well-born man, an able man, a biologist, a child, a carpenter.[60]

It is then to the collectivist whole—not individuals—to which the fully developed liberal dogma looks, and it opts for a managerial bureaucratic elite to exercise control of the collectivist mass through a central national government with vastly enhanced powers of regulation and taxation. In his concluding paragraph of analysis on the basic tenets of contemporary American liberalism, Meyer wrote:

> Emotionally, it prefers psychoanalysis to the dark night of the soul, "adjustment" to achievement, security to freedom. It preaches "the end of ideology," admires experts and fears prophets, fears above all commitment to value transcending the fact.[61]

## V

In Meyer's thinking, the most pernicious form of collectivism is modern totalitarianism. It was Communist totalitarianism with which Meyer himself was personally familiar and about which he wrote most extensively. Meyer also strongly opposed Fascism.[62] For more than a decade during the era of the 1930s, Meyer had been a Communist and had worked for the Party in England and in the United States. Only after a long period of self-examination did he reject Communism and commence the journey that would lead him to Christianity and ultimately to his embracing Roman Catholicism immediately prior to his death. Meyer's classic work in this area is *The Moulding of Communists*. This major work, along with his *In Defense of Freedom*, must be considered his principal contribution to political thought in general and to American conservatism in particular.

In *The Moulding of Communists*, Meyer lays bare the ideological character of the Communist mind, and he brings into sharp focus the profound conflicts between Communism and Meyer's philosophical ideal of the free, Christian man pursuing his destiny within the limited political state. Communism rejects Meyer's ideal on every count: for Christianity it substitutes a virulent atheism; instead of the concept of the free individual person, it is predicated upon the theory of an elite relentlessly molding a collectivist whole; and, as opposed to Meyer's limited state, Communism creates a state totalist in its scope and depth. At the highest theoretical level, in Meyer's view, the fundamental conflict between Communism and his ideal is a religious one; in essence, then, the issue is a struggle between two irreconcilable faiths. Concerning the origins of his ideal, Meyer wrote:

The Hellenic and Hebraic traditions of the dignity of the individual man, fused by Christianity in the self-sacrifice of a divine Person, imbue the deep consciousness of the West with that view of the human person as ultimately sacred which takes ethical form in the Golden Rule.... Very few men actually live always by this maxim; but most men in the

West accept it in some form or other as the way they *ought* to live.[63]

Regarding the matter of the basic philosophical difference between Communism and the Western ideal, Meyer observed, "What is intrinsic to the religious outlook—piety, humility, love—is missing from the Communist outlook."[64] The religious temper of the West is rooted in an abiding sense of awe and reverence—piety—for the mystery and majesty of creation; there is an undeniable sense of the meaning and the reality of the transcendent; there is an awareness of the chasm between man and his Creator; and there is a profound appreciation that the chasm can be bridged only through the Incarnation. The religious mind of the West has no illusions about the perfectibility of the human condition; when used to describe the human situation, it understands the meaning and relevance of the ancient concepts: sin, evil, tragedy, frailty, and finitude. In a word, there is intellectual humility before the ineffable creation. This humility is a precondition to the acquisition of faith and ultimately of that faith "working through love": love of God the Creator, and love of one's neighbor.

In contrast, "Communism is the child of unbelief."[65] To the Communist there is no sense of mystery concerning the indescribable wonder of creation; there is no awareness of the transcendent; rather, from the Communist vantage point, "man is self-produced." With no sense of mystery, with no awareness of the transcendent, the Communist mind is incapable of piety, humility, and ultimately of love: "Communism lives in the conviction that, having mastered the secrets of Necessity and History, power over nature and man is in its hands."[66] Or as one young Russian Communist, whom Meyer quoted, put the matter:

We are believers. Not as you are. We do not believe either in God or in men. We manufacture gods and we transform men. We believe in Order. We will create a universe in our image, without weaknesses, a universe in which man, rid of the old rags of Christianity, will attain his cosmic grandeur, in the supreme culmination of the species. We are not fighting for a regime, or for power, or for riches. We are the instruments of Fate.[67]

As Marx himself had instructed, "The philosophers have only *interpreted* the world, the point however is to *change* it"; the end sought, to borrow Eric Voegelin's phrase, is to gain "dominion over being"; or as Meyer described it, the Communist goal is "to seize the wheel of history, to wipe out the heavens, to remake the world and man..."[68] Concluded Meyer, "It is not with consumers' durable goods that [Communists] appeal, but with the concept of collectivist man as the maker of heaven and earth."[69] Because Communism rejected the philosophical and religious heritage of the West with their emphasis upon intellectual humility and the pursuit of knowledge, and substituted hubris, utopian ideology, and a fanatical commitment to action to that ideology, Meyer observed:

There probably has existed nowhere in history so widespread and powerful a doctrine without a systematic statement of its principles. Marxism-Leninism has no *Summa*, no *Institutes*, no *Discourse on Method*, no *Essay concerning Human Understanding*—not even an *Il Principe* or a *Leviathan*. All its foundation stones are occasional polemics. (*Capital* and *The Communist Manifesto* might be considered possible exceptions, but they too are full of polemics and their essential inspiration is polemical.)...The authoritative political texts are all directed to a particular action or a particular controversy.... Thought for thought's sake or for the sake of pure knowledge is, from the Marxist-Leninist viewpoint, not merely sterile; in the last analysis it is impossible.... Virtue, full-bodied existence, resides only in the apprehension of life as action "to change the world."[70]

In this call for action "to change the world," Communism perpetrates a massive "assault upon the autonomy of the person," upon the "innate and unique value of the person which lies at the heart of the Western ethos."[71] Communist ideology demands elimination of the autonomous person; it requires the casting of a new collectivist mold into which the human personality, no matter how unique and distinctive, will be compelled to fit. The "molding" of the Communist cadre is the remaking of the individual man as the West has traditionally known him. As Meyer had personally experienced it, the new collectivist man is forced into total subservience to the will of the Party:

> For, "soul of a soulless universe" and god of a godless world, the Party idolatrously takes to itself the stance of God to Job: "Where wert thou when I laid the foundations of the earth? declare if thou hast understanding." Only by a god can such acceptance be demanded and only to a god can it be given without the utter destruction of self-respect. And this is the goal of the process: to force a transformation of the person in such a way as to preserve his necessary self-respect and at the same time make of him a loyal and driving microcosm of the Party.[72]

Because of the powerful ideological grip the Communist Party achieves upon its cadre through the transformation of the human personality, Meyer noted that defection of the *bona fide* Communist cadre is a rare phenomenon. He agreed with Whittaker Chambers observation:

> Thirty years after the Russian Revolution, after the known atrocities, the purges, the revelations, the jolting zigzags of Communist politics, there is only a handful of ex-Communists in the whole world.... By an ex-Communist, I mean a man who knew clearly why he became a Communist, who served Communism devotedly and knew why he served it, who broke with Communism unconditionally and knew why he broke with it. Of these there are very few—an index of the power of the vision and the power of the crisis.[73]

Meyer noted, "Communist theory is powerful not because it is true; most obviously it is not. It is powerful because *it is believed*."[74] Moreover:

It is in men, Communist men, that theory and practice fuse. Thus they become History: "We are the future." Arrogating to themselves a quality, the unity of thought and action, which is manifestly absurd in men—which Western thought has always attributed as a distinguishing quality of God— they acquire a strength and confidence which, like the fearful evil they bring into being, can only be described as Luciferian.[75]

What will loosen this satanic grip? According to Meyer, to find the answer one must probe to the deepest level of under standing: "[T]he Communist personality is like that transparent sphere of legend which no sword or axe could mar, but which flew apart in a thousand pieces at the playing of the right note of music."[76]

What is "the right note of music"? It manifests itself when the Communist cadre recognize "with a power that could not be denied that something was true and real which, by its truth and reality, shattered the foundations on which their life was built."[77] The will to change "rests in the end on belief": belief in the transcendent, and in the right order of things; belief in the sacredness and dignity of each individual personality as a unique product of God's creative capacity; and belief in the limited state where the individual can order and direct his own life—to virtuous ends. Such change in belief must take place "in the recesses of men's souls."[78] The journey of change in belief can be triggered by what would appear on first examination to be inconsequential matters: in the case of Whittaker Chambers, it was "the emotional impact of an infant daughter on him"; in Meyer's case, it was the simple fact of physical separation from Communist Party activity during his service in the Army.[79] As dissimilar as the triggering factors are in these two cases, the common denominator is a slight cracking of the ideological crust by a fleeting glimpse of the real and concrete, and a temporary distraction and disengagement from a world powerfully bound by abstraction and ideology. A new sensitivity is subtly sparked; there is a slight but perceptible turning from the Communist perspective which "examines an individual very much as a carpenter examines a piece of lumber."[80]

The new sensitivity instills an appreciation for the mystery and complexity of life; it generates a sense of piety the marvel of creation; it arouses respect for the reality of the transcendent. Here one comes full circle with a commencing change in belief. In essence, as Meyer had contended, the crucial point of difference between traditional Western philosophy and the ideology of Communism is a religious one.

Meyer greatly lamented the inability of the American liberal (with rare exception) to understand the ideological underpinnings of Communist actions, and to appreciate that this ideology is unalterably hostile to the historical intellectual foundations of the West. In response to that perennial plank of liberal foreign policy that implores us to find a *modus operandi* with the Communists and to "compromise" with them, Meyer wrote, "[C]ompromise with Communism is the historical equivalent of a Norman Crusader proposing to a Moslem lesser acceptance of the doctrine of the Trinity as the basis for agreement between them."[81] Meyer further lamented:

> This utter lack of understanding of the phenomenon of Communism and of the extreme challenge it poses to the West is the foundation of the structure of Liberal foreign policy... [The Liberal] can conceive the Communists only as rougher and cruder species of Liberal, with whom we can have "common interests." This conflict between us, in [Liberal] ideology, does not spring from the principled devotion of Communism to the destruction of Western Civilization (the civilization of the free person and the transcendental moral law) and of the American Republic (the polity based upon the sanctity of the free person and the norm of the moral law). It is the result of a parallel guilt on both sides: *"We are both caught up in a vicious and dangerous cycle, with suspicion on one side breeding suspicion on the other, and new weapons begetting counterweapons."*[82]

In summary, Meyer warned, "This radical failure to understand the historical significance of Communism as an alien and inimical force bearing down upon the West is central to the suicidal program...[of American liberalism]."[83] Until contemporary American liberalism could instruct itself on the deep ideological and heretical cast of Communism, Meyer saw little opportunity to check the steady, strategic erosion of the West's position. American liberalism itself seemed to have fallen prey to that insidious virus (albeit an infinitely milder strain than that of the Communist infection) of secular collectivism; checking the course of the disease was precisely the crucial challenge facing the Western world.

Meyer left no doubt that the overriding reality of international politics in the twentieth century was "formed by the drive of the Soviet Union [undergirded by Communist ideology] toward world domination."[84] Furthermore, he argued:

> Nor can the danger be averted by Metternichian games of ...[playing power politics]. Metternich's policies were valid and effective for the settlement of Europe—but after Napoleon was defeated. *Our Napoleon has not yet been defeated.* It is not time for the machinations of a Metternich, but for the determination and fortitude of a Pitt.[85]

To put it bluntly: "[D]etente is an illusion."[86] Finally, Meyer admonished:

> The parallel between the course we are following and that which England has followed since World War II is sad to contemplate. Welfare and comfort, the decay of armaments, devaluation, withdrawal from a leading status in the world—all in one degree or another are here. But England followed this course safeguarded by the United States. If we continue on our present course, there is no greater power to shield us. The future, in the most literal sense, depends upon our recovery from the disease that grips us.[87]

In his last *National Review* column, written just before his death,

Meyer observed, "The true issue...is whether we face up to the sheer threat of survival, whether our leaders make clear the danger of Communism and the need to refurbish our armaments before it is too late."[88]

From the time he broke with Communism toward the close of World War II until his death in 1972, Meyer never relented in his opposition to Communism. To him it was the total antithesis of what the best of the religious and philosophical traditions of the West represented. Communism was secular elitist collectivism raised to the nth power; it represented a faith in satanic forces: omnicompetent man was elevated to the status of Creator; the ultimate in heresy had been perpetrated. As Meyer viewed the historical development of our time, it was the particular responsibility of the American conservative to resist in mind, body, and spirit the encroachments of this totalist ideology and to remind his fellow countrymen (and those elsewhere who would listen) that there was a great tradition of Western thought, inherent in the order of being, that needed restoration: a tradition arising from the mutual interdependence of Christian virtue, human freedom, and the limited state.

## VI

In his writings, Meyer spent considerable effort defining the type of conservatism for which he labored. He expressly rejected what he called the American "New Conservatism" as represented by such diverse writers as Peter Viereck, Clinton Rossiter, Robert A. Nisbet, John H. Hallowell, and Russell Kirk.[89] As different as these New Conservatives might be on various points of philosophy, emphasis, and interpretation, their common denominator, as Meyer viewed it, was a subordination of individualism to tradition and community; consequently, the New Conservatives were offering no opposition to the collectivist spirit of our time:

> It is at this point—in its attitude towards the person and society—that the New Conservatism fails most signally to offer resistance to collectivist liberalism.

Putting the individual person at the center of political thought is to them the greatest of political and social evils. Caught within the pattern of concepts inherited from classical political theory, they cannot free themselves from the doctrine that men find their true being only as organic parts of a social entity, from which and in terms of which their lives take value. Hence the New Conservatives cannot effectively combat the essential political error of collectivist liberalism: its elevation of corporate society, and the state which stands as the enforcing agency of corporate society, to the level of final political ends.[90]

The error of the American New Conservatism, Meyer reasoned, lay in its uncritical embrace of Burkean conservatism: "However, much one may respect [Edmund] Burke's stand as a practical statesman, it is impossible to derive a firm political position from him."[91] In Meyer's view, Burke must be admired for his eloquent denunciation of the philosophical enormities of French revolutionary thinking; however, it would be a cardinal error—and this was the error of the New Conservatives—to accept the Burkean reaction to the French Revolution as a theoretical premise from which an overall, general theory of the state could be extracted. Burke's thinking in the *Reflections* is heavily rooted in a perspective that is "historicist," and "expediential."[92] That is, given the historical setting of England in 1790 it was expedient (and understandable and appropriate) that Burke should defend the existing political institutions of England against the mindless fanaticism of the French revolutionaries and their English disciples; however, in defending the existing institutions of that time Burke tied himself to a historical period and his theories are not of general and universal applicability unless one is defending an existing good state against the encroachments of malevolent forces of revolution. In practical, historical terms, Burke's *Reflections*, although appropriate for the England of 1790, would have been inappropriate at the time of the Glorious Revolution of 1688: "His reliance upon tradition, upon prescription, upon prejudice in the circumstances of 1790 would, in the crisis of 1688, have made him the supporter of a very different policy and of very different principles."[93]

The Burkean conservative's preoccupation with "tradition," "prescription," and "prejudice" is at the core of his philosophical error. With Burke, this preoccupation is understandable: he is defending an existing good system against a potentially evil one. The error of the New Conservatives is to take a theory valid under the conditions in response to which Burke wrote and to elevate that theory to one of general and universal application. In making tradition the ultimate first principle of politics, the New Conservatives have unwittingly allowed to slip away the crowning first principle of Western political thought: that vision of the free individual pursuing Christian virtue within the framework of the limited state. If this ideal exists in a given society, "traditionalism" would be appropriate; if that ideal were nonexistent or had been subverted, then either creation or restoration respectively, rather than tradition, would be in order. With traditionalism as the guiding, universal first principle, the New Conservatives had come to look for final fulfillment of the human condition in the life of the community rather than in the dignity and fulfillment of each individual. In its obsession with tradition and community, the New Conservatism developed "an ethos tightly swaddled in the multitudinous wrappings of code and custom."[94] This brand of conservatism, Meyer argued, had sacrificed individual reason and genius to the collective, prudential judgment of the community; likewise, the crucial matter of individual free will and choice of virtue over vice were subordinated to the dictates of an ineffable, mystical Providence, and that vision of the free man seeking the transcendent was eclipsed by a fixation upon the immanent within the community."[95]

The "vindication of the person"—that primal theory of Western thought, wrought out of the experience of the Greek and Judaic heritages and given permanence and universality through the Incarnation—was not, Meyer concluded, well served by the New Conservatism:

Persons as such are anathema to the New Conservative doctrine, unless they are mere symbols for orders and ranks and hierarchies, stiffly disposed as in a Byzantine mosaic, signifying the abstract virtue of diversity. But Heaven forfend that they be actually diverse, individual human beings, unranked and uncontrolled. There is no place in the New Conservative conspectus for the person as such, for those who live as individuals—"humble to God, haughty to man"—scoring the bounds of a predetermined estate, vindicating the glory of the person as person.[96]

Or as Meyer explained it on another occasion:

[The New Conservative] is shaped by such words as "Authority," "order," "community," "duty" "obedience." "Freedom" is a rare word: "the individual" is anathema. The qualities of this suggested society are a mixture of those of eighteenth-century England and medieval Europe—or perhaps, more aptly, they are those of Plato's Republic with the philosopher-king replaced by the squire and the vicar.[97]

Meyer did not challenge the classical premise that "man is a social animal" nor did he attempt to refute the notion that society is inherent in the human condition: "I am not therefore proposing a Robinson Crusoe social theory or maintaining that the person is a monad-like atom, cut off and isolated from other persons."[98] Rather, he was challenging the ideology of collectivism (in whatever guise it might travel, including that of the New Conservatism) which went beyond the natural and commonsense observation that man is a social creature and proclaimed the ancient heresy that society is a living, organic, spiritual entity in its own right with rights antecedent and superior to those of the individual person.[99] The New Conservatism had made estimable contributions in the vital effort to restore an appreciation for value, virtue, and civility in an age which too often had succumbed to relativism, decadence, and boorishness; however, Meyer contended, the New Conservatism, with its roots in the

Burkean perspective, with its preoccupation with "community," "tradition," and "society," and with its subordination of the individual to the prerogatives of society, had failed on the crucial test of offering resistance to modern collectivism: "The New Conservatives are neither the champions of Leviathan that the collectivist liberals are, nor the enemies of Leviathan that the principled conservatives are, but mere critical observers of Leviathan undiminished."[100] Moreover, Meyer declared,

> The "liberals" are well aware of all this. They realize that the New Conservatives, with their emphasis on tone and mood, with their lack of clear principle and their virulent rejection of individualism...threaten no danger to the pillars of the temple.... The New Conservatism, stripped of its pretensions, is, sad to say, but another guise for the collectivist spirit of the age.[101]

In contrast to the "natural conservatism" of the New Conservatives, which accepts, in the tradition of Burke, the existing order as right and proper because dictated by Providence, Meyer offers a "principled" or "conscious conservatism."[102] By "conscious" he means that reason will be employed to discern fundamental and universal principles grounded in the nature of things. In addition, regardless of place and circumstance, reason will be used to instruct and guide men toward the realization of the principled ideal:

> Today's conservatism cannot simply affirm. It must select and adjudge.... We cannot simply revere; we cannot uncritically follow tradition, for the tradition presented to us is rapidly becoming—thanks to the prevailing intellectual climate, thanks to the schools, thanks to the outpourings of all the agencies that mold opinion and belief—the tradition of a positivism scornful of truth and virtue, the tradition of the collective, the tradition of the untrammeled state.[103]

We must then hold steady on course with our philosophical eye on "basic principle," upon "the truth of the great tradition of the

West."[104] As Meyer viewed it, that truth, of course, is symbolized in the Incarnation: it is through this symbol that the individual becomes the "central moral entity" and society and community are seen merely as matters of convenience and utility, not ends in themselves. Meyer noted a subtle but significant point; namely, that only individualism, not collectivism, is compatible with the symbol of the Great Commandment:

> Only the independence and autonomy of the person makes love or any other valid relationship between persons possible; were human beings but parts of a larger whole, their love, all their reachings out one to another, would be but the cellular interactions dictated by the tropisms of the larger organism.[105]

From any perspective in Meyer's thinking, the Incarnation is the primordial principle to which the "conscious" or "principled" conservative will turn in commencing the formidable task of restoration.

## VII

As a contributor to American conservative thought, Meyer was essentially a political theorist. Out of the twelve possible choices in the *Biographical Directory* of the American Political Science Association, Meyer listed his "field of interest" as "political theory and philosophy." As opposed to a literary, journalistic, or historical approach, Meyer thought, analyzed, and wrote in terms of theory. His style of writing reflects this quest for underlying theory: little concern for flair and effect, so characteristic of literary efforts; little preoccupation with elaborate presentation of detail and fact, so characteristic of the historian; and there is no concern for shock or entertainment value as is often found with journalistic styles. To Meyer, theory dealt with fundamentals, essences, ultimates; reflecting that fact, his writing is uncomplicated in construction, and in substance it moves unhesitatingly and unerringly to theoretical roots. Meyer sought theoretical truth and everything, including style, yielded to the achievement of that end.

It is curious that among some observers Meyer should have come to personify the pragmatic conservative, the "fusionist" who attempts to find a place for all in the house of conservatism. This is to misconstrue the essential Meyer. Careful analysis of his writings yields up a theoretical position that is unflinchingly principled. Meyer is not a "traditionalist" or a "libertarian," nor is he a "fusionist": the essential Meyer is a Christian theorist. The Incarnation is the point of departure in all of his serious theoretical works; remove that symbol as the foundation of his theoretical structure, and the entire edifice falls. If the Incarnation is invalid, if it does not inhere in the order of being, Meyer would concede—indeed, he would have to concede—his entire theoretical position is negated. Without the Incarnation, the individual *qua* individual can lay no claim to transcending personal dignity and worth. Similarly, a conception of virtue embedded in a transcendent nature of being becomes impossible, and a notion of individual freedom, whereby choice is to be exercised to choose the virtuous end, becomes meaningless. If the Incarnation has no validity, then no case can be made for the need of the limited state wherein the free man can seek virtue; without the Incarnation, the specter of the total state emerges whereby Man the Creator can erect the Earthly Eden.

In 1958 in a letter to William F. Buckley, Jr., Whittaker Chambers warned

> The Republican Party [and by implication the conservative movement] will become like one of those dark little shops which apparently never sell anything. If, for any reason, you go in, you find, at the back, an old man, fingering for his own pleasure some oddments of cloth (weave and design of 1850). Nobody wants to buy them, which is fine because the old man is not really interested in selling. He just likes to hold and to feel. As your eyes become accustomed to the dim kerosene light, you are only slightly surprised to see that the old man is Frank Meyer.[106]

In a sense, Chambers was correct in this observation. Meyer was confronting a world overwhelmingly secular, relativistic, and collectivist, and there is no trace in his writings that he is willing to relinquish one inch of ground to these tragic developments; rather, he erects as his impenetrable fortress against them an unalloyed Christian fundamentalism (fundamentalist in the best sense of the word), and that position he will not compromise.

Meyer would dissent categorically from those contending that conservatism need not be religious in its basic character; that conservatism can be built upon theoretical bits and pieces selected to suit individual taste. If conservatism seeks to attune itself to the ultimate essences, it must be not only religious in character, Meyer held, but unashamedly Christian in its basic theoretical premise. Meyer's conversion to Catholicism at the time of his death is evidence that he maintained this unyielding position to the end of his life. Meyer is a Christian theorist, and, as a result, his conservatism is a principled one of the highest order.

# Willmoore Kendall

By any reasonable standard of measurement, as Professor Jeffrey Hart in 1971 noted, Willmoore Kendall remains "the most important political theorist to have emerged in the twenty-odd years since the end of World War II."[1] Moreover, as regards the American political tradition, it can be argued that Kendall is the most original, innovative, and challenging interpreter of any period. Born in Oklahoma in 1909, Kendall received his undergraduate degree from the University of Oklahoma (B.A., 1927), and his graduate degrees from Northwestern University (M.A., 1928), Oxford University (B.A., 1935; M.A., 1938), which he attended as a Rhodes Scholar, and the University of Illinois (Ph.D., 1941). Kendall taught at various universities, including fourteen years at Yale. At the time of his death in 1967, he was Chairman of the Department of Politics and Economics at the University of Dallas. Kendall was a prime mover in the American conservative movement. His major works include *John Locke and the Doctrine of Majority-Rule* (1941), *The Conservative Affirmation* (1963), *The Basic Symbols of the American Political Tradition* (1970), and *Willmoore Kendall Contra Mundum* (1971). Among his more prominent students were William F. Buckley, Jr. and Professor George W. Carey.

## I

With his penchant for political basics and fundamentals, coupled with his keen interest in the American experience, it is not surprising that Willmoore Kendall was drawn to a study of John

Locke. John Locke invariably is considered the central figure of the American political tradition. Indeed, when speaking of the American experience we often speak of the "Lockean tradition" or the "Lockean heritage," and every schoolboy knows (or is supposed to know) that Thomas Jefferson, the patron saint of American democracy, borrowed extravagantly from Locke in drafting the Declaration of Independence, considered by conventional wisdom the most authoritative and eloquent statement of the theoretical foundations of the American tradition.

Kendall's classic work is perhaps *John Locke and the Doctrine of Majority-Rule.* In the world of political philosophy, Kendall was the inveterate dissenter from "accepted interpretations," and this book is part of the legacy. Kendall contended that the conventional interpretation of Locke, depicting him as an exponent of individualism and natural rights that transcended majority sentiments, was in error. Why had conventional scholarship on Locke been in error? According to Kendall, it was "an illustration of what happens when scholars abdicate responsibility for reading the books they criticize."[2] To put it otherwise (in one of Kendall's favorite phrases): "[T]he thesis of the present study is precisely that Locke did not say the things he is supposed to have said...."[3]

In the tradition of Leo Strauss, Kendall insisted on reading the original materials and the "universal confrontation of the text." In Kendall's words, this approach "demands, in principle at least, that we accept no sentence or paragraph from the *Second Treatise* as Locke's 'teaching' without first laying it beside every other sentence in the treatise, and attempt to face any problem, regarding the interpretation of that sentence or paragraph, posed by the presence within the text of those other sentences."[4] Kendall contended that conventional Lockean interpreters had operated upon the invalid assumption that the *Second Treatise* "will yield up its meaning to a hasty reader," whereas in fact he insisted the Second Treatise was "a book that wants months and months, or even years and years, of poring over."[5] After close textual analysis of this classic, Kendall challenged the conventional interpretation of Locke. Rather than a thinker wedded to notions of transcendent abstract natural rights and discrete individualism, Kendall found an exponent of absolute majoritarianism who contended that the individual had only those rights that society, through the political majority, wished to bestow upon him. The nature and form of those rights will depend upon social needs as defined by society. Thus individual rights are functional and changeable, not transcendent and absolute.

Kendall argued that Locke's state of nature was expository, not historical.[6] He expressly accepted G. E. G. Catlin's observation that

> It is irrelevant to enter into a full discussion of how far the theorists of social contract ever thought of the contract as having taken place at any historical epoch. A study of these writers would seem to lead to the conclusion that...they were never guilty of this *naivete*[7]

Kendall wrote, "[F]or Locke the law of nature and the law of reason are the same thing," and he noted Locke's statement that "no *rational* creature can be supposed to change his condition with an intention to be worse"; therefore, Kendall concluded, "The [Lockean] law of nature is, in short, a law which commands its subjects to look well to their own interests."[8] With Kendall's Locke, in pursuing its perceived interests through reason, society will define the rights, duties, and obligations of the individual. In this regard, society is antecedent to and controlling over any claimed inalienable or transcendent rights of the individual. Kendall found the following representative quotation from the *Second Treatise* unequivocal:

> To conclude, the power that every individual gave the society when he entered into it can never revert to the individuals again as long as the society lasts, but will always remain in the community, because without this there can be no community, no commonwealth....[9]

Kendall's Locke not only rejected any notion that individuals have rights superior to society's demands, but in addition embraced majoritarianism as the means by which society should order and express its interests and desires. Kendall found the following statements from the *Second Treatise* clear and unmistakable:

> When any number of men have so consented to make one community or government, they are thereby presently incorporated and make one body politic *wherein the majority have a right to act and conclude the rest.*

> For when any number of men have, by the consent of every individual, made a community, they have thereby made that community one body, with a power to act as one body, *which is only by the will and determination of the majority* ..., and it being necessary to that which is one body to move one way, it is necessary the body should move that way whither the greater force carries it, which is *the consent of the majority,* or else it is impossible it should act or continue one body, one community, which the consent of every individual that united into it agreed that it should; and so every one is bound by that consent to be *concluded by the majority.* And therefore we see that in assemblies impowered to act by positive laws, where no number is set by that positive law which improves them, *the act of the majority passes for the act of the whole* and, of course, determines, as having by the law of nature and reason the power of the whole.[10]

In sum, Kendall's Locke turned out to be the majority-rule democrat, and the majority had *unlimited* political power. Although not obligated under any notions of inalienable individual rights, is there any guarantee that Locke's majority will be respectful in some form of the individual integrity of the person? In the final chapter of *John Locke and the Doctrine of Majority-Rule,* Kendall discusses Locke's "latent premise," by which Kendall meant that with effort one can tease out of the *Second Treatise* some evidence of limits upon majoritarian action; however, Kendall cautioned that Locke never fully developed the point, and he called Locke's failure to deal in depth with this central issue the "capital weakness" of the *Second Treatise.*[11]

Throughout the *Second Treatise,* Locke offered such limitations on governmental action as "reason and common equity," "the public good," and the avoidance of "absolute arbitrary power" or "tyranny."[12] Similarly, Locke concluded, "It [the legislative] is a power that has no other end but preservation, and therefore can never have a right to destroy, enslave, or designedly to impoverish the subjects."[13] In these cases it is essential to understand that Locke was referring to limitations placed upon *governmental* institutions, such as the legislature or the executive, and not upon "the people." In the *Second Treatise,* "the people" as a whole is the ultimate and "supreme power," and *everything* else is subordinate.[14] In Locke's words, "Who shall be judge whether the prince or legislative act contrary to their trust. . . . To this I reply: The people shall be judge. . . ."[15] Lest there be any lingering doubt, Locke put the matter unequivocally in the final sentence of the *Second Treatise:*

> But if they have set limits to the duration of their legislative and made this supreme power in any person or assembly only temporary, or else when by the miscarriages of those in authority it is forfeited, upon the forfeiture, or at the determination of the time set, it reverts to the society, and the people have a right to act as *supreme* and continue the legislative in themselves, or erect a new form, or under the old form place it in new hands, *as they think good.*[16]

Furthermore, on the ultimate matter of revolution, in Locke of the *Second Treatise,* it was not individuals flaunting abstract rights who were granted the right of revolting. In Locke's words, "But if a long train of abuses, prevarications, and artifices, all tending the same way, make the design visible to *the people,* and *they* cannot but feel what *they* lie under and see whither *they* are going, it is not to be wondered that *they* should then rouse themselves and endeavor to put the rule into such hands which may secure to *them* the ends for which government was at first erected . . . ."[17] How do "the people" express their preferences in the matter? We are back to majoritarianism, for as Locke wrote, "Nor let anyone think this lays a perpetual foundation for disorder; for this operates not till the inconvenience is so great that *the majority feel it* and are weary of it and find a necessity to have it amended"[18]

It was Kendall's contention in his discussion of the "latent premise" that having placed ultimate power in the majority will of the people, Locke did not give explicit guidelines as to what shall limit the majority in exercising its power. That is, individuals and governmental institutions are limited, but what prevents the majority with unlimited power from trampling on the rights of individuals or minorities? In the *Second Treatise* there are no express limitations, according to Kendall, there is only the "latent premise" that the majority is "rational and just."[19]

Kendall published no article on Locke between 1941, the publication date of *John Locke and the Doctrine of Majority-Rule,* and 1966, when his article "John Locke Revisited" appeared in *The Intercollegiate Review.*[20] In this article, which is among the most intensely reasoned and intellectually challenging he has written, Kendall re-evaluated his positions on Locke. Kendall adhered to the basic thesis of his earlier work that Locke is not the abstract natural rights theorist of conventional wisdom, but rather is a "majority-rule authoritarian." In Kendall's words, "I find in Locke...no limit on the power of the majority to set up any form of government that meets its fancy, and thereby to withdraw any and every supposed individual right."[21] On this crucial point the Kendall of 1966 stands firmly with the Kendall of 1941.

Regarding the problem of "the latent premise," Kendall reversed his position on this matter, and admitted his "embarrassment" at having proposed this premise in his earlier work.[22] Kendall rejected the "latent-premise" argument that the majority can be counted on to respect individual natural rights and absolute standards of morality because it is "rational and just." He contended that the "latent premise" is simply not in the *Second Treatise,* and "is produced out of thin air, and *attributed* to Locke in a fashion that can only be called wholly gratuitous."[23] In his analysis of the text, the Kendall of 1966 refused to *read into* the text something that is not there solely for the purpose of giving a "sympathetic" treatment to an author in trouble. Thus by dropping the "latent-premise" contention of natural political virtue in the majority, the Kendall of 1966 sealed permanently Locke's fate as a majority-rule authoritarian, who placed no restrictions on majority will.

The Kendall of 1966 went beyond the Kendall of 1941 and expressly put Locke in the camp of the enemies of the great tradition of politics—in the camp of Machiavelli and Hobbes.[24] Kendall concluded that Locke is a progenitor of modern ideology and not of the enduring tradition of political philosophy. This results from Locke's basic premise in the *Second Treatise* that man "is willing to join in society with others who are already united, or have a mind to unite, for the mutual preservation of their lives, liberties, and estates, which I call by the general name 'property.' The great and chief end, therefore, of men's uniting into commonwealths and putting themselves under government is the preservation of their property."[25] It is the "right of self-preservation," then, that is at the center of Lockean thought. With this "right of self-preservation" being the first principle of Locke's political science, it naturally follows, Kendall argued, that consent alone becomes the basis of governmental legitimacy. That is, man owes no binding *obligation* or *duty* to anyone or anything, for the *right* of self-preservaton is the center and measure of all things political, and society will express and advance this right collectively through unlimited majoritarianism. Kendall contended that this Lockean philosophy contributed to the birth of modern ideology and the death of the normative tradition of political philosophy, which had made rights correlative to duties. Modern ideology knows nothing of duties, morality, ethics, and obligations; it knows only of the "right of self-preservation," and thereby it is at odds with the biblical and great traditions in political philosophy. This was Kendall's final analysis of Locke; he died a year after the important 1966 article was published.

*John Locke and the Doctrine of Majority-Rule* is generally

considered a classic in the literature on Locke. It is invariably cited in any discussion on Locke and in any bibliography relating to him. Kendall's view of Locke as absolute majoritarian was unique and clearly at odds with conventional interpretations which pictured Locke as master exponent of the inalienable natural rights of the individual. Kendall's thesis, although always cited, is generally ignored by writers on political thought. The well-known texts of George Sabine and William Ebenstein are typical. Sabine wrote:

> Locke set up a body of innate, indefeasible, individual rights which limit the competence of the community and stand as bars to prevent interference with the liberty and property of private persons....The foundation of the whole [Lockean] system was represented as being the individual and his rights, especially that of property. On the whole this must be regarded as the most significant phase of his political theory, which made it primarily a defense of individual liberty against political oppression.[26]

Similarly, Ebenstein stated, "The text of the Declaration [of Independence] is pure Locke, and the main elements of the American constitutional system—limited government, inalienable individual's rights, inviolability of property all directly traceable to Locke."[27]

Sabine and Ebenstein cited Kendall in their bibliographies; however, and this is the crucial point, they did not accept or refute Kendall—they simply ignored him. In that everyone concedes *John Locke and the Doctrine of Majority-Rule* is a classic among works on Locke, this is a troublesome point for students of political philosophy, and it deeply concerned Kendall. In his 1966 article on Locke he wrote:

> Judging from...the 'mainstream' of political theory scholarship, Kendall's 1941 Locke [has not] had any perceptible impact on the mine-run political theory scholars. The latter's general practice would seem to be either first, to ignore

[Kendall's Locke] altogether, or second, to mention [him] *en passant*, . . . but never, third, to enter into public debate with [him][28]

Kendall observed, "I conclude that the political theory profession is suffering from a mortal sickness."[29]

Kendall has a valid point. It is difficult to explain why an admittedly classic and seminal work and the substantive ideas it offered would be cited but ignored. To accept or refute would be permissible but to ignore is mystifying. Kendall was not protesting an imagined slight upon himself; rather, he was questioning why a glacial freeze should make the profession of political theory impervious to serious innovation.[30] Kendall was warning that the study of political philosophy may have succumbed to ideology, and that the inertia of ideology had left us only with ancient symbols which we are expected to accept without challenge. In particular, Locke is the ideological symbol of individualism and abstract natural rights, and the raising of points to the contrary is declared out of order. As to the validity of Kendall's thesis, it does challenge anyone to read with care the *Second Treatise* and conclude that it stands as the supreme call for individualism and abstract natural rights. It simply will not yield up that conclusion. At most, the *Second Treatise* presents a mixed picture of individualism and majoritarianism, but to find natural-rights individualism as anterior to and transcending society, government, and the majority will is to base conclusions on ideological assumption and not on careful textual analysis.

II

The related problems of "the public orthodoxy" and "the open society" were major concerns of Kendall throughout his professional career. In the reappraisal of 1941, Kendall's Locke emerged as an exponent of the public orthodoxy as expressed through the majority. As Kendall sees it, in Lockean thought, "In consenting to be a member of a commonwealth, therefore, he [the individual] consents beforehand to the acceptance of obligations which he does not approve, and it is right that he should do so because such an obligation is *implicit in the nature of community life.*"[31] Throughout *John Locke and the Doctrine of Majority-Rule,* the reader can discern Kendall's deep skepticism about constructing an ongoing political system on the foundations of abstract natural-rights individualism; to attempt to do so would be unnatural, contrary to the realities of human nature and the human condition.

In Kendall's political science, the public orthodoxy is a "way of life," identical with the Greek *politeia,* which refers to "the 'character' or tone of the community."[32] More particularly, the public orthodoxy is

> [T]hat matrix of convictions, usually enshrined in custom and "folkways," often articulated formally and solemnly in charter and constitution, occasionally summed up in the creed of a church or the testament of a philosopher, that makes a society The Thing it is and that divides it from other societies as, in human thought, one thing is divided always from another.

> That is why we may (and do) speak intelligibly of a Greek and Roman, or an American "way of life."[33]

From Kendall's perspective, "the existence of the *politeia* [i.e., the public orthodoxy] is the unquestioned point of departure for political philosophy," for it is the primordial fact of social and political existence.[34] The public orthodoxy is antecedent to all other political matters:

> Not only can society not avoid having a public orthodoxy; even when it rejects an old orthodoxy in the name of "enlightenment," "progress," "the pluralist society," "the open society," and the like, it invents, however subtly, a new orthodoxy with which to replace the old one. As Aristotle is always at hand to remind us, only gods and beasts can live alone—man, by nature, is a political animal—whose very political life demands a *politeia* that involves an at least im-

plicit code of manners and a tacit agreement on the meaning of man within the total economy of existence. Without this political orthodoxy...the state withers; contracts lose their efficacy; the moral bond between citizens is loosened; the State opens itself to enemies from abroad; and the *politeia* sheds the sacral character without which it cannot long endure.[35]

Since the state is founded upon the public orthodoxy, if the orthodoxy decays and disintegrates, the state itself will inevitably falter. It is an unyielding reality: The good and health of the political state are dependent upon the vitality and character of the public orthodoxy. In Kendall's political theory, not only is the public orthodoxy inescapably rooted in the order of being, but it is a positive good. Without it there is no society, no state, and civilized man, as we traditionally know him, is destroyed.

Kendall was strongly at odds with the dogmatic proponents of the "open society," who seemed to be contending that all public orthodoxies are evil—except, of course, the public orthodoxy that there are no public orthodoxies. One of Kendall's principal *bêtes noires* was John Stuart Mill, who was leading, as Kendall saw it, the attack of the open-society proponents on the concept of the public orthodoxy.[36] In his analysis of *On Liberty,* Kendall concluded that Mill was in fact an absolutist on the matter of freedom of expression. It is true that Mill made certain concessions on such matters as libel and slander, situations where children were involved, and incitement to crime; however, once these peripheral matters were conceded, Mill assumed an absolutist and dogmatic posture on the question of freedom of expression. Kendall considered the following representative quotations from *On Liberty* as dispelling any possible doubt on the matter:

> Protection, therefore, against the tyranny of the magistrate is not enough; there needs protection also against the tyranny of the prevailing opinion and feeling, against the tendency of society to impose, by other means than civil penalties, its own ideas and practices as rules of conduct on

those who dissent from them. [In short, the prevailing public orthodoxy is by definition "tyranny"and must be displaced.]

This, then, is the appropriate region of human liberty. It comprises, first, the inward domain of consciousness, demanding liberty of conscience in the *most comprehensive sense,* liberty of thought and feeling, *absolute freedom of opinion* and sentiment on *all subjects,* practical or speculative, scientific, moral, or theological.... No society...is completely free in which [these liberties] do not exist *absolute* and *unqualified.*[37]

Mill was unequivocal that his call for "absolute freedom of opinion"included freedom of thought, speaking, and writing.[38] It was Mill's unrelenting disdain for the public orthodoxy or, as he called it, "the despotism of custom" that led him to make his best-known remark: "If all mankind were of one opinion, and only one person were of the contrary opinion, mankind would be no more justified in silencing that one person, than he, if he had the power, would be justified in silencing all mankind."[39]

Kendall rejected categorically Mill's absolutist position on the "open society," and he repudiated its theoretical underpinnings. Hardly less than Machiavelli, and more than Hobbes, Mill is in full rebellion against both religion and philosophy, and so in full rebellion also against the traditional society that embodies them.[40] Kendall charged that Mill's position is at odds with elementary facts of the human condition. It is unnatural and perverse to ask mortal men to accept a posture of absolute relativism, for in fact men do have values, in fact they do think some questions are settled, and they do not accept the position that all points of view are relative and equal in value. Kendall contended Mill erred in proposing that any society should and would make absolute freedom of expression its supreme and only value:

Mill's proposals have as one of their tacit premises a false conception of the nature of society, and are, therefore, unrealistic on their face. They assume that society is, so to speak, *a debating club* devoted above all to the pursuit of truth, and capable therefore of subordinating itself—and all other considerations, goods, and goals—to that pursuit.... But we know only too well that society is *not* a debating club—all our experience of society drives the point home—and that, even if it were one...the chances of its adopting the pursuit of truth as its supreme good are negligible. Societies ...cherish a whole series of goods among others, their own self-preservation, the *living* of the truth they believe themselves to embody already, and the communication of that truth (pretty much intact, moreover) to future generations, their religion, etc.—which they are not only likely to value as much as or more than the pursuit of truth, but *ought* to value as much as or more than the pursuit of truth, because these are *preconditions* of the pursuit of truth.[41]

As Kendall viewed it, Mill failed to understand that the *politeia* is the condition precedent to society, and that it is only within the frame of reference or consensus established by the *politeia* that debate, or discussion as Kendall would prefer to call it, can take place. To deny the *politeia,* and to ask for unlimited debate in the abstract as Mill does, is to request what is not only impossible of achievement—human nature and the human condition dictate otherwise—but indeed, even if attainable, would be undesirable:

For the essence of Mill's freedom of speech is the divorce of the right to speak from the duties correlative to the right; the right to speak is a right to speak *ad nauseam,* and with impunity. It is shot through and through with the egalitarian overtones of the French Revolution, which are as different from the measured aristocratic overtones of the pursuit of truth by discussion, as understood by the tradition Mill was attacking, as philosophy is different from phosphorus.[42]

If the doctrine of Mill is the right to speak *ad nauseam,* without correlative duties or obligations, we are installing the cult of individual eccentricity as our supreme value; if this is followed to its logical and final conclusion, society will be brought to the brink of disintegration. Mill was an advocate of the cult of individual eccentricity. "In this age, the mere example of nonconformity," he wrote, "the mere refusal to bend the knee to custom, is itself a service. Precisely because the tyranny of opinion is such as to make eccentricity a reproach, it is desirable, in order to break through that tyranny, that people should be eccentric.... That so few now dare to be eccentric marks the chief danger of the time."[43]

In Mill's "open society," the individual with his absolute right of expression is then instructed that eccentricity is a positive good and that there is a duty to pursue it. That is, there emerges a public orthodoxy of eccentricity and, in Kendall's critique, this will drive individuals to the making of exorbitant and impossible demands upon society. This in turn will lead to confrontation and the disintegration of society, for there is no center that can hold; more importantly, there is no obligation or duty for anybody to have since all things political are conceived wholly in terms of individual rights and demands. Into the vacuum created by disintegration will move force and coercion—in a word, tyranny. As Kendall succinctly put it, "I next contend that such a society as Mill prescribed will descend ineluctably into ever-deepening *differences of opinion,* into progressive breakdown of those common premises upon which alone a society can conduct its affairs by discussion, and so into the abandonment of the discussion process and the arbitrament of public questions by violence and civil war."[44] Kendall queried, "[I]s there any surer prescription for arriving, willy nilly, in spite of ourselves, at the closed society, than is involved in current pleas for the open society?"[45] And he answered: "By asking for all, even assuming that all to be desirable, we imperil our chances of getting that little we might have got had we asked only for that little."[46]

Inexorably, then, Kendall argued, Mill's position of dogmatic relativism leads to the emergence of the coercive state. Kendall reasoned, "The proposition that all opinions are equally—and hence infinitely—valuable, said to be the unavoidable inference from the proposition that all opinions are equal, is only—and perhaps the less likely—of two possible inferences, the other being: All opinions are equally—and hence infinitely—without value, so what difference does it make if one, particularly one not our own, gets suppressed?"[47] He concluded with this admonition: "We have no experience of unlimited freedom of speech as Mill defines it, of the open society as [Karl] Popper defines it, unless, after a fashion and for a brief moment, in Weimar Germany—an experience no organized society will be eager to repeat."[48]

Kendall accused the "open-society" proponents, such as John Stuart Mill and Karl Popper, of presenting us with false choices. That is, they force us to choose between the "closed" or the "open" society. As Popper stated it, "We can return to the beasts [meaning the closed society]. But if we wish to remain human, then there is *only one way,* the way into the open society."[49] Kendall challenged that assumption:

> Mill would have us choose between never silencing and declaring ourselves infallible, as Popper would have us believe that a society cannot be a little bit closed, any more than a woman can be a little bit pregnant. All our knowledge of politics bids us not to fall into that trap. Nobody wants all-out thought-control or the closed society; and nobody has any business pretending that somebody else wants them. For the real question is, how open can a society be and still remain open at all?[50]

To Kendall choices between the "open society" and "closed society" are false choices; indeed, they are not our only alternatives. In the real world of being there is "an infinite range of possibilities." The great irony is that by offering these false choices, proponents of the open society actually nudge us closer to the closed society. Because the attainment of a completely open society is impossible, and undesirable to boot, the advocates of the open society, by their own process of elimination, leave us with no other alternative than that of the closed society, which unfortunately is attainable. It was Kendall's contention that political philosophers should be seeking realistic and moderate solutions in that "infinite range of possibilities" lying between those purist concepts of the open and closed societies, which political ideologists have been wrongly informing us are our only options.

As a political philosopher, Kendall was always pushing to deeper levels of meaning and understanding. One of the most impressive illustrations of this is his carefully honed and brilliantly argued article, "The People Versus Socrates Revisited."[51] Kendall contended that the advocates of the open society had converted Socrates-before-the-Assembly into their fundamental symbol. For example, in *On Liberty* Mill wrote:

> Mankind can hardly be too often reminded, that there was once a man called Socrates, between whom and the legal authorities and public opinion of his time there took place a memorable collision....This acknowledged master of all the eminent thinkers who have since lived—whose fame, still growing after more than two thousand years....[52]

Similarly, throughout *The Open Society and Its Enemies,* Karl Popper spoke glowingly of Socrates and concluded, "The new faith of the open society, the faith in man, in equalitarian justice, and in human reason, was...beginning to take shape.... The greatest contribution to this faith was to be made by Socrates, who died for it."[53]

Regarding the Mill-Popper symbol of Socrates-arrayed-against-the-Assembly, Kendall wrote:

> What symbol? The symbol, of course, of Socrates the Bearer of the Word standing with unbowed head in the presence of his accusers and judges, who hold the Word in contempt of the Servant of Truth being punished, murdered rather, for the truth that is in him; that of the Wise Man being sacrificed by fools who, had they but listened to him, would have been rescued from their folly. That symbol, I contend, lies at the root of the simon-pure doctrine [of the

open society]...of the Mill-Popper position.[54]

It was Kendall's position that a close reading of the *Apology* and the *Crito* will reveal this to be a spurious symbol. The political theory of the *Crito* does not endorse a limitless open society of the Mill-Popper version; rather, argued Kendall, it offers a society in which the individual is accorded a reasonable opportunity to convince society of the failings and errors of its public orthodoxy. When that reasonable opportunity has been exhausted, and society chooses not to alter its values or orthodoxy, the individual is expected to desist or emigrate. Furthermore, after his hearing the dissenter may encounter punishment for ideas or methods found by society to be utterly repugnant to those things it treasures as fundamental. In short, the teaching of the *Crito* is not that offered by the open society advocates, for it does not propose a society in which the individual has the absolute and unlimited right to talk *ad nauseam* until society converts itself to the preachment of the dissenter. According to Kendall, this latter theory is, as has been previously noted, unworkable, unattainable, and undesirable; it is a political theory which has its roots in *On Liberty,* not in the *Crito.*

In addition, Kendall charged the open-society advocates with misunderstanding the political lessons of the *Apology.* The lesson is not that Socrates has been denied the opportunity for a reasonable hearing as required by the *Crito.* Indeed, the Athenians had been listening to Socrates for several decades. Nor was the major issue raised between Socrates and the Assembly a demand by Socrates that the Athenians keep all questions open questions and modify the public orthodoxy here or enlarge it there. The heart of the matter was that Socrates wished the Athenians to reorder their entire public orthodoxy and to bring it into conformity with his own. In pressing his case, Socrates is instructing the Athenians that their present way of life is "not worth living." Not only is their way of life foolish and frivolous; it is also base and immoral, and Socrates will settle for nothing less than a total rejection of the Athenian public orthodoxy. As Kendall summed it up,

"There is the model..., the situation of every society over against every revolutionary agitator; nor could there be better evidence of the poverty of post-Platonic political theory than the fact that it has received so little attention."[55]

It was Kendall's contention that students of political philosophy in their understanding of the forces inherent in human society will recognize the unyielding realities that leave the Athenians and the Assembly no choice:

> The Athenians are running a *society,* which is the embodiment of a *way of life,* which in turn is the embodiment of the *goods* they cherish and the *beliefs* to which they stand committed....The most we can possibly ask of them ... is that they shall keep their minds a little open to proposals for this or that improvement, this or that refinement.... To ask of them, by contrast, that they jettison their way of life, that they carry out the revolution demanded of them by the revolutionary agitator, is to demand that they shall deliberately do that which they can only regard as irresponsible and immoral—something, moreover, that they will seriously consider doing only to the extent that their society has ceased, or is about to cease, to be a society.[56]

As laudable as the thought might seem in certain situations, to ask a society to condemn and repudiate itself is unnatural and contrary to what political philosophy has learned about the *politeia,* that condition antecedent to society and government. In fine, a being, be it an individual or a society, cannot be asked to repudiate itself and to declare its nothingness, for that is unnatural, perverse, and contrary to elementary first principles on the nature of being we have culled out of our accumulated experience and wisdom.

It was Kendall's belief that we had best understand those unrelenting realities, and thereby be better able to develop the realistic open society, the society of the *Crito.* To ignore those realities, and to attempt to construct the perfected, limitless, and utopian open society of the Mill-Popper school, is to build on infirm foundations and to court society's disintegration with the resulting potential of the closed societies of the authoritarian or totalitarian stripe. In their fervor to obtain everything, the exponents of the open society will end up getting nothing. It is that disastrous end Kendall wished to avoid.

As Kendall viewed it, the Mill-Popper proponents have read their own *de novo* theories, spun out of wholly new cloth, into the works of the ancients—such as the *Crito* and the *Apology* and they deceive themselves in contending that they are extracting their theories out of a proper reading of these classics. As Kendall would see it, Publius read Plato more accurately: "Had every Athenian citizen been a Socrates, every Athenian citizen would still have been a mob."[57]

## III

In his analysis of the Socrates of the *Apology,* Kendall was hinting strongly at the probability that the contemporary Mill-Popper school in the United States is using the argument of the purist open society as an instrument or weapon to unhinge the existing orthodoxy, not for the alleged purpose of then ushering in the wholly limitless open society, but rather, after having dislodged the existing *politeia* of American society, for instituting their own orthodoxy, which is antithetical on fundamental points to basic values of the American tradition.[58] In Kendall's view there are in contemporary America two fundamentally different orthodoxies, one liberal and one conservative, competing for dominance.[59] The contemporary liberal orthodoxy traces its history to Abraham Lincoln's heretical position on the Declaration of Independence, while the meaning and the spirit of the conservative orthodoxy are expressed in *The Federalist,* a document Kendall considered the finest expression of the essence of the American political tradition.

Kendall asserted that the primary and distinguishing mark of the modern American liberal is his ardent desire for an egalitarian society.[60] This liberal genre seeks not merely a society based upon political equality, but, in addition, this "commitment to equality means that government should assume the role of advancing equality by pursuing policies designed to make 'all men equal' socially, economically, and politically." Kendall concluded, "There is, then, so far as one can learn, no reasonably definite stopping point for liberal egalitarianism...."[61] It was Kendall's position that Lincoln wrenched the equality clause—"all men are created equal"—from the Declaration of Independence and gave it this egalitarian meaning, which the contemporary liberal has seized upon. This symbol of equality was not that intended by the drafters of the Declaration. Kendall elaborated:

> What does it [i.e., the equality clause] mean? Our best guess is that the clause simply asserts the proposition that all peoples who identify themselves as one—that is, those who identify themselves as a society, nation, or state for action in history—are equal to others who have likewise identified themselves.... The Declaration asserts that Americans are equal to, say, the British and French.... Specifically, the drafters of the Declaration are maintaining that the Americans are equal to the British and are, therefore, as free as the British to establish a form of government [of their own choosing].[62]

In Kendall's interpretation, the equality symbol of the Declaration is an equality-of-societies symbol employed for the purpose of justifying separation by the American colonies. The Lincolnian heresy lies in "internalizing" the symbol, thereby perverting it into a symbol for domestic egalitarianism and leveling.[63]

Moreover, claimed Kendall, the legacy of the Lincolnian heresy is the modern liberal concept that it is the responsibility of the central national government to promote leveling, and, in particular, it is the solemn duty of the President to lead the attack. A succession of strong Presidents, each looking more deeply into the ultimate meaning of an American tradition rooted in leveling, will launch the nation on a continuing series of missions.[64] These missions will entail marshaling majoritarian mandates for the long-term purpose of bringing us finally to the perfected egalitarian society. Those opposing the egalitarian New Jerusalem will have to be seen for what they are—selfish recalcitrants and obstructionists. With the unrelenting pressure of exposure and "education," their resistance can be overcome.

An integral part of liberal egalitarianism is unshakable confidence in majoritarianism. Majoritarianism is integral to a leveling philosophy, for it is rooted in the concept of political equality— one man one vote. In Kendall's view, by modern liberal hands a corollary had been added to majoritarianism that demands the abolition of all obstacles to the instant expression of the majority will. In the American experience, this means the elimination of the seniority system, the filibuster, staggered elections, the amending process, nonprogrammed political parties, and in general anything that inhibits instant expression of majority preferences.[65] Liberal ideology seeks to establish a system based upon plebiscitary mandates, and it is a cardinal tenet of liberal ideology that if the majority will can be unshackled it will approve an egalitarian society. Thus in Kendall's analysis, all liberal thinking ultimately returns to the touchstone of leveling.

Kendall concluded in 1966 that he was "dead wrong" in his 1941 conclusion in *John Locke and the Doctrine of Majority-Rule* that the Framers were concerned about inalienable, abstract, natural rights.[66] It is in Kendall's analysis of the political thinking of the Framers of the American constitution that we find his final articulation of the meaning of American conservatism. His last and major work, *The Basic Symbols of the American Political Tradition,* co-authored with his student and close friend George W. Carey, is the single best expression we have of Kendall's ideas on the Framers. It is clear that this book is the culmination of years of reading, reflection, and thought.

Kendall declared that it is not in abstract, natural rights wrenched out of the Declaration of Independence or the Bill of Rights that one finds the core of American political thought envisioned by the Framers. It is to the Preamble and *The Federalist* that one must look. From Kendall's perspective, the Preamble is the "finest statement of purpose" of the American experiment.[67] Instead of speaking of rights, equality, power, and demands, the Preamble speaks of union, justice, tranquility, the common defense, the general welfare, and the blessings of liberty.[68] As Publius said of the Preamble in *The Federalist:* "Here is a better recognition of popular rights, than volumes of those aphorisms which make the principal figure in several of our State bills of rights, and which would sound much better in a treatise of ethics than in a constitution of government."[69]

How are the goals of the Preamble to be attained? As Kendall analyzed the Framers' intentions, they are to be attained by way of self-government. In the eloquent words of Publius: "The fabric of American empire ought to rest on the solid basis of THE CONSENT OF THE PEOPLE. The streams of national power ought to flow immediately from that pure, original foundation of all legitimate authority."[70] Taking his cue from Publius, Kendall wrote in the year of his death: "[W]hat I do take sides on is the thesis of the *Federalist Papers,* namely: That America's mission in the world is to prove to the world that self-government—that is, government by the people through a representative assembly which, by definition, calls the plays—is possible."[71]

It is from careful analysis of *The Federalist* that Kendall extracted the basic symbols of the American political tradition, which over and against contemporary liberalism, is the conservative tradition, and the principal competitor of the modern liberal orthodoxy. As indicated, the goals are symbolized in the Preamble and are to be achieved through self-government. The supreme symbol that Kendall extracted from *The Federalist* is that which shows in what manner we are to achieve self-rule. As Kendall read Publius, self-government is to be achieved by "the deliberate sense of a virtuous people."[72] Publius spoke of the "cool and deliberate sense of the community," of the importance of "reflection and choice," and of the "fullest and most mature deliberation."[73] The deliberative process, then, is the supreme symbol of *The Federalist.* And the end of the deliberative process is consensus on how best to deal with concrete problems at specific points in history, in order to achieve, in the words of Publius, "the safety and happiness of society [which] are the objects at which all political institutions aim...."[74]

In achieving consensus on how to maintain "the safety and happiness of society" through the deliberative process, Publius deplores utopian visions rooted in such doctrinaire abstractions as rights, equality, and mandates. In eschewing utopian schemes, Publius cautioned:

> Have we not already seen enough of the fallacy and extravagance of those idle theories which have amused us with promises of an exemption from the imperfections, weaknesses, and evils incident to society in every shape? Is it not time to awake from the deceitful dream of a golden age and to adopt as a practical maxim for the direction of our political conduct that we, as well as the other inhabitants of the globe, are yet remote from the happy empire of perfect wisdom and virtue?[75]

According to Kendall, even the pen name "Publius" is a product of a deliberative process. Kendall believed that the controversy over who wrote which Federalist paper was a "red herring" and demonstrated that modern scholarship had missed the point of *The Federalist*. The significant point is that Hamilton, Madison, and Jay were not seeking to force their pet theories of government on one another and on the country as a whole; rather, they were attempting to achieve a consensus of viewpoints, through the deliberative process, that would contribute to "the safety and happiness of society."[76] They were creating the supreme symbol of the American political tradition.

Kendall noted that the deliberative process, as developed by Publius, is characterized by discussion, not debate. The latter conjures up visions of rights, demands, mandates, and winning or losing, while discussion connotes, in Kendall's words, "a cooperative quest for common premises from which discourse can begin, and...a cooperative striving not for triumph over an opponent, but for truth."[77] In the tradition of Publius, Kendall concluded:

> I do not like debates—if by a debate we mean the confrontation of two diametrically opposed positions, the trading and parrying of argument and the chalking up of points, in the fashion in which prize-fighters trade and parry blows and chalk up points. I strongly believe that such debates merely confuse issues, that their prevalence in our time is a frightening symptom of a worldwide breakdown of the discussion process, and most important of all, that our only hope lies in rediscovering the art and ethic of discussion as distinguished from debate.[78]

Kendall contended that Publius preferred discussion over elections for the same reasons he preferred it over debate. Elections, which unfortunately have become "the central ritual of American politics," elicit visions of bitter debates, confrontations between squared-off political antagonists, winners and losers, not-to-be-denied mandates, and the heavy hand of abstract majoritarianism. In contrast, discussion suggests deliberation, accommodation, moderation, harmony, consensus, and the long-term pursuit of those elusive first principles essential to the well-ordered society.

In seeking consensus through the deliberative process, Publius does not lust after unanimity: "To have required the unanimous ratification of the thirteen States would have subjected the essential interests of the whole to the caprice or corruption of a single member. It would have marked a want of foresight in the convention, which our own experience would have rendered inexcusable."[79] In addition, Publius noted, "the history of every political establishment in which this principle [of unanimity] has prevailed, is a history of impotence, perplexity, and disorder."[80] Hence, unanimity is rejected as unattainable, impractical, unworkable—and utopian.

Similarly, in Kendall's interpretation, Publius rejected majoritarianism as antithetical to the deliberative process. In contrast to the deliberative process, which fosters discussion, accommodation, and consensus, the philosophy of majoritarianism demands a losing minority. This minority has lost the "debate" and the "election"; now it must submit to the "mandate" of "majority rule." Such theories do violence to the deliberative process, in Publius's conception of it. "Pockets of irredentism" will arise if the majority forces its mandate upon the minority. That is, if the minority is intensely opposed to the mandate, it will dig in its heels and dream of reclaiming its lost cause. In the political theories of Publius and Kendall this undermines the well-ordered commonwealth, for it contributes to the ripping and tearing of the social fabric. The deliberative process prevents "pockets of irredentism" from forming by stressing at every stage of discussion the importance of adjustment, accommodation, assimilation, and consensus.[81]

Moreover, as interpreted by Kendall, Publius opposed majoritarianism because it is abstract and inflexible; it has no theoretical capacity to deal with the real and fluid problems of "intensity." Under traditional majoritarian theory, there is an assumed uniformity of commitment on the part of the majority and the minority, and there is also a presumed equality of conviction. But often the real world of majority-minority relations is otherwise. In a given situation, the majority may not feel intensely committed to its position, whereas the minority may feel quite intent or the reverse could be true. In any case, as traditionally conceived, majoritarian theory has no capacity for accommodating that kind of situation; it can only add up raw figures to fifty percent plus one, and then enforce its mandate. As a consequence, majoritarianism can think only in one-dimensional, quantitative terms, while the real world of majority-minority relations must deal with the multifaceted problems presented by the intensity factor. Only the deliberative process, with its suppleness and flexibility, can accommodate and ameliorate the intensity problem, and thereby avoid pockets of irredentism, which those persons, along with Publius, committed to the well-ordered society wish to avoid.[82]

As the deliberative process of Publius eschews unanimity and majoritarianism, it also rejects minoritarianism. Specifically, minorities flaunting rights and demands are not allowed to badger and coerce society as a whole. If the majority cannot run roughshod over the minority (and in Publius's view it cannot), certainly the reverse is not tolerable either. The minority can expect a sympathetic and reasonable hearing for its position, but, that having been achieved, it cannot go on *ad nauseam* in an attempt to intimidate society into submission through obnoxious and offensive methods. Minoritarian coercion, similar to majoritarianism and resulting irredentism, will tear the social tissue by putting men at each other's throats, and such a condition is antithetical to Publius's consensus-seeking deliberative process. Kendall stated Publius's position concisely: "What I do take sides on is government by consensus, which, I repeat, requires of minorities demanding drastic change that they bide their time until they have pleaded their case successfully before the bar of public—not merely majority—opinion.... They must...cool their heels in the ante-room of our basic law until they are admitted to the inner sanctum by a consensus."[83]

In Kendall's analysis, the differences between the American liberal and conservative orthodoxies (and let it be remembered that *every* society has a matrix of values called an "orthodoxy") are fundamental. The conservative orthodoxy, rooted in *The Federalist,* is based on the idea that the American people will seek their "safety and happiness" through self-government, which means, in the eyes of Publius, consensus achieved through the deliberative process. In contrast, the liberal orthodoxy, based on the Lincolnian distortion of the Declaration of Independence, seeks egalitarianism and leveling through mobilized majoritarian mandates. Publius, said Kendall, had nothing to do with equality as the final end of political society. Indeed, Publius nowhere even suggested (the Preamble would have been a fitting place to do so), let alone demanded, that leveling be the ultimate political value. Publius and American conservatives even reject the concept of "equality of opportunity." Why this rejection? In his inimitable style Kendall observed:

The equality of opportunity goal, they would say, is unrealistic, impossible to achieve, *utopian*—and because utopian, *dangerous*. In order to equalize opportunity in any meaningful way you have, first of all—as clearheaded political philosophers have always seen—to neutralize that great carrier and perpetuator of unequal opportunity, the *family*, and you can do that, really do it, only by abolishing the family, which we will not let you do because that would be wrong.[84]

To those nurtured in the tradition of Publius, equality means "leaving people free to equalize their own opportunities. . . to the extent that they have the ability, the energy, and the determination to do it."[85]

Similarly, the tradition of Publius rejects the egalitarian implications of the liberals' "open-society" interpretation of the Bill of Rights and, in particular, of the First Amendment. As previously noted, Kendall took issue with the Mill-Popper school, which contends for the equality of ideas and thus lays the basic theoretical foundation for the unlimited "open society." And as Kendall pointed out, Publius never proposed or intended for the Bill of Rights to be interpreted and applied as the contemporary liberal orthodoxy has done. Nor did Publius ever intend for the Bill of Rights to serve as an egalitarian springboard for proponents of the "open society." Kendall and Carey argued, "We can only conclude as follows concerning the Bill of Rights and the First Amendment: Their adoption did not alter the mainstream of the American tradition which, as the Preamble and *The Federalist* would have it, comes down to rule by the deliberate sense of the community."[86]

What did Publius intend by the First Amendment? He intended, argued Kendall, to give each state within its jurisdiction a monopoly on regulating matters encompassed within the Amendment.[87] That is, Publius never intended for the Supreme Court to impose a national standard on all of the states, and he certainly would be shocked to see that development as it has unfolded in this century. Kendall reasoned that the whole thrust of the Madisonian argument for the Bill of Rights was to "bring aboard the Masonite irredentists."[88] This goes to the supreme symbol of *The Federalist*—the symbol of the deliberative process. Madison meant that if the Masonites felt strongly on the importance of the Bill of Rights—strong enough to create a pocket of irredentism— then Madison, in the spirit of Publius, argued for accommodation. In sum, Madison never intended by the addition of the Bill of Rights to supersede "the deliberate sense of the community"; rather, he meant to support it by accommodating a minority. Modern liberalism, by wrenching the Bill of Rights out of context and bringing it into the service of egalitarianism, has again weakened the supreme symbol—the deliberative process—of the American political tradition.

## IV

It is clear that Publius's deliberative process, with its emphasis on accommodation, harmony, and consensus, is antithetical to the conflict-oriented majoritarianism of the egalitarians. As a corollary, it is essential to note that as a result of the supreme symbol of the deliberative process, the followers of Publius, with Kendall as their guide, resist those fundamental institutional changes demanded by levelers. To illustrate, Publius and his political descendants are negative on the modern liberal conception of the presidency. In one of his classic pieces, Kendall reasoned that in American national politics we have "two majorities": the presidential and the congressional.[89] The former majority is rooted in the Lincolnian heresy and is the focal point of liberal leveling; the latter majority is a product of the conservative tradition as expressed in *The Federalist*. Because of the size of the presidential constituency, and because of the presidency's remoteness from local realities and concretes, presidential politics, Kendall insisted, lends itself to a campaign style, to generalities and idealism.

In contrast, members of Congress represent comparatively small constituencies, which forces them to deal with specifics and eschew the quixotism of presidential politics. Consistent with the emphasis on the deliberative process, solving specific case-by-case policy questions, the tradition of Publius considers Congress the pre-eminent branch. In Kendall's words: "The plain language of the Constitution tells us unambiguously that Congress . . . *is* supreme, and just can't help being supreme because the Constitution places in its hands weapons with which, when and if it chooses to use them, it can completely dominate the other two branches."[90] Kendall reasoned that Congress is "the very heart of the system," and although it has the power to emasculate the other two branches, it restrains itself from doing so because of Publius's "constitutional morality" with the emphasis on harmony and accommodation, and the rejection of harsh and brittle conceptions of powers and rights, which invariably play havoc with the development of a sound social fabric.[91]

Likewise, Publius and his contemporary admirers will reject out of hand the liberal call for programmed political parties.[92] Liberal theoreticians have considered the "doctrine of responsible party government" as indispensable to facilitate equality through majoritarian mandates. In restructuring our two-party system, the liberal ideologists would create a "liberal" and "conservative" party. The new parties would be centralized and disciplined, and would offer the electorate a clear-cut choice on matters of philosophy and policy. In liberal thinking, it is anticipated (erroneously in Kendall's view) that when the American people are confronted with these dramatic choices, they will overwhelmingly pick those candidates favoring liberal egalitarianism. Hence, under the "doctrine of responsible party government" one of our major parties would become the vehicle for harnessing and implementing liberal egalitarian mandates. In liberal thought, the current decentralized and "undisciplined" parties are "irresponsible" because they serve as institutional obstacles to leveling.

Drawing his nourishment from Publius, Kendall wrote, "Contemporary theories of party discipline and responsibility represent . . . the most comprehensive and systematic possible assault upon the Madisonian system [that is, the system of Publius]."[93] Programmed political parties do violence to that supreme symbol of the deliberative process. Because of commitment to the spirit of Publius, Kendall found, there are "no raging seas" of egalitarianism in the American experience "to hold back."[94] Publius would be repelled by an institutional change whose admitted purpose is to create sharp cleavages and to pit the majority against the minority. To structure an institution for the avowed purpose of promoting division, and thereby deliberately tearing the social fabric, is the ultimate affront to Publius and to his latter-day disciple, Willmoore Kendall.[95]

Nor would Kendall's Publius be pleased with the assertive egalitarian role of the modern Supreme Court. Indeed, the modern activist court has short-circuited the deliberative process and frequently acts in conscious opposition to it. The modern liberal has perverted the doctrine of judicial review as articulated by Publius. Concerning judicial review, Publius wrote:

> The complete independence of the courts of justice is peculiarly essential in a limited Constitution. By a limited Constitution, I understand one which contains certain specified exceptions to the legislative authority; such, for instance, as that it shall pass no bills of attainder, no *ex-post-facto* laws, and the like. Limitations of this kind can be preserved in practice no other way than through the medium of courts of justice, whose duty it must be to declare all acts *contrary to the manifest tenor of the Constitution* void.[96]

It is clear from this quotation, and from a careful analysis of all of *Federalist* 78, that Publius intended the Court, in its capacity of exercising judicial review, to have a modest role of declaring void *only* those acts of Congress (for example, as Publius stated, bills of attainder and *ex-post-facto laws*) clearly "contrary to the manifest tenor of the Constitution." Moreover, Publius expressly noted that the Court will have "neither FORCE nor WILL, but merely judgment," and "The courts must declare the sense of the law: and if they should be disposed to exercise WILL instead of

JUDGMENT, the consequence would equally be the substitution of their pleasure to that of the legislative body."[97] Expressly warning on the need "to avoid an arbitrary discretion in the courts," Publius explained:

> Nor does this conclusion by any means suppose a superiority of the judicial to the legislative power. It only supposes that the power of the people is superior to both; and that where the will of the legislature, declared in its statutes, stands in opposition to that of the people, declared in the Constitution [a product of "the deliberate sense of the community"], the judges ought to be governed by the latter rather than the former.[98]

Publius returns us to the touchstone of the supreme symbol—the deliberative process—and his position on judicial review can only be understood in that context. Unequivocally, no one can extract from *The Federalist* a conception of the role of the Supreme Court which would justify the egalitarian excursions and excesses of the modern court, where in fact the court has launched into areas manifestly beyond the scope envisioned by Publius, and where in fact "WILL" has been substituted for "JUDGMENT." The constitutional morality of *The Federalist,* resting on "the deliberate sense of the community," would not sustain such harsh impositions of judicial "WILL" as the abortion decision of *Roe v. Wade* (1973), which is based on the "arbitrary discretion in the courts" and in clear defiance of "the deliberate sense of a virtuous people."[99]

## V

As Kendall read *The Federalist,* the supreme symbols of the American tradition are "rule by the deliberate sense of a virtuous people."[100] It will not suffice merely to have the deliberative process, for a process alone cannot guarantee a moral and just result. To ensure the integrity of policy decisions, it is essential that "virtue" be the basic characteristic of a people employing the deliberative process. Commencing with *John Locke and the Doctrine of Majority-Rule,* Kendall had expressed an enduring concern for the moral quality of society. He lamented that "the capital weakness of Locke's *Second Treatise*" was Locke's failure to address himself explicitly to the problem of how we are to ensure "rational and just" decisions by the majority.[101] Similarly, Kendall considered the principal defect of *The Federalist* to be its failure to explore this crucial problem of how to keep the people virtuous in order to guarantee the integrity and justice of those decisions made through the deliberative process.[102] In short, if the public orthodoxy is lacking in virtue, the deliberative process cannot produce a virtuous result.

With profound relief, Kendall proclaimed that this "missing section" of *The Federalist,* a section dealing with how to keep the people virtuous, is provided in Richard M. Weaver's final book, *Visions of Order.*[103] Kendall spared no superlative in his praise of this work. *Visions of Order,* he wrote, must be placed upon the shelf beside *The Federalist,* and, as with *The Federalist,* it must have conferred on it "the political equivalent of biblical status."[104] Kendall further declared "Then go read—nay, *live with*—the book, until you have made its contents your own. It will prepare you, as no other book, not even *The Federalist* will prepare you, for your future encounters with the protagonists of the Liberal Revolution, above all by teaching you how to drive the debate to a deeper level than that on which our present spokesmen are engaging the Liberals."[105] To understand *Visions of Order* is to understand Willmoore Kendall's commitment as a political philosopher to the great tradition of the study of politics, to that search for the moral, the good, and the just in things political. Kendall is unequivocal: if men believed as Weaver did, the people would indeed be virtuous, and the product of the deliberative process would thereby itself be virtuous.

No less than Publius and Kendall, Weaver was anti-egalitarian, and this attitude pervades his book. Illustrative is the following insight:

Democracy [that is, political equality] is not a pattern for all existence any more than a form of economic activity is a substitute for the whole of living.... When democracy is taken from its proper place and is allowed to fill the entire horizon, it produces an envious hatred not only of all distinction but even of all difference.... The fanatical democrat insists upon making [men] equal in all departments, regardless of the type of activity and vocation. It is of course the essence of fanaticism to seize upon some fragment of truth or value and to regard it as the exclusive object of man's striving. So democracy, a valuable but limited political concept, has been elevated by some into a creed as comprehensive as a religion or a philosophy, already at the cost of widespread subversion.[106]

Kendall would agree with Weaver that cultural equality involves more than the "consulting of opinions and [the] counting of votes," and he would concur that "[c]ulture is thus by nature aristocratic, for it is a means of discriminating between what counts for much and what counts for little...."[107] In addition, Kendall and Weaver were in agreement that the canker of egalitarianism was traceable to the quest for the secular utopia. In Weaver's words, the utopians are those "who think that human nature and history can be laid aside" and that "equality must reign, *ruat caelum!*"[108] Utopians, Weaver cautioned, are forever "postulating an equalitarian natural man as the grand end of all endeavor."[109] Finally, Weaver warned of the utopian visions "dreamed up by romantic enthusiasts, political fanatics, and unreflective acolytes of positive science."[110]

When we turn to Weaver's alternatives to utopianism and egalitarianism, we see emerging those subtle, but profound themes which so attracted and fascinated Kendall. Weaver turned to the great tradition of politics, to those fundamental and enduring principles he perceived as rooted in the structure of reality. Pervasive in Weaver's analysis was the classical concept from the great tradition of politics instructing us that, in establishing societies and honing out civilization, it is essential we maintain a sense of proportion, balance, harmony, and tone. "Function," signifying change, and "status," suggesting position, form, memory, tradition, and permanence, must be held in balance. Where function exists without status, there is generated a momentum of mindless change, which wrenches and undermines those qualitative things so indispensable to society worthy of the name "civilized" or "virtuous." Similarly, where status exists without function, there is the risk of stagnation and sterility, and thereby a fatal blow is struck against civilization, for it is deprived of those essential elements of dynamism and creativity.

Likewise, in Weaver's analysis, it is imperative that an equilibrium be maintained between "dialectic" and "rhetoric." Where dialectic denotes reason, the abstract, and dialogue—Socrates was a dialectician—rhetoric refers to a sense of the unspoken, the felt, the intuitive, and the organic. Dialectic alone will distort reality and magnify alleged virtues and vices, and it will lead to the arid world of the logician and geometer, while rhetoric in isolation will lead to excessive reliance upon the given and the mystical, and society loses the capacity to re-examine continually in a rational method its own basic premises. Similarly, there must be a proportioned relationship between "aesthetics" and "ethics." Aesthetics refers to that sensitivity to created beauty, which without an ethical basis can degenerate into the banal and frivolous at best, and possibly into the sordid and debased. Ethics, suggesting commitment to moral principle, without the balancing effect of aesthetics, is in danger of running aground upon the bleakness and harshness of puritanism, and even of erupting into fanaticism.

In addition to these themes reflecting the classical concern for proportion, balance, harmony, and tone, which contribute to the virtue of the populace, and thereby to the integrity of the deliberative process, Weaver added religion as the ultimate foundation for a virtuous society. With uncommon eloquence, Weaver wrote:

The Greeks could out-argue the Christians and the Romans

could subject them to their government, but there was in Christianity an ethical respect for the person which triumphed over these formalizations. Neither the beauty of Greek culture nor the grandeur of the Roman state system was the complete answer to what people wanted in their lives as a whole.

But the road away from idolatry remains the same as before; it lies in respect for the struggling dignity of man and for his orientation toward something higher than himself which he has not created.[111]

In full accord with Weaver, Kendall (through George W. Carey) stated in the final paragraph of his last book:

The false myths produce the fanatics amongst us. They are misrepresentations and distortions of the American political tradition and its basic symbols which are, let us remind you, the representative assembly *deliberating* under God; the virtuous people virtuous because deeply religious and thus committed to the *process* of searching for the transcendent Truth. And these are, we believe, symbols we can be proud of without going before a fall.[112]

At another point, in this his major and final work, Kendall asked: "What is to keep the virtuous people virtuous? The question is as old as Greek philosophy, and Greek philosophy offered, on one level at least, the decisive answer: The people will be virtuous only to the extent that the souls of its individual components are rightly ordered...."[113] Kendall cautioned against the error "of forgetting that the truth of the soul and the truth of society are transcendent truths, and that the function of the basic symbols is to express the relations between political society and God."[114] Failure to understand that basic proposition "represents a very fundamental derailment [of the American political tradition] and the most dangerous one."[115] The religious dimension is the ultimate guarantee of a virtuous people, or as Kendall wrote:

But where the public orthodoxy is guaranteed by transcendence, by the Word of God, then the truths of the soul and of society, the first principles of the *politeia* and of metaphysics (that is the very being of both), are theoretically guaranteed. Beyond this guarantee, which can be had only as a gift and as a blessing, there is no other for any human society born upon this earth.[116]

In Kendall's view the tradition of modern American utopianism commenced by wrenching the equality symbol from the Declaration of Independence and perverting that symbol into an instrument for constructing the egalitarian New Jerusalem. This tradition is secular in its philosophical foundations. It has no conception of "sin," "evil" and "tragedy," nor does it concede the imperfectibility of the human condition; rather, it argues that human nature is wholly malleable, and that the perfected good life is attainable through institutional and environmental manipulation. Driven on by this mind's eye view of the perfected egalitarian utopia, this tradition becomes restive, anxious, and on occasion fanatical, when society seems impervious and indifferent to its hortatory. When confronted with the failure to attain the worldly City of Man, instead of reappraising the soundness of their secularism and their false view of the nature of man, the exponents of the utopian tradition double their efforts and attribute their continued failures to the ignorance of the populace ("more education is needed"), to the sinister machinations of reactionaries and recalcitrants ("greater political organization and effort is needed"), and to the general failure of society to appreciate the clarity of insight and vision of egalitarian utopianism.

From Kendall's perspective, the tradition of Publius, as enhanced by Weaver, draws its nourishment from strikingly different roots. As opposed to the secularism of the egalitarian utopians, this tradition is undeniably religious in temper. Unlike the secularist, the follower of this tradition is impressed (indeed, awed) with the wonder of creation and the mystery of being. He appreciates the relevance of such concepts as "original sin," "evil," and the "tragic sense of life." With Saint Augustine, he understands that "pride" is the ineradicable canker contributing to the imperfectibility of the human condition in this earthly sojourn. He loves and reveres man as the creature and child of God, but he has no illusions about the erection of a worldly utopia, for basic human nature precludes it—Man is not God, and the infinite complexity of life, thought, and matter, as the handiwork of God, will not yield to the iron-cast molds of man-made uniformity, that the egalitarians seek to impose.

By inoculating against utopianism, this religious temper produces a continuing political mood of moderation, restraint, conciliation, civility, and contributes immeasurably to the deliberative process and the pursuit of consensus, which are, according to Kendall, the foundations of the American political tradition. Where, in its zeal to create *now* the Worldly Paradise, the secular egalitarian tradition sometimes sees its petulance and impatience erupt into a shrill fanaticism, the other tradition—the tradition of Publius and Weaver, by rejecting the reconstruction of society from wholly new cloth, holds steady on course with confidence in the capacity of society for self-government through "the deliberate sense of the community" composed of a "virtuous people"—a people virtuous because religious.

The conservatism of Willmoore Kendall is grounded in the deliberative process, as expounded by Publius in *The Federalist,* and in that concept of a "virtuous people," as articulated by Weaver in *Visions of Order.* It is wide of the mark to conceive of Kendall's conservatism in terms of such conventional contemporary labels as "traditionalist," "libertarian," or whatever. His conservatism is an *American* conservatism, which Kendall contends is *the* American political tradition. From Kendall's vantage point, it is the egalitarian utopians (whether liberals or radicals) who are the "outsiders." It is they who are waging war against the tradition of Publius and of Weaver to subvert the American tradition to the man-made idol of Equality.

The lasting significance of Kendall lies not in whether one accepts or rejects his revisionist theories, for that would cast the issue in too narrow a mold. Indeed, in view of Kendall's own methods as a political philosopher, he would expect—demand— that his theories be carefully examined and tested. Rather, Kendall's basic contribution is in demonstrating the technique of critical analysis: the desire to read, to question, to rethink, and to challenge. We should read the ancients and the moderns and should try to understand them as they understood themselves. Only then are we able to evaluate critically their major premises. No one is too sacred to escape examination and challenge: not Mill, not Publius, not Locke, not even Socrates. This emphasis upon careful textual analysis and upon critical evaluation of method and value is the enduring contribution of Willmoore Kendall, a needed antidote to the intellectual climate of our time, which seems to have succumbed to the narrowness of positivism and the dogmatism of ideology.

# Leo Strauss

Leo Strauss (1899-1973) was a native of Germany. "I was," he reported near the end of his life, "brought up in a conservative, even orthodox Jewish home somewhere in a rural district of Germany."[1] Strauss received his doctorate from Hamburg University in 1921. To escape the Nazi holocaust, in 1938 he emigrated to the United States and commenced teaching political science and philosophy at the New School for Social Research. Joining the faculty of the University of Chicago in 1949 as a professor of political philosophy, Strauss subsequently was named Robert Maynard Hutchins Distinguished Service Professor at the institution. After his retirement in 1968 from the University of Chicago, Strauss held teaching positions at Claremont Men's College in California and at St. John's College in Maryland. At the latter institution he was named Scott Buchanan Distinguished Scholar-in-Residence, and he held that position at the time of his death.

A prolific scholar, Strauss authored a dozen books and more than eighty articles. Moreover, he spawned a generation of admiring students who have attained the highest ranks in the academic profession. As one admirer declared, "At the University of Chicago his lectures at the Hillel Foundation were events. In a university that prided itself on intellectual distinction, he was widely regarded as most distinguished."[2] Another admirer said, "He surely was the most learned man of our time in the great writings...."[3] In particular, conservative intellectuals were enamored of Strauss's work. For example, to Walter Berns "He was the greatest of teachers."[4] In his assessment, Dante Germino concluded, "Strauss's impact on American philosophy and political science has been one of almost astonishing proportions."[5] With unreserved praise, Harry V. Jaffa wrote, "For us who have had the privilege of knowing him as a teacher and as a friend, we can only say that of the men we have known, he was the best, and the wisest and most just."[6] William F. Buckley, Jr. observed that Strauss was "unquestionably one of the most influential teachers of his age," while the always exacting Willmoore Kendall referred to Strauss as "*the* great teacher of political philosophy, not of our time alone, but of any time since Machiavelli."[7] Among Strauss's books, those having the greatest influence upon American conservative thought were *The Political Philosophy of Hobbes* (1936), *Natural Right and History* (1953), *Thoughts on Machiavelli* (1958), and *What Is Political Philosophy?* (1959). Concerning the latter two works, Kendall exclaimed, "Both of these should be not required reading but scripture for everyone who likes to think of himself as a conservative."[8]

What was this powerful spell Strauss cast over his students—nay, his disciples? His message was disarmingly simple. He commenced with this admonition:

> However much the power of the West may have declined, however great the dangers of the West may be, that decline, that danger, nay, the defeat, even the destruction of the West would not necessarily prove that the West is in a crisis: the West could go down in honor, certain of its purpose. The crisis of the West consists in the West's having become uncertain of its purpose.[9]

The key to the resolution of the crisis lay in a restoration of vital ideas and faith that in the past had sustained the moral purpose of the West. It was necessary to go back to the origins and to explore deeply the fundamental problems. Specifically, it was imperative to study the great thinkers of the past, be they teachers of good or evil, and to study their enduring works; it was essential to understand these thinkers as they understood themselves, and from that base the task of revitalization could begin. Who are the teachers of Good? They will be found, Strauss responded, in the classical Greek and biblical heritages; inescapably, the soul of the historical West is rooted in these intellectual traditions, and here are found the metaphysical foundations of what Strauss called "The Great Tradition" of Western politics.

## II

Strauss's affection for classical Greek political philosophy is a pervasive characteristic of all his work. Strauss cautioned that when a person "engages in the study of classical philosophy he must know that he embarks on a journey whose end is completely hidden from him. He is not likely to return to the shores of our time as exactly the same man who departed from them."[10] Why study the classics? Strauss instructed, "It is not...antiquarianism nor...romanticism which induces us to turn...toward the political thought of classical antiquity. We are impelled to do so by the crisis of our time, the crisis of the West."[11] The fact that classical political philosophy had been replaced by modern utopian ideologies was, according to Strauss, "the core of the contemporary crisis of the West"; consequently, "the indispensable starting point" for rekindling the idea of "the very possibility of high culture" lay with a return to the classics.[12] Indeed, Strauss concluded, "After the experience of our generation, the burden of proof would seem to rest on those who assert rather than on those who deny that we have progressed beyond the classics."[13]

A subtle yet key point in Strauss's affinity for the classical heritage is his preference for the Platonic emphasis over that of the Aristotelian. Although generally laudatory of Aristotle, it is in Plato that Strauss finds the *summum bonum* of classical political thought. Strauss elaborated: "Plato never discusses any subject ...without keeping in view the elementary Socratic question, 'What is the right way of life?'...Aristotle, on the other hand, treats each of the various levels of beings, and hence especially every level of human life, on its own terms."[14] Or as Strauss wrote on another occasion, "Aristotle's cosmology, as distinguished from Plato's, is unqualifiedly separable from the quest for the best political order. Aristotelian philosophizing has no longer to the same degree and in the same way as Socratic philosophizing *the character of ascent.*"[15]

"The character of ascent," Strauss contended, leads to the Great Tradition of political philosophy:

> The Great Tradition of political philosophy was originated by Socrates. Socrates is said to have disregarded the whole of nature altogether in order to devote himself entirely to the study of ethical things. His reason seems to have been that while man is not necessarily in need of knowledge of the nature of all things, he must of necessity be concerned with how he should live individually and collectively.[16]

The ascent commences with acknowledgment that the highest calling of man is in the role of philosopher, for he alone relentlessly pursues "knowledge of the whole"— and it is essential to stress that the quest is for knowledge (*episteme*), not opinion (*doxa*). The philosopher perceives a "nature of things" that is "intelligible" and "knowable," and to a comprehension of the Truth of this whole he bends his will and talents. In keeping with the Socratic heritage, to Strauss the first step in seeking comprehension is *piety:* "The beginning of understanding is wonder or surprise, a sense of the bewildering or strange character of the subject matter."[17] More simply, "[P]iety...emerges out of the contemplation of nature," and in so doing man learns "to see the lowliness of his estate."[18] In perceiving his lowliness, man is acknowledging a hierarchy of being. At the pinnacle of this hierarchy is transcendent Truth, or the Good. To know Truth, to go out of the Platonic cave and to know fully the essence of the sun, would be inexpressibly exhilarating and would be the ultimate in attainment and satisfaction for the philosopher. Needless to say, total comprehension of the whole, including Truth at the pinnacle, eludes the full grasp of mortal man; yet, it is from knowing in the marrow of his intellectual being that the hierarchy of the whole exists that the philosopher is driven unrelentingly in pursuit of knowledge of the whole. To the philosopher the logic of the matter is inexorable: Man is not self-produced; he is a part of a larger scheme of things; and no greater challenge lies before man than to attempt to discern, however dimly, the essence of that whole.

As imperfect as our knowledge is, from the Platonic-Straussian perspective, we have learned some truth; that is, there is such a thing as human knowledge, and, in fact, knowledge about important matters. For example, we know in our understanding of the whole that things have unalterable essences; more particularly, we know "that there is an unchangeable human nature."[19] Similarly, individual men have fixed natures that are not amenable to fundamental alteration or change. The initial task is to know ourselves, to perceive our fixed natures, and to attune ourselves accordingly. To the extent that we know our inner beings and accept our fixed essences as integral parts of the hierarchy of the whole, we have glimpsed the essence of classical Justice: "We shall then define justice as the habit of giving to everyone what is due to him according to nature."[20] Conversely, "Justice means attending to one's own business, bringing oneself into the right disposition with regard to the transcendent unchanging norm."[21]

The political implications of classical Platonic thinking are profound. As a consequence of the general concern for ascent, piety, knowledge, truth, justice, and kindred concepts, the Platonic tradition stresses the quest for "the best political order"— the summit of the political hierarchy. As Strauss explained, the best political order entails government by "good men":

> The claim to rule which is based on merit, on human excellence, on "virtue," appeared to be least controversial [in thought].... Good men are those who are willing, and able, to prefer the common interest to their private interest and to the objects of their passions, or those who, being able to discern in each situation what is the noble or right thing to do, do it because it is noble and right and for no ulterior reason.[22]

Virtue emerges as the controlling ingredient in establishing the best political order: "[T]he chief purpose of the city is the noble life and therefore the chief concern of the city must be the virtue of its members...."[23] And what is the hallmark of virtue?: "Pseudovirtue seeks what is imposing and great, true virtue what is fitting and right."[24] Moreover, "Virtue is impossible without toil, effort, or repression of the evil in oneself."[25] As Strauss maintained, "The classics had conceived of regimes (*politeiai*) not so much in terms of institutions as in terms of the aims actually pursued by the community or its authoritative part. Accordingly, they regarded the best regime as that regime whose aim is virtue...."[26] It is, then, "the character, or tone, of a society" that is the key datum to the classical thinkers in the quest for the best regime. The cornerstone in building the best political order is the character of the individual. As the society is only the individual writ large, it is "the formation of character" in the individual that preoccupied the classical thinkers. Neither institutions, environmental changes, nor science, according to classical thought, were capable of redeeming man and ushering him into the political promised land. Indeed, it was beyond the potential of mortal man to redeem himself; however, he could seek the best attainable by aspiring to ascend, and this required developing the intellectual and moral character of the individual.

There is the element of universalism in classical political thought: "By the best political order the classical philosopher understood that political order which is best always and everywhere .... 'The best political order' is, then, not intrinsically Greek: it is no more intrinsically Greek than health."[27] This quest for the finest is not to be confused with egalitarianism; in fact, it is the antithesis of egalitarianism: "But just as it may happen that the members of one nation are more likely to be healthy and strong than those of others, it may also happen that one nation has a greater natural fitness for political excellence than others."[28] The concept of the hierarchy of things—the movement from lower to higher—was an immutable component of classical thinking, and it indelibly etched an anti-egalitarianism into classical political thought. Strauss observed, "The basic premise of classical political philosophy may be said to be the view that natural inequality of the intellectual powers is, or ought to be, of decisive political importance."[29] Similarly, he wrote, "The founding of the good city started from the fact that men are by nature different and this proved to mean that they are by nature of unequal rank."[30]

Although classical political thought searched for an understanding of the ideal or best political order in order that man might aspire to ascend, it was categorically antiutopian. As Strauss explained it: "The classics thought that, owing to the weakness or dependence of human nature, universal happiness is impossible, and therefore they did not dream of fulfillment of History. . . . [T]hey saw how limited man's power is. . . ."[31] In contrast to the utopian, Strauss noted, "[T]he philosopher. . .is free from the delusions bred by collective egoisms. . . . [H]e fully realizes the limits set to all human action and all human planning. . . he does not expect salvation or satisfaction from the establishment of the simply best social order."[32] Concisely stated, "The best regime and happiness, as classical philosophy understood them, are impossible."[33]

"Perhaps Socrates," Strauss speculated, "does not primarily intend to teach a doctrine but rather to educate human beings— to make them better, more just or gentle, more aware of their limitations."[34] In sum, classical political philosophy "is free from all fanaticism because it knows that evil cannot be eradicated and therefore that one's expectations from politics must be moderate. The spirit which animates it may be described as serenity or sublime sobriety."[35] We return to that originating principle of piety, or as Strauss explained, "Classical political philosophy was liberal in the original sense."[36] Conversely, "The classics were for almost all practical purposes what now are called conservatives."[37]

## III

In Strauss's thinking the Judaeo-Christian heritage is the second pillar of the Great Tradition of political philosophy. Unequivocally, he found the religious tradition of the West as vital to the

Great Tradition as he did the classical heritage. Revealing of Strauss's affinity for the religious basis of Western thought is his intense admiration of Moses Maimonides, described by Strauss as the "greatest Jewish thinker of the Middle Ages."[38] Maimonides' major work was *The Guide for the Perplexed,* which is directed, Strauss explained, "[T]o those believing Jews who have, by reason of their training in philosophy, fallen into doubt and perplexity...."[39] or as Maimonides himself wrote, "I address those who have studied philosophy and have acquired some knowledge, and who while firm in religious matters are perplexed and bewildered on account of the ambiguous and figurative expressions employed in the holy writings."[40] Did Strauss feel that Maimonides had been successful in resolving this perplexity? Strauss answered, "*The Guide* as a whole is not merely a key to a forest but is itself a forest, an enchanted forest, and hence also an enchanting forest: it is a delight to the eyes. For the tree of life is a delight to the eyes."[41]

Maimonides "is the Jewish counterpart" of Saint Thomas Aquinas: "Maimonides reconciles reason and revelation by identifying the distinctive aim of...divine law, with the aim of philosophy."[42] Regarding their respective emphasis upon the classical heritage, Strauss noted a basic difference between Aquinas and Maimonides:

> For Thomas Aquinas, Aristotle is the highest authority...in political philosophy. Maimonides, on the other hand, could not use Aristotle's *Politics,* since it had not been translated into Arabic or Hebrew; but he could start, and he did start, from Plato's political philosophy.[43]

Thus Maimonides did out of necessity what Strauss had done by choice: both drew more heavily from Platonic than Aristotelian thought. Maimonides was able to harmonize the Platonic and Judaic tradition, Strauss observed, since both heritages sought the Ideal; specifically, Judaism became the "perfect law in the Platonic sense" of the Ideal.[44]

Strauss's admiration for Maimonides takes on a particularly

important dimension in view of the deep religious orthodoxy of Maimonides. In Strauss's words: "The remedy for this perplexity [the perplexity the philosopher has about religion] is the...explanation...that restores the faith in the truth of the Bible, that is, precisely what Maimonides is doing in *The Guide*."[45] The basic tenet of Maimonides' thinking is rooted in Platonic and biblical piety: "Maimonides finds...that given man's insignificance compared with the universe man's claim to be the end for which the world exists is untenable."[46] According to Maimonides, "human reason is inadequate for solving the central problem"; consequently, he affirms the indispensability of revealed religion.[47] As Strauss concisely stated the matter: "Maimonides defines his position by two frontiers. In the face of orthodoxy he defends the right of reason, in the face of philosophy he directs attention to the bounds of reason."[48]

Maimonides's recommended approach to the study of scripture had a profound effect on Strauss. Maimonides offered these maxims: "The *deeper sense* of the words of the holy law are pearls, and the literal acceptation of a figure is of no value in itself." "Their *hidden meaning,* however, is profound wisdom, conducive to the recognition of real truth." "Your object should be to discover...the general idea which the author wishes to express."[49] As to reading *The Guide,* Maimonides requested, *"Do not read superficially,* lest you do me an injury, and derive no benefit for yourself. You must study thoroughly and read continually; for you will then find the solution to those important problems of religion, which are a source of anxiety to all intelligent men."[50] Maimonides concluded with an observation Strauss could only relish:

Lastly, when I have a difficult subject before me—when I find the road narrow, and can see no other way of teaching a well established truth except by pleasing one intelligent man and displeasing ten thousand fools—I prefer to address myself to the one man, and to take no notice whatever of the condemnation of the multitude; I prefer to extricate that intelligent man from his embarrassment and show him the cause of his perplexity, so that he may attain perfection and be at peace.[51]

The technique of study advocated by Strauss in his teaching career is unmistakenly vintage Maimonides. There is that emphasis upon careful textual analysis in which one eschews literalism and looks for the "deeper sense" and "the hidden meaning." In addition, as noted, there is that strong Platonic and biblical willingness, if necessary, to ignore "the multitude" and "to address" oneself to "one intelligent man." Indeed, the point is compelling: Strauss not only drank deeply of the substance of Maimonides's thought, he not only attempted to reconcile the classical and biblical views, but in addition he borrowed considerably from Maimonides's method of study, and it is not too much to say that he cast himself in the role of a modern Maimonides.

Further underscoring Strauss's commitment to the biblical heritage is his disdain for Spinoza. Maimonides and Spinoza were both of Jewish heritage. The former was devoted to preserving the biblical roots, while the latter, through his major work, *Theologico-Political Treatise,* sought to free himself and his readers from biblical guidance. Strauss was lavish in his praise of Maimonides and unsparing in his criticism of Spinoza: "Spinoza rejects both Greek idealism and Christian realism.... Spinoza's God is simply beyond good and evil.... Good and evil differ only from a merely human point of view; theologically the distinction is meaningless."[52] Spinoza's initial error is to reject the classical-biblical concept of piety: "To humility Spinoza opposes composure of mind as the joy that springs when man contemplates himself and his power of action."[53] Having rejected piety, Spinoza called for "an open attack on all forms of orthodox biblical theology."[54] Spinoza "denies revealed religion" and rejects the biblical conception of sin:

> Does there exist [in Spinoza's thinking], apart from all humanly constituted law, a law plainly imposed on all men, and of which transgression is sin? Is there human action

which contravenes the will of God? For Spinoza, this is the question regarding the *lex divina,* and to the question understood in this sense his answer is No.[55]

As Strauss explained even more succinctly, "Spinoza's real view [is that] every man and every being has a natural right to everything; the state of nature knows no law and knows no sin."[56]

Strauss continued, "Spinoza...charges full tilt...with the wholehearted scorn of the realist free of illusions who knows the world."[57] According to Spinoza the error of religion is that it causes man to place "his trust in others rather than in himself, rather than in his own powers of rational reflection...."[58] Unlike Maimonides, Spinoza was "convinced...of the adequacy of human capacities for the guidance of life," and he demanded of "Judaism that it should justify itself before the tribunal of reason, of humanity."[59] In sum, Spinoza, "taking his stand on the unambiguous evidence and of reason," points directly to the mind and spirit of the Enlightenment:

> Interest in security and in alleviation of the ills of life may be called the interest characteristic of the Enlightenment in general. This movement sought in every way open to it to assure greater security and amelioration of life...Nothing could be more odious to the Enlightenment than the conception of God as a terrible God, in which the severity of mind and heart, and the spirit of the Book of Deuteronomy, finds its ultimate justification.[60]

What is the result of Spinoza's view?: "[T]he humanitarian end seems to justify every means; he plays a most dangerous game; his procedure is as much beyond good and evil as his God."[61] More specifically, Strauss wrote, "The explicit thesis of the *Theologico-Political Treatise* may be said to express an extreme version of the 'liberal' view," and thus Spinoza ultimately "found his home in the liberal secular state."[62]

Not only in his differing reactions to Maimonides and Spinoza does one see the religious facet of Strauss's thinking. In stating directly his personal views, Strauss reveals a deeply religious dimension. Note this somewhat cryptic remark: "It is true that the successful quest for wisdom [that is, philosophy] might lead to the result that wisdom is not the one thing needful."[63] Throughout his work Strauss employs this biblical phrase, "the one thing needful." This phrase is used by Christ in the story of Martha and Mary wherein He said to Martha, "Martha, you are anxious and troubled about many things, one thing is needful." Is there any doubt as to the religious implications of this statement by Strauss? "The insecurity of man and everything human is not an absolutely terrifying abyss if the highest of which a man knows is absolutely secure."[64] Strauss contended that reason is inadequate for a comprehensive explanation, for it "knows only of subjects and objects."[65] Similarly, naturalism is inadequate, for it "is completely blind to the riddles inherent in the 'givenness' of nature," and finally "humanism is not enough.... Either man is an accidental product of a blind evolution or else the process leading to man, culminating in man, is directed toward man. Mere humanism avoids this ultimate issue."[66]

The answer lies, Strauss reasoned, "Only by surrendering to God's experienced call which calls for one's loving Him with all one's heart, with all one's soul and with all one's might can one come to see the other human being as one's brother and love him as oneself."[67] In addition, Strauss cautioned, "The absolute experience will not lead back to Judaism...if it does not recognize itself in the Bible and clarify itself through the Bible...."[68] Concerning the Bible, Strauss wrote, "[I]t is true...I believe... that the Bible sets forth the demands of morality and religion in their purest and most intransigent form...," and he further reflected, "[T]he orthodox answer rests upon the belief in the superhuman origin of the Bible."[69] Strauss claimed that without "biblical faith" it was not possible to see "human beings...with humility and charity...."[70] Men of "unbelief" are "haunted men. Deferring to nothing higher than their selves, they lack guidance. They lack thought and discipline. Instead they have what they call sincerity."[71] Strauss continued with this profoundly religious observation: "One can create obstinacy by virtue of some great villainy, but one needs religion for creating hope."[72] Compelling is this final observation, "The genuine refutation of orthodoxy would require the proof that the world and human life are perfectly intelligible without the assumption of a mysterious God."[73] There is no question that Strauss looked upon biblical knowledge of this "mysterious God" as an indispensable step toward "knowledge of the whole."

Although his personal heritage was Jewish, there is not a trace of antagonism in Strauss's writing toward Christianity; indeed, probably the most moving dimension of Strauss's thinking was his effort to afford "recognition of that common ground" between Judaism and Christianity:

> What can such recognition mean? This much: that Church and Synagogue recognize in each the noble features of its antagonist. Such recognition was possible even during the Christian Middle Ages: while the Synagogue was presented as lowering its head in shame, its features were presented as noble.... Even the pagan philosophers Plato and Aristotle remained friends...because each held the truth to be his greatest friend. The Jew may recognize that the Christian error is a blessing, a divine blessing, and the Christian may recognize that the Jewish error is a blessing, a divine blessing. Beyond this they cannot go without ceasing to be Jew or Christian.[74]

In pursuing his "common-ground" theme, Strauss argued:

> The common ground on which Jews and Christians can make a friendly *collatio* to the secular state cannot be the belief in the God of the philosophers, but the belief in the God of Abraham, Isaac, and Jacob—the God who revealed the Ten Commandments or at any rate such commandments as are valid under all circumstances regardless of the circumstances.[75]

As Strauss viewed it, "The agency of the Jew and the agency of the Cross belong together; 'they are aspects of the same agony.' Judaism and Christianity need each other."[76] To Strauss it was essential to understand that "over against scientism and humanism Judaism and Christianity are at one."[77]

Beyond "the common-ground" argument, Strauss wrote admiringly of Christian contributions to Western thought. For example, regarding Catholicism he observed:

Anyone who wishes to judge impartially of the legitimacy or the prospects of the great design of modern man to erect the City of Man on what appear to him to be ruins of the City of God must familiarize himself with the teachings, and especially the political teachings, of the Catholic church, which is certainly the most powerful antagonist of that modern design.[78]

Be it in their "common ground" or in their separate contributions, he spoke approvingly of the Jewish and Christian heritages. It is to be cautioned that Strauss was not advocating a maudlin ecumenical synthesis of Judaism and Christianity. Strauss insisted, as noted, that beyond "the common ground" neither faith could proceed "without ceasing to be Jew or Christian." Strauss did not conceive it as the task of mortals to dilute the essence of either faith. To attempt to do so would reflect impiety in its worst form.

## IV

To Strauss the issue was clear: "Western man became what he is and is what he is through the coming together of biblical faith and Greek thought. In order to understand ourselves and to illuminate our trackless way into the future, we must understand Jerusalem and Athens."[79] As had Maimonides and Aquinas, Strauss saw, in spite of certain irreconcilable antagonisms, a mutuality of interest between "Plato and the prophets." To begin with, both the classical and biblical heritages renounced human pride or *hubris* and commended piety as the key virtue: "According to the

Bible, the beginning of wisdom is fear of the Lord; according to the Greek philosophers, the beginning of wisdom is wonder."[80] Moreover, as a corollary premise, Strauss noted both traditions "made very strict demands on self-restraint. Neither biblical nor classical morality encourages us to try, solely for the sake of our preferment or our glory, to oust from their positions men who do the required work as well as we could."[81] Similarly, "Neither biblical nor classical morality encourages all statesmen to try to extend their authority over all men in order to achieve universal recognition."[82]

In addition to emphasizing the virtues of piety and self-restraint, "Plato teaches, just as the Bible, that heaven and earth were created or made by an invisible God whom he calls the Father, who is always, who is good and hence whose creation is good."[83] Furthermore, in biblical and classical thought "justice is compliance with the natural order" of creation.[84] The wisdom of Jerusalem and Athens requires discernment of the natural order of things and man's attuning himself to that order. That is, man is not the Creator, he is the creature; he is not the potter, he is the clay. It is then man who adapts to creation, not creation to man—to propose the latter is to propose perverting the natural order of things. On the essence of God, creation, and justice, Plato and the prophets were as one.

In his analysis of the "coming together" of the wisdom of Jerusalem and Athens, Strauss cautioned, "Yet the differences between the Platonic and the biblical teaching are no less striking than the agreements."[85] First, there is the inescapable problem of "the opposition of Reason and Revelation." By its essence Reason accepts as true only that which has withstood the probing power of human logic and scientific understanding. In contrast, by its nature Revelation assumes there are truths beyond the intelligence of man to grasp. Man is finite and limited in his understanding; hence, those ineffable truths are knowable only through Revelation. Thus the philosopher yields: from the human vantagepoint, because of their respective essences, Reason and Revelation are not fully reconcilable.

Jerusalem and Athens take opposing positions on the fundamental question of whether we are pursuing truth or whether we already possess truth. Strauss explained:

> The philosopher is the man who dedicates his life to the quest for knowledge of the good, of the idea of the good.... According to the prophets, however, there is no need for the quest for knowledge of the good: God "has shewed thee, o man, what is good; and what doth the Lord require of thee, but to do justly, and to love mercy, and to walk humbly with thy God.[86]

Plato and the prophets are agreed that truth is the goal, but by the very nature of their differing perspectives, the clear thinker again concedes that from the standpoint of human understanding complete reconcilability is not possible; differing essences cannot be forced into a common mold; to attempt to do so does violence and irreparable harm to the vital nature of each.

As he had done in his efforts to find "the common ground" between Judaism and Christianity, so Strauss had done in his analysis of the classical and biblical views. He looked for the mutual foundations and artfully defined and boldly asserted them; however, he resolutely refused to force either component into an unnatural synthesis of human design. The essence of things had to be respected. The philosopher-theologian could carry the matter of synthesis to the highest level possible consistent with his understanding of the nature of things; yet it was gross error—perversion—to force the unnatural union of differing essences. We would have to learn to reconcile ourselves to the irreconcilable. This was acceptable to learned men, for classical and biblical piety had disclosed that it was not in the nature of things that mortal man should have total knowledge of the whole.

## V

The cardinal error of modern ideologies was to war against the nature of things, and to attempt to superimpose a strictly new design solely human in origin. With the thinking of the Renaissance, Strauss wrote, commenced the heresies of modernity: "[W]ithin the Renaissance an entirely new spirit emerged, the modern secular spirit. The greatest representative of this radical change was Machiavelli. . . ."[87] In Machiavelli, Strauss contended, lay the theoretical foundations of the modern age:

> The founder of modern political philosophy is Machiavelli. He tried to effect, and he did effect, a break with the whole tradition of political philosophy. He compared his achievement to that of men like Columbus. He claimed to have discovered a new moral continent. His claim is well founded; his political teaching is "wholly new." The only question is whether the new continent is fit for human habitation.[88]

Machiavelli launched the "first wave of modernity" as he broke sharply with the classical and biblical heritages, and as he also broke with the Great Tradition of Western political thought. Regarding Machiavelli's break with the classical tradition, Strauss observed, "Machiavelli refers so rarely to philosophy and philosophers: in the *Prince* and the *Discourses* taken together there occurs only one reference to Aristotle and one reference to Plato."[89] Concerning the key concept of piety in classical thinking, Strauss noted, "[O]ne does not find a trace of pagan piety in Machiavelli's work."[90] Similarly, "Wisdom is not a great theme for Machiavelli because justice is not a great theme for him"; consequently, there is "a movement from excellence to vileness" as Machiavelli, in departing from the classical view, "denies that there is an order of the soul, and therefore a hierarchy of ways of life or of goods."[91] In repudiating the classical view, Machiavelli denied "the possibility of a *summum bonum,*" and thereby "Machiavelli abandoned the original meaning of the good society or of the good life."[92] The "character of ascent," characteristic of classical thought, is destroyed by Machiavelli.

Nor, Strauss continued, is Machiavelli any less devastating in his attack upon the biblical tradition. In his clever and subtle attack on the biblical legacy, Machiavelli employs a conspiracy of silence: "He silently makes superficial readers oblivious of the biblical teaching."[93] "As one would expect," Strauss said, "Machiavelli is silent about God's witnessing or the relation between the conscience and God."[94] In neither *The Prince* nor *The Discourses* does Machiavelli make a "distinction between this world and the next, or between this life and the next; nor does he mention in either work the devil or hell; above all, he never mentions in either work the soul."[95] On this latter point, Strauss concluded, "[H]is silence about the soul is a perfect expression of the soulless character of his teaching: he is silent about the soul because he has forgotten the soul, just as he has forgotten tragedy and Socrates."[96] Thus "Machiavelli unambiguously reveals his complete break with the biblical tradition, and...he ascribes to all religions a human, not a heavenly, origin."[97] In short, Machiavelli "is certain that the Christian religion will not last forever. It is [merely] 'the present religion.' "[98]

The cleavage between Machiavelli and Christianity is sharply reflected in fundamentally differing attitudes on the meaning of "virtue." To Machiavelli virtue (*virtu*), properly understood, meant the pursuit of worldly power and honor. As Strauss elaborated, "Not trust in God and self-denial but self-reliance and self-love is the root of human strength and greatness."[99] In other words, "God is with the strongest battalions."[100] To Machiavelli, Christian virtue had "led the world into weakness...by lowering the esteem for worldly glory [and by] regarding humility, abjectness and contempt for things human as the highest good."[101] In summing up Machiavelli's position, Strauss wrote, "The sins which ruin states are military rather than moral sins. On the other hand, faith, goodness, humility, and patience may be the road to ruin, as everyone understanding anything of the things of the world will admit."[102] Machiavelli was indifferent to the truth of the biblical view; he proceeded to substitute politics for religion. In his "spiritual warfare" on the historical faiths of the West he raised a banner which proclaimed that "there is no sin but ignorance."[103] Had Machiavelli's assault on the established faiths succeeded? Strauss retorted, "The problem posed by biblical antiquity remains behind him like an unconquered fortress."[104]

Yet Strauss acknowledged the powerful effect Machiavelli has had upon the modern mind. Machiavelli was a bold "innovator" who sought to discover "new modes and orders" in the moral realm. He was "a rebel against everything that is respected," and he "liberated himself completely from belief in any authority."[105] Indeed, he attempted to establish a new authority spun from wholly new cloth. This new authority was rooted in Machiavelli's well-known proclamation "that all armed prophets have conquered and unarmed ones failed." This meant, Strauss explained, that "the primacy of Love must be replaced by the primacy of Terror. . . . Therefore the perfection envisaged by both the Bible and classical philosophy is impossible. . . . Man cannot rise above earthly and earthy humanity and therefore he ought not even to aspire beyond humanity."[106] In Machiavelli is found, then, an "attempt to replace humility by humanity," and the practical result is "to lower man's goal."[107] The purpose in lowering the goal is "to increase the probability of its attainment."[108] The new standard is "low but solid" and "its symbol is the Beast Man as opposed to the God Man: it understands man in the light of the sub-human rather than of the super-human."[109] Machiavelli's conception of the Beast Man leads to the threshold of modern tyranny, which "has its roots in Machiavelli's thought."[110] Ironically, Strauss observed, "A stupendous contraction of the horizon appears to Machiavelli and his successors as a wondrous enlargement of the horizon."[111]

In, *The Prince,* Strauss wrote, "The characteristic feature of the work is precisely that it makes no distinction between prince and tyrant: it uses the term 'prince' to designate princes and tyrants alike."[112] In Machiavelli's own words, "[F]or how we live is so far removed from how we ought to live, that he who abandons what is done for what ought to be done, will rather learn to bring about his own ruin than his preservation. . . . Therefore it is necessary for a prince, who wishes to maintain himself, to learn how not to be good. . . ."[113] In pursuing worldly honor and the praise of men, Machiavelli further instructed that the prince "must imitate the fox and the lion," must, that is, alternate between cunning and violence; "in the actions of princes, from which there is no appeal, the end justifies the means. Let a prince therefore aim at conquering and maintaining the state...."[114] Strauss summed up Machiavelli's instructions to the fledgling prince-tyrant: "He must pursue a policy of iron and poison, of murder and treachery .... [T]he patriotic end hallows every means however much condemned by the most exulted traditions both philosophic and religous."[115] "There can be no doubt regarding the answer," Strauss concluded, "the immoral policies recommended throughout the *Prince* are not justified on grounds of the common good but exclusively on grounds of the self-interest of the prince, of his selfish concern with his own well-being, security and glory."[116]

An additional result in Machiavelli's "lowering the goal" is that he "replaces God...by Fortuna."[117] "Fortuna is malevolent," Strauss explained, and she "mysteriously elects some men or nations for glory and others for ruin or infamy."[118] Furthermore, "[T]he end which Fortuna pursues is unknown, and so are her ways toward that end."[119] Fortuna is what is conventionally called chance, and she is the essence of human existence. Unlike the classical and biblical views, Machiavelli sees no hierarchy of order, nor does he perceive that things have essences and substances, that there is a "nature of things" independent of man's will. From the classical-biblical perspective man is a vital component of the whole, but he is not creator of the whole, nor does he have full dominion over it. The matter is otherwise with Machiavelli, Strauss noted, for "Fortuna is like a woman who can be vanquished by the right kind of man." Thus "if Fortuna can be vanquished, man would seem to be able to become the master of the universe. Certainly Machiavelli does not recommend that Fortuna be worshipped: she ought to be beaten and pounded."[120] As Machiavelli himself explained, in the case of "great men...fortune holds no sway over them."[121]

If fortune holds no sway over man and "if there is no natural end of man" in the Machiavellian view, then, as Strauss maintained, "[M]an can set for himself almost any end he desires:

162

man is almost infinitely malleable. The power of man is much greater, and the power of nature and chance is correspondingly much smaller, than the ancients thought."[122] And what are the practical implications of the notion that man is "infinitely malleable"? Strauss elaborated:

Machiavelli takes issue with those who explain the bad conduct of men by their bad nature: men are malleable rather than either bad or good; goodness and badness are not natural qualities but the outcome of habituation.

[Thus] what you need is not so much formation of character and moral appeal, as the right kind of institutions, institutions with teeth in them. The shift from formation of character to the trust in institutions is the characteristic corollary of the belief in the almost infinite malleability of man.[123]

It was to "the young" that Machiavelli took his call to join with him, as with a bold Columbus, in establishing "new modes and orders" and in settling a new "moral continent." Machiavelli stated, "I certainly think that it is better to be impetuous than cautious, for fortune is a woman.... And therefore like a woman, she is always a friend to the young, because they are less cautious, fiercer, and master her with greater audacity."[124] "Machiavelli tries," Strauss continued, "to divert the adherence of the young from the old to the new teaching by appealing to the taste of the young," and consequently "he displays a bias in favor of the impetuous, the quick, the partisan, the spectacular, and the bloody over and against the deliberate, the slow, the neutral, the silent, and the gentle."[125] In Machiavelli's thought, Strauss reasoned, "Reason and youth and modernity rise up against authority, old age, and antiquity." The result is "the birth of that greatest of all youth movements: modern philosophy...."[126]

In *The Prince* Machiavelli instructed youth with this superficial and callow doctrine: "Only those defences are good, certain and durable, which depend on yourself alone and your own ability."[127] "Machiavelli thus establishes," Strauss wrote, "a kind of intimacy with his readers par excellence, whom he calls 'the young,' by inducing them to think forbidden or criminal thoughts."[128] Strauss asked, "How can we respect someone who remains undecided between good and evil or who, while benefiting us, benefits at the same time and by the same action our worst enemies?"[129] "If it is true" Strauss maintained, "that only an evil man will stoop to teach maxims of public and private gangsterism, we are forced to say that Machiavelli was an evil man."[130] After all, Machiavelli himself had proclaimed in *The Discourses* that "evil deeds have a certain grandeur."[131] The Florentine, then, is "a teacher of evil," and it is only "the incredibility of his enterprise which secures him against detection, i.e., against the detection of the intransigence and awakeness with which he conducts his exploration of hitherto unknown territory and thus prepares the conquest of that territory by his brothers."[132]

## VI

Although Machiavelli laid the primary theoretical foundations, Strauss considered Thomas Hobbes one of those "brothers" assisting in launching the "first wave of modernity." In fact, earlier in his writing career Strauss had viewed Hobbes as the key figure in introducing modern Western thought; subsequently he wrote, "Hobbes appeared to me [earlier] as the originator of modern political philosophy. This was an error: not Hobbes, but Machiavelli, deserves this honor."[133] "It was Machiavelli, that greater Columbus," Strauss decided, "who had discovered the continent on which Hobbes could erect his structure."[134] To understand this "structure" erected by Hobbes, it was imperative, Strauss instructed, that "the fundamental difference" between Hobbes's thinking "and the classical as well as the Christian attitude should be grasped."[135] Succinctly stated, it was essential to understand that "the shifting of interest from the eternal order of man ...carried to its logical conclusion...leads to Hobbes's political philosophy."[136] As had Machiavelli, Hobbes broke completely with the Great Tradition of Western thought.

Under the tutelage of Plato, the classical perspective yearned for "the truth hidden in the natural valuations and therefore [sought] to teach nothing new and unheard-of"; rather, it sought to discover and articulate the "old and eternal." In contrast, Hobbes lusted after the "future and freely projected"; he searched for the "surprising new, unheard-of-venture."[137] At war with the classical legacy, Hobbes unleashed a violent outpouring of the modern spirit. He denied the notion of the soul, and he rejected the idea that there was a supreme good. Moreover, he denied the concept of the natural law; he repudiated the notion that there was an order of being and that there was a hierarchy of value and gradation in the nature of things. Likewise, Hobbes renounced any ideal of an objective moral order, that justice could be perceived, and that there was a natural end of man. As Strauss viewed it, Hobbes was "elated by a sense of the complete failure of traditional philosophy."[138]

Hobbes turned with comparable vehemence on the biblical heritage, preaching a doctrine of "political atheism." As to the Christian tradition, Hobbes differed with it "by his denial of the possibility that just and unjust actions may be distinguished independently of human legislation."[139] To Hobbes man "has no reason to be grateful to the 'First Cause' of [the] universe," and "there is then no reason for believing in the authority of the Bible."[140] Thus "unbelief is the necessary premise of his teaching about the state of nature."[141] In Hobbes's hands impiety is converted into a virtue.

According to Strauss, Hobbes taught a corollary doctrine of "political hedonism." In the Hobbesian scheme of things, death is "the primary and greatest and supreme evil, the only and absolute standard of human life, the beginning of all knowledge of the real world."[142] As death is the primary evil, it follows that "self-preservation" is the most basic of all rights, particularly self-preservation against violent death. In effect Hobbes upended the classical and biblical heritages and made self-preservation the *summum bonum* of the human experience; thus the ultimate sacrifices of self by Socrates and Christ in the pursuit of truth become odious perversions—evil—in the Hobbesian view. Self-preservation is the supreme right; it is the foundation of political morality, and it is antecedent to all things political. Classical and biblical notions of duty, service, and sacrifice to higher transcendent callings are summarily rejected. The Hobbesian goddess is sovereign power, for she alone can offer security against violent death, the supreme evil. Strauss wrote, "[O]ne may call Hobbes's whole philosophy the first philosophy of power."[143] He did find a measure of difference between Hobbes and Machiavelli: "[W]hereas the pivot of Machiavelli's political teaching was glory, the pivot of Hobbes's political teaching is power."[144] Power and glory emerge as key pillars of modern thought; they stand in stark contrast to the classical-biblical notions of piety and service.

After Machiavelli and Hobbes, Strauss maintained, "The second wave of modernity begins with Rousseau. He changed the moral climate of the west as profoundly as Machiavelli."[145] Rousseau unleashed the romantic radical spirit of modern Jacobinism. Whereas Machiavelli and Hobbes had subtly (and even on occasion gracefully) undermined the Great Tradition, Rousseau with glee and bravado wielded the ideological sword against the classical-biblical heritage. He was obscenely impious: he repudiated God and reason and declared human passion as the center and measure of all things. Through Rousseau's concept of the General Will, which is no more than collectivized human passion, we see erected the modern idol of collective man. The wreckage lies all around and the end of the destruction is not yet in sight. Strauss concluded, "[T]he restitution of a sound approach is bound up with the elimination of Rousseau's influence."[146]

Upon the heels of Rousseau, Strauss asserted, Nietzsche ushered in "the third wave of modernity." At least in Rousseau there had been the potentially redeeming virtue of the "noble savage" exuding compassion in his tranquil and blissful state of nature. Nietzsche offered no redeeming virtue; rather, he raised the preaching of evil to the nth power. He struck savagely at the twin pillars of the Great Tradition; with barbaric frenzy and sadistic pleasure he openly and explicity condemned Jerusalem and Athens. The heritage of Plato was rejected out-of-hand because of its emphasis upon reason in the pursuit of the Good. As had Rousseau, Nietzsche turned from reason to sentiment and passion, and he repudiated categorically any notion of a transcendent Good. Rather than the "character of ascent" of the classical view, Nietzsche led to descent into the world of the animal—the beast. Of man, Nietzsche wrote, "[The] hidden core needs to erupt from time to time, the animal has to get out again and go back to the wilderness."[147] In the same breath, Nietzsche renounced the biblical view by declaring that "God is dead." In addition, he uttered the heretofore unthinkable blasphemy that "man is god in the making," and he dismissed Christianity as no more than a "slave morality."

In place of the classical Good and Christian love, Nietzsche offered the "will to power." He wrote, "A living thing seeks above all to discharge its strength—life itself is will to power; self-preservation is only one of the indirect and most frequent results."[148] In the Nietzschean view, Strauss observed, "Man derives enjoyment from overpowering others as well as himself. Whereas Rousseau's natural man is compassionate, Nietzsche's natural man is cruel," and the result is that the "harmony and peace" of the classical-biblical view are replaced by "terror and anguish."[149] Nietzsche prefers Dionysus to Apollo, prefers the egotistic and orgiastic to the humble and contemplative. In converting man, the creature, into God, the creator, Nietzsche commits the ultimate blasphemy. As a result, Strauss wrote, "Man is conquering nature and there are no assignable limits to the conquest."[150] As God, Nietzschean man knows no authority higher than himself. He repudiates all authority and guidance provided by traditional theology, philosophy, and history. When released from the restraining forces of classical reason and biblical love, with a frenzy Nietzschean man grasps for the levers of power and deliberately directs that power to the destruction of man—to the obliteration of self. Nietzsche "thus has grasped a more world-denying way of thinking than that of any previous pessimist," and the result is the "adoration of the Nothing."[151]

## VII

In breaking with the Great Tradition of the classical and biblical legacies, Machiavelli, Hobbes, Rousseau, Nietzsche, and kindred spirits spawned the modern "isms." Foremost among these are positivism and historicism. "These are the two most powerful schools in the West today," Strauss observed.[152] Strauss underscored the positivist dimension in Machiavelli's thinking: "He may be said to exclude dogmatically all evidence which is not ultimately derived from phenomena that are at all times open to everyone's inspection in broad daylight."[153] Precisely stated, "Positivism is the view according to which only scientific knowledge, as defined by modern natural science, is genuine knowledge."[154] Positivism looked only to the factual and the material; it refused to think in terms of the transcendent and the spiritual—in sum, the essences of the Great Tradition were beyond its comprehension.

"Positivism," Strauss declared, "necessarily transforms itself into historicism."[155] From the viewpoint of the historicist, "History...became the highest authority.... [N]o objective norms remained."[156] Strauss elaborated, "The typical historicism of the twentieth century demands that each generation reinterpret the past on the basis of its own experience and with a view to its own future. It is no longer contemplative, but activistic...."[157] To the historicist, values "change from epoch to epoch; hence it is impossible to answer the question of right and wrong or of the best social order in a universally valid manner."[158] Historicism led its followers to the pursuit of temporal honor and glory as successful "sons-of-the-times." In substance, the modern historicists were ancient sophists in new garb. Machiavelli was a historicist in his pursuit of "power," "realism," and "new modes and orders"; similarly, Hobbes and Rousseau in their respective pursuits of "sovereign power" and the "General Will" were historicist in orientation; and Nietzsche's individual "will to power" was, Strauss maintained, no more than an extreme form of "radical historicism." Although varying in technique, in all cases these thinkers had repudiated notions of the transcendent and enduring; they sought solace and understanding in the mortal clay of specific times and places; and in so doing they broke with the Great Tradition and laid the foundations of modern historicism.

Historicism fragmented into corollary isms. The "radical historicism" of Nietzsche led to existentialism: "[I]t became clear that the root of existentialism must be sought in Nietzsche...."[159] Existentialism rejected "the assumption that being is as such intelligible," and it pitted the "will to power" of each individual against an indifferent, sometimes hostile, and always meaningless universe. It was a pathetic mismatching of power; the individual invariably lost, for in searching solely within himself for the resources to prevail, man found his stock of private resources woefully inadequate, and he inevitably succumbed to his infinitely more formidable opponent, blind fate. Under these despairing circumstances, the ineluctable end was nihilism. "Let us popularly define nihilism," Strauss wrote, "as the inability to take a stand for civilization against cannibalism."[160] Indeed, to those caught up in the depressing web of existentialism and nihilism, cannibalism was an acceptable alternative, for it offered escape even though through self-destruction.

Finally, the "three waves of modernity" led to the great heresy of utopianism. The classical and biblical traditions were rooted in piety, and thus though they strove powerfully to perceive the transcendent Ideal, there were no illusions that the human condition was perfectible; it was not inherent in the nature of things: from the classical perspective mortal man could never expect to escape completely the limitations of the Platonic cave, and in the biblical view only God's grace, not human effort, could fully redeem. The philosophical founders of the modern age contended otherwise; they did promise an earthly utopia. Machiavelli had proclaimed that Fortuna or chance could be conquered, and that man could be "master of the universe." Hobbes assured his listeners that "not divine grace, but the right kind of human government" would allow man to escape the limits of nature; Rousseau likewise maintained that man was "infinitely perfectible" and that there were "no natural obstacles" to human progress. And Nietzsche brazenly asserted, in Strauss's words, "that man is conquering nature and there are no assignable limits to that conquest."[161] As Strauss assessed the impulse of modern utopianism, he found it predicated on the notion of "man's conquest of nature for the sake of the relief of man's estate."[162] Hence "[t]he modern project...demands that man should become the master and owner of nature," and it holds out the promise not only of "emancipation" but of "secular redemption."[163] This was a powerful ideology that had come to grip the modern imagination, and it moved with confidence and relentlessness.

To Strauss modern utopianism was little more than ancient tyranny. Its essentials were well known to classical and biblical thinkers (after all, "there is nothing new under the sun"), and it was antithetical to the Great Tradition of Western political thought. While the latter tradition stressed piety, the order of things, truth, justice, love, service, hope, and the attunement of man to the ordained nature of things, the legacy of tyranny was founded upon pride, egalitarianism, relativism, perversion, terror, power, despair, and the rebuilding of the human condition from new foundations of a strictly human design. Strauss summarized, "In limitless self-love, in frenzied arrogance, the tyrant seeks to rule not merely over men but even over gods."[164] Tyranny was a massive heresy; its roots were Machiavelli; and it found its fullest expression in modern totalitarianism, in National Socialism and Communism.

The armed ideology of National Socialism had been halted by World War II, and in that Strauss rejoiced. It was the relatively unchecked growth of contemporary Communism, the ultimate in tyranny, that deeply troubled him. "The victory of Communism would mean," Strauss wrote, "the victory of the most extreme form of Eastern despotism."[165] What of those "new" political scientists who expected Communist regimes "to transform themselves gradually into good neighbors?"[166] They were "criminally foolish," retorted Strauss; they knew nothing of the immutable ideological character of the Marxist-Leninist mind; and because these thinkers had ceased to draw intellectual and spiritual nourishment from the Great Tradition, as "old fashioned political scientists" had done, they appeared incapable of discerning tyranny, let alone condemning it. In probably his most famous statement, Strauss lamented:

> Only a great fool would call the new political science diabolic: it has no attributes peculiar to fallen angels. It is not even Machiavellian, for Machiavelli's teaching was graceful, subtle, and colorful. Nor is it Neronian. Nevertheless one may say of it that it fiddles while Rome burns. It is excused by two facts: it does not know that it fiddles, and it does not know that Rome burns.[167]

## VIII

Although Strauss saw contemporary society gravely threatened by the modern "isms," he was not a teacher of despair. "Not anguish but awe is 'the fundamental mood'," Strauss advised, and he added that it is false to assume "that a prophet is true only if he is a prophet of doom; the true prophets are also prophets of ultimate salvation."[168] Even when confronted with the monstrous evils of contemporary totalitarianism, Strauss counseled, "There will always be men who will revolt against a state which is destructive of humanity or in which there is no longer a possibility of noble action and of great deeds."[169] This rich prophecy, perhaps now symbolized in the figure of a Solzhenitsyn, gives assurance that out of the very crucible of degradation springs hope and thereby power; thus out of evil itself emerges good. If this is the case, and Strauss contended that it was, hope inhered in the nature of things. There is cause then for joy, not despair. The ultimate metaphysical center in Strauss's thinking is one of affirmation, not negation.

Building successfully on the foundations of hope is not likely to be accomplished by merely offering alternative "isms" of more alluring and comforting nature. John Locke, whom conventional wisdom considers the theoretical patron saint of American democracy, does not point to the needed solution, for "Locke is closer to Machiavelli than he is generally said or thought to be": "Locke enlarged self-preservation to comfortable self-preservation and thus laid the theoretical foundation for the acquisitive society."[170] The Lockean tradition negated notions of duty and service, of excellence and virtue, and offered instead tantalizing visions of ever-expanding rights which fostered egoism. Locke was a "political hedonist." Nor, continued Strauss, did libertarianism in general possess the theoretical strength and depth to withstand the evils of the modern "isms." Rooted also in hedonism and egoism, libertarianism soon produced cloying and aimlessness, and life degenerated into "the joyless quest for joy."[171] Libertarianism left the "ultimate sanctity of the individual as individual unredeemed and unjustified."[172] Similarly, there was no redemptive power in modern statist liberalism. Its ethical foundations were appallingly thin: it challenged no one to virtue and service; rather, it openly, unrelentingly, and arrogantly pandered to hedonism by promising material surfeit through governmental planning and edict. Knowledge no longer had "the character of ascent" in relation to the transcendent and enduring; it existed exclusively to serve the ever escalating material demands of the unrestrained human ego. Strauss concluded, "There is undoubtedly some kinship between the modern liberal and the ancient sophist."[173]

Moreover, it was unlikely that some form of traditionalism alone could restore the needed metaphysical foundations. Strauss was not hostile to traditionalism if it were properly understood as a corollary to a deeper metaphysic. As a corollary theorem, it had the value of restraining men from engaging in mindless and reckless innovation; it served as a preventive to impiety, the rankest and most ancient of heresies. However, the potential error of unassisted traditionalism was its equating "the good with the ancestral."[174] Strauss warned, "But not everything old everywhere is right."[175] "Prudence," Strauss cautioned, "cannot be seen properly without some knowledge of 'the higher world'—without genuine *theoria*."[176] In sum, the ultimate goal is ascent to the Truth, and unexamined traditionalism frequently serves as a deterrent to that upward thrust.

The only course open to restoring the essential theoretical foundations seemed clear. Contemporary man had succumbed to the petty dogmas and harsh ideologies of the modern thinkers. To restore the intellectual vitality of the Western tradition, to alleviate the crisis of modernity and to avert disaster, it was imperative to reject the modern "isms" and to repair to the restorative powers of the classical and biblical heritages—to the Great Tradition of Western politics. Strauss never defined his intellectual position as "conservative"; perhaps there was the risk that any newly spawned "ism," no matter how nobly conceived, would degenerate into another fleeting variant of historicism. Yet American conservatives happily accepted Strauss on his terms; they drew incalculable sustenance from him; many shared his belief in the restorative powers of the Great Tradition; and finally, conservatives instinctively knew that Strauss, the teacher, was correct: to endure and to prevail it was imperative to escape the stifling clutches of historicism.

# Eric Voegelin

Eric Voegelin was born in Cologne, Germany in 1901. Receiving his doctorate from the University of Vienna in 1922, he served on the law faculty of that institution. To escape the Nazi regime he came to the United States in 1938. Subsequently he taught at Harvard University, Bennington College, the University of Alabama, and Louisiana State University, where he was Boyd Professor from 1952 to 1958. Voegelin returned to Germany in 1958 where he became Professor of Political Science and Director of the Institute for Political Science at the University of Munich until his retirement in 1966. Following his retirement Voegelin was affiliated with the Hoover Institution at Stanford University until his death in 1985. Voegelin was a prolific writer of books, articles, and reviews. His major works include *The New Science of Politics* (1953), *Science, Politics and Gnosticism* (1968), *From Enlightenment to Revolution,* (1975), and his multi-volume work, *Order and History,* commenced in 1956.

Although he did not label himself a conservative, nor write specifically for a conservative audience, Voegelin's work has been sympathetically received by many Americans of conservative persuasion, and his impact on conservative thought in America since World War II has been considerable. For example, Peter Stanlis has spoken of Voegelin's writing as "a great monument to the spirit of both Hellenic and modern man."[1] Ellis Sandoz has lauded Voegelin as "the leading political scientist and thinker of our time," while Frank S. Meyer spoke of the "towering genius of Eric Voegelin."[2] Indeed, Meyer asserted that Voegelin may well be "remembered as one of the foremost of those who defeated the forces of infamy."[3] Finally, Russell Kirk described Voegelin as "the most influential historian of our century, and certainly the most provocative."[4] Kirk concluded: "Yes, the climate of opinion among historians is clearing; and the work which may do more to effect a general revision of learned opinion than any other historical production of this century is Voegelin's."[5]

Permeating Voegelin's work is the theme that "spiritual regeneration is the burning problem of the age."[6] In the West, Voegelin finds a "crisis of the spirit" precipitated by the growth of gnosticism. As defined by Voegelin, gnosticism assumes that through human knowledge man can fulfill himself within history. It is not that gnosticism is new—it is a perspective with a long history in the Western experience. Rather, what precipitates the crisis is the emergence of gnosticism in the modern age as probably the dominant intellectual tone. Modern "progressivism" or statist liberalism is gnosticism in its mildest form: the emphasis is upon the earthly perfection of the human condition through gradual "reform." Through education and institutional manipulation and restructuring, coupled with increasing governmental involvement, regulation, and control, mankind in the mass will be gently coerced into conformity with the vision of the perfected life as divined and articulated by progressivist political elites.

Gnosticism is seen in its most virulent form in modern totalitarianism, Fascism and Communism. The totalitarian mind lusts for total control of all facets of human life, thought, and behavior. Its vision is boundless and its alleged wisdom knows no limits. The totalitarian proclaims to have unraveled the mystery of history, and he proceeds to ensconce himself as the self-appointed elite who will direct mankind in the creation of an instant worldly paradise. Not surprisingly, an insatiable pride and a fascination for violence are his hallmarks. To Voegelin, totalitarianism is the ultimate in the crisis of the spirit of the modern age.

In the Western experience, are there intellectual and theoretical tools to overcome this predicament? Voegelin answered unequivocally in the affirmative: there are the enduring resources of the Hellenic and biblical philosophical heritages. Notwithstanding key philosophical differences between these traditions, both share a common commitment to the pursuit of human dignity and the humane society through an appreciation that man is first and foremost a dependent creature with a spiritual dimension.

## II

Voegelin lamented that the modern climate of opinion was unfavorable to classical studies, for "[i]n its essentials the classical foundation of political science is still valid today."[7] More particularly, Voegelin wrote, "Political science, *politike episteme,* was founded by Plato and Aristotle."[8] Throughout Voegelin's works is found a deep affection for the classical Greek heritage; however, as Voegelin cautioned, "By restoration of political science [of the classical Greek tradition] is meant a return to the consciousness of principles, not...a return to the specific content of an earlier" historical era.[9]

This "consciousness of principles" commences with the mood of contemplation and the desire for discovery. The "life of contemplation," which Aristotle described as the *bios theoretikos,* results in an "understanding of man himself and of his place in the universe," and it is "a fundamental spiritual obligation quite independent of its contribution to 'useful activities.'"[10] In sum, the ultimate goal is the discovery of the "unchangeable order of the soul and the world."[11] The "spiritual obligation" of the contemplative mind stems from an "openness toward transcendence."[12] As Voegelin viewed it, in Hellenic thought the dominant emphasis is upon the quest for the *summum bonum,* for the transcendent Good, in a word, for God.

Voegelin explained that Greek "philosophy by definition has its center in the experience of transcendence."[13] The consciousness of transcendence produces a profound sensitivity to the "constitution of being." In fact, the essence of classical Greek philosophy is the "exploration of the constitution of being."[14] "The constitution of being is what it is," Voegelin continued, "and cannot be affected by human fancies."[15] He elaborated,

"The constitution of being remains what it is—beyond the reach of the thinker's lust for power. It is not changed by the fact that a thinker drafts a program to change it and fancies that he can implement that program."[16] Within the constitution of being there is a "hierarchy of existence, from the ephemeral lowliness of man to the everlastingness of the gods."[17] In view of this hierarchy of existence, anti-egalitarianism was an immutable principle of the classical mind; it was understood "that not all men were equal, that the creation and maintenance of civilizational order was the work of minorities, of the excellent, and...this was the insight on which Plato based his conceptions of the philosopher-king and...Aristotle his conception of the mature man, the *spoudaios,* who was the carrier of moral excellence as well as order in the polis."[18]

Understanding the hierarchy of existence and "attunement" thereto is the central task of the classical philosopher. Specifically, from the Hellenic view "[r]estoration of order could only come from the soul that had ordered itself by attunement to the divine measure."[19] Essential to achieving attunement was the cultivation, through training and discipline, of the "ordering powers" of wisdom, courage, temperance, and justice. Concerning the latter, Voegelin stated, "Justice, the keystone of the system of ordering powers, is that disposition of the well-ordered soul by virtue of which each part fulfills its proper function."[20] In the hierarchy of existence, then, there are parts or elements that have their differing essences or natures, and justice is achieved when the innateness of those essences and natures is respected and allowed to reach its intended level of development and fulfillment. According to the classical view, "The nature of a thing cannot be changed; whoever tries to 'alter' its nature destroys the thing."[21] Concerning human nature, Voegelin observed that in the classical mind "the very idea of a history of mankind presupposes that constancy of nature." Thus "[h]uman nature is constant in spite of its unfolding in the history of mankind," and "the discernible stages of increasing truth of existence are not caused by 'changes in the nature of man' that would disrupt the unity of mankind and dissolve it into a series of different species."[22]

The theoretical premise of "attunement to the divine measure" reflected in the Hellenic mind a deep sense of humility or piety about man and his position in the total hierarchy of being. Voegelin explained, "Man is not a self-created, autonomous being carrying the origin and meaning of his existence within himself."[23] There is an appreciation in the classical mind that "[t]he difficulties [of life] fall apart when the burden of fate and responsibility is accepted with humility."[24] This humility lent itself to a strongly antiutopian element in classical thinking: "A theory of the best order must be based on a study of the limiting factors."[25] Accordingly, the Hellenic spirit "was not obsessed by the superstition that the blueprint of a constitution will deliver the world from evil."[26] Similarly, there was no "eschatological desire to escape the world," nor were there any illusions about "the collective salvation of a people through a mediator-king, halfway between God and mankind."[27] In brief: "There is a nature of man, a definite structure of existence that puts limits on perfectibility"; therefore, "it is beyond a man's ability to translate the mystery of the cosmos into perfection in history."[28]

To the classical spirit, the greatest heresy is to ignore attunement to the order of things and to pursue the illusions of the utopian rebels, who contend human nature is malleable and the human condition perfectible. This course produces disorder and disintegration in society. In the utopian rebellion, Voegelin advised, there results "the process of gradual corrosion in which the elements of the psyche are one after the other loosened from their 'just' position in the integrated, well-ordered soul, until the passions without a higher ordering principle range freely without restraint."[29] Disorder and passion are the sustaining pillars of the degenerate society, and their presence in ancient Athens became the principal factor in the reaction "that culminated in the work of Plato and Aristotle."[30]

The concept of philosophy, Voegelin claimed, is the underlying premise of the classical mind, and through an understanding of its essence a return to ordered existence might be accomplished. What is philosophy? "Philosophy springs from the love of being; it is man's loving endeavor to perceive the order of being and attune himself to it."[31] From another perspective, "Philosophy is the endeavor to advance from opinion (*doxa*) about the order of man and society to science (*episteme*)."[32] The goal of philosophy is, then, the pursuit of wisdom and knowledge about the true nature and order of being—that order decreed and created by God. In this quest for understanding the *"modus operandi* is not revolution, violent action, or compulsion, but Persuasion...."[33] Concerning the vital characteristics of the philosopher, Voegelin wrote, "[T]he nature of the true philosopher is distinguished by the virtues of justice, temperance, courage, love of wisdom, unrelenting zeal in the search for true being, greatmindedness, ability to learn, and good memory."[34] To Voegelin, the classical principles are patently relevant to the modern age.

A subtle but significant facet of Voegelin's thinking is his assessment of the relative merits of Plato and Aristotle as the crucial figures in the development of the Hellenic mind. On occasion he treats them as philosophers of equal stature: "The spiritual sensitiveness and the magnificent realism, both of Plato and Aristotle...preserved them from the catastrophic derailment which characterizes modern politics...."[35] Elsewhere, suggesting a parity, he wrote, "The validity of the standards developed by Plato and Aristotle depends on the conception of a man who can be the measure of society because God is the measure of his soul"[36] Indeed, he singled out Aristotle for this accolade: "Aristotle is a philosopher; he is not an intellectual flunkey for the historically inevitable."[37] However, in spite of occasional intimations of parity, Voegelin articulated a position in which Plato emerged as the superior thinker.

Voegelin cautioned that there is no philosophical "gulf" between the two thinkers; on the contrary, there is an undeniable intellectual continuity between the two.[38] Nevertheless, in comparing Plato and Aristotle, Voegelin found "an intellectual thinning out" in the case of the latter. There emerges a difference in emphasis that approaches a difference in kind: "[With Aristotle there] is a curious transformation of the experience of transcendence which can perhaps be described as an intellectual thinning-out. The fullness of experience which Plato expressed in the richness of his myth is in Aristotle reduced to the conception of God as the prime mover...."[39] In addition, the Platonic love for the ultimate Good in Aristotelian thinking "is reduced to... the delight in cognitive action for its own sake."[40] "Moreover," Voegelin concluded, "no longer is the soul as a whole immortal but only that part in it which Aristotle calls active intellect...."[41] As Aristotle had lowered the spiritual sights, the result was a lessening of philosophical depth:

> Plato understood that the nature and acuteness of the [Athenian] crisis required an extraconstitutional government of men; this insight makes him a philosopher...superior to Aristotle, who, with a sometimes inconceivable complacency, could describe the...Hellenic polis and give shrewd recipes for dealing with revolutionary disturbances at a time when the polis world came crashing down all around him....[42]

"In Plato's work," Voegelin continued, "we feel the somber tension that stems from his theocratic will to achieve the impossible and to restore the bond between spirit and power," while in "Aristotle we feel a coolness and serenity which stems from the fact, if we may express it drastically, that he has 'given up.'"[43] Aristotle was content with surveying political phenomena, collecting data, classifying it, and dealing with problems on a pragmatic and prudential basis as they presented themselves in the existing environment. Unlike Plato, Aristotle no longer had "dreams of a spiritually reformed" Hellenic civilization.[44] The result of the Aristotelian emphasis was the encouragement of a philosophical "derailment which, though present in Aristotle, was still restrained by his genius."[45] Although Aristotle avoided disaster, "the derailment has become one of the principal modes of philosophizing after Plato—so predominant indeed that the history of philosophy is in the largest part the history of its derailment."[46] A turning from the Platonic quest for the spiritual to an exclusive preoccupation with the material and fleeting is the essence of the derailment.

With Voegelin, then, Plato emerged as the preeminent thinker: "[A] new epoch of order began with Socrates and Plato."[47] Plato is, in Voegelin's analysis, "the founder of the community of philosophers that lives through the ages."[48] Plato was not only a "great philosopher who knows what he is doing," but in addition, "Plato...became the religious founder, marking an epoch in the spiritual history of mankind."[49] The preeminence of Plato lay in his preoccupation with the spiritual dimension in man: "The opposition to a world of thought without spiritual order was repeatedly expressed by Plato at critical junctures of his work."[50] Succinctly stated, "Plato especially was very much aware that man...was open toward a depth of divine reality."[51] It was a key Platonic premise that society was man writ large: consequently, the well-ordered society was dependent upon proper spiritual order in the souls of its individual members: "The restoration of social order...will require the restoration of spiritual persuasion. And this has, indeed, become one of the great themes of Platonic politics."[52] "Platonism in politics," Voegelin concluded, "is the attempt...to regenerate a disintegrating society spiritually by creating the model of the true order of values."[53] Thus Platonism was founded upon the deepest philosophical "insight that the end of all human action does not lie with this world but beyond it."[54]

Voegelin believed that Plato was not a visionary or idealist in the modern utopian sense. Plato did not seek to escape reality; rather, he strove to understand it and man's place therein. From the Platonic view, it was an irrefutable datum that man was not self-produced: man owed his being and existence to an ineffable transcendent Being. This was not an ideal or a vision; this was an undeniable reality—a theoretical first principle. Man existed in what Plato termed the *metaxy*, the arena of "in-between," which suggested a human existence with all of the attendant tensions and burdens experienced by mortal beings: "good and evil, order and disorder, perfection and imperfection, life and death."[55] The fact of tension was not cause for despair, anxiety, and utopian revolts against the order of being; instead, it was cause for contemplation and reflection about the nature of man and his predicament. Reflection yielded up the premise that man was inescapably dependent on "the unseen measure" and was an integral part of its creation. This unseen measure was the source of being and order, and men of philosophical bent turned their talents to ascending toward it, for, if even dimly perceived, the foundations of a well-ordered society would have been laid, and there would be considerable cause for hope.

## III

In addition to his affection for the classical temper, Voegelin's writings reveal a deep affinity for the biblical view. On one occasion, when discussing the modern disdain for the biblical heritage, Voegelin wrote, "I do not intend to rush to the aid of the outcasts—Judaism and Christianity need no defense...."[56] He has not written an article or book dealing exclusively with a defense of the biblical perspective; however, such an effort possibly is not needed—indeed, might be anticlimactic—for throughout the corpus of his work is reflected a constant and unquestionable affinity for the essence of the biblical conception and its pivotal significance to the Western experience.

Voegelin maintained that Judaism represented a "leap in being" over the thinking of the "cosmological empires" of the ancient Near East. The Egyptian, Babylonian, Assyrian, and Mesopotamian civilizations were forms of cosmological empires whose theoretical centers were rooted solely in collective experiences. There was an impenetrable rhythm to the physical cosmos which set the pattern and the form for collective human experience. There was not the "differentiated" experience of the individual person; there was only the "compact" experience of undulating civilizations. This compactness suggested the ebb and flow of civilizational cycles, and it foreclosed any possibility of a personal spiritual experience arising out of sensitivity to the transcendent force that was not only the physical creator, but in addition, was the ordering spiritual force in individual lives. Israel and Judaism broke sharply with the theoretical premises of the cosmological view: "Through the leap in being, that is, through the discovery of transcendent being as the source of order in man and society, Israel constituted itself the carrier of a new truth in history."[57] "Through the divine choice," Voegelin explained, "Israel was enabled to take the leap toward more perfect attunement with transcendent being. The historical consequence was a break in the pattern of civilizational courses."[58] A wholly new conception of the human situation emerged: "History as the present under God was the inner form of Israel's existence."[59] Accordingly, Voegelin observed, "At the time when Egyptians themselves strained their cosmological symbolism to the limits without being able to break the bonds of its compactness, Moses led his people from bondage under Pharaoh to freedom under God."[60]

This new bond was based upon the "insight that existence under God means love, humility, and righteousness of action rather than legality of conduct."[61] The new relationship was predicated upon the notion that the "human personality" itself is "the authoritative source of order in society."[62] In contrast to the views of the cosmological empires, which offered no differentiated conception of the dignity or worth of the individual person, nor perceived a spiritual dimension to the single personality, "the Mosaic leap in being" asserted unequivocally the preeminence of the individual spiritual dimension as the fundamental datum of the human experience.

An affection for Christianity is reflected in Voegelin's admonition that a mature thinker will be "transcendentally oriented by grace and love."[63] Similarly, Voegelin advised, "The *only* thing a spiritual realist can do is to . . . return to the original sources of order in the soul, that is to the experiences of faith."[64] The Christian acknowledges "the mystery" of being and realizes that understanding of the human predicament is exceedingly limited. Man can acknowledge his being, can confirm that he is not self-produced, and he is intensely aware of his limitations and the imperfectibility of his condition. Furthermore, Christian man is aware of "the inscrutable mystery of evil in the world."[65] Compounding the mystery and the agony of evil, is man's realization that evil inheres in his condition; that is, evil can be lessened sometimes, but never fully eradicated. The Christian knows that man cannot escape this unsettling reality of his nature and being, and in fact, "one can discern the component of cruelty in the spiritual hardness even of Jesus and Saint Francis."[66] They were not maudlin and sentimental; on the contrary, in opposition to the ever-present agony of evil, they posited a spiritual steeliness. This steeliness was not callousness nor indifference; rather, it reflected an intense sense of realty which acknowledged and accepted through faith the whole of God's creation, including the inescapable presence of evil.

In the Christian view, education is not capable of eradicating evil, nor are new institutions and manipulations of the environment. Unavoidably, then, must crushing anxiety and despair be permanent and immutable features of the human predicament? The enduring quality of Christianity is in answering that question in the negative, for in place of anxiety and despair it offers the ineffable joy of hope through faith. "From such negations," Voegelin explained, "arose the idea of the God who would return as our Redeemer into history in order to rectify a condition of man beyond hope."[67] There was infinite potential for hope in "the fact that Western Civilization...contain[s] as a positive force—however diluted and weak it may have become—the Christian idea of the singularity and spiritual dignity of the human soul."[68] In sum, "Christianity discovered the faith that saves man from the death of sin and lets him enter, as a new man, into the life of the spirit."[69]

Christianity taught that "[m]an is no longer...a mere link in the chain of generations" but is a "spiritual center." [70] "The truth ...of Christianity," Voegelin stated, "[b]reaks with the rhythm of existence; beyond temporal successes and reverses lies the supernatural destiny of man, the perfection through grace in the beyond. Man and mankind now have fulfilment, but it lies beyond nature."[71] Christianity asserted this compelling moral first principle: "A man cannot fall back on himself in an absolute sense, because, if he tried, he would find very soon that he has fallen into the abyss of his despair and nothingness...."[72] Antiquity had suffered through that cruel lesson. "But the order of the ancient world was renewed by that movement which strove through loving action to revive the practice of the 'serious play' (to use Plato's expression)—that is, by Christianity."[73] Voegelin warned, "The atrophy of Christianity on a socially relevant scale causes a primitivization of intellectual and spiritual culture—the quite normal consequence of the breakdown of a spiritual order."[74] Moreover, he admonished, "[I]f in practice Christianity is successfully driven out of men, they become not rational liberals but ideologues."[75] The conclusion was inescapable: The "life of the spirit is the source of order in man and society."[76]

Of considerable value in underscoring Voegelin's affinity for Christianity are his frequent and invariably commendatory references to Saint Augustine. On the introductory page of each volume of *Order and History*, Voegelin offers this quotation from the Bishop of Hippo: "In the study of creature one should not exercise a vain and perishing curiosity, but ascend toward what is immortal and everlasting." Voegelin contended that Saint Augustine's *City of God* was a "great literary" event "in the West."[77] The Augustinian conception of history impressed Voegelin: "History no longer moved in cycles,... but acquired direction and destination...toward the understanding of the end as a transcendental fulfillment. In his elaboration of this theoretical insight Saint Augustine distinguished between a profane sphere of history in which empires rise and fall and a sacred history which culminates in the appearance of Christ and of the church."[78] For Saint Augustine, "[T]he universality of history lies in the providential guidance of mankind toward the true religion."[79] As a consequence, "The history of Israel, the appearance of Christ, and the history of the Church are the meaningful history of mankind, while profane history with its revolutions of empire has only the function of providing educative tribulations for Israel and the Church preparatory to the ultimate triumph."[80]

In his admiration for Saint Augustine, Voegelin wrote, "I want to give you Saint Augustine's formulation of the problem of exodus, for it very probably will never be surpassed. It is philosophically perfect, and hence it is still a valid category today." Voegelin elaborated, "According to Saint Augustine, in man, in the soul, there are organizing centers. The principal centers are the love of self and the love of God; these are the emotional orienting centers in the soul." Concerning "the problem of exodus," Voegelin explained, "Exodus is defined by Saint Augustine as the tendency to abandon one's entanglements with the world, to abandon the love of self, and to turn toward the love of God. So you see," Voegelin concluded, "it is a perfect formulation of the problem. It is not only perfect philosophically, it is also extremely beautiful."[81] Where there is departure from the Augustinian view, Voegelin lamented, "[T]he human personality has lost the integrating spiritual center with its phenomena of love, faith, hope, contrition, penitence, renovation and acquiescence. The only human faculty that is left is thought...."[82] A select position for Saint Augustine in Voegelin's thinking appears secure.

## IV

Voegelin's affection for the Hellenic, Judaic, and Christian heritages can be easily documented. They are the crucial strands in the formation of his thought. Yet the matter goes deeper than this. Subtly, but irrefutably, in the corpus of his writing, Christianity emerges as the preeminent achievement of the Western experience. For example, Voegelin spoke of "our own historical form of maximal clarity, which is the Christian."[83] On another occasion, he wrote, "There emerge [in the study of history] the contours of a giant cycle, transcending the cycles of the single civilizations. The acme of this cycle would be marked by the appearance of Christ; the pre-Christian high civilizations would form its ascending branch; modern, Gnostic civilization would form its descending branch."[84]

Regarding Judaism, Voegelin inquired, "Who was Moses?" He answered, "[He was] a symbolization of man who stands between the compactness of the Egyptian and the lucidity of the Christian order."[85] Judaism had made its enduring contribution: "The radical break with the cosmological myth was achieved only by Israel."[86] Nevertheless, "Israel...still had to carry the 'mortgage' of its revelation in so far as the universalism of existence under God was still narrowed down to a particular people. The existence of the Chosen People, therefore, prefigured the universal history of mankind under God through Christ."[87] "The imperial symbolism flickered for the last time in the Messianic hopes of the Solomon Psalms," Voegelin explained, "Then it was extinguished by the theology of the Epistle to the Hebrews."[88] As a consequence, "The Son of God, the Messiah of Yahweh, was no longer the head of a Judaite clan; and the cosmic god no longer presided over a mundane empire. The house of David has been transformed into the house of God the Father, to be built with man as the material, by the Son."[89] "[I]n no period of Jewish history before the appearance of Christ," Voegelin asserted, "had the articulation of the life of the soul, as well as the way of truth, reached an intenseness and a precision of symbolism" comparable with that represented in the life of Jesus: "Only with Jesus does the symbol of the Way of Truth appear in the Jewish orbit."[90] Voegelin elaborated, "[T]he history of Israel as the people under God is consummated in the vision of the unknown genius, for as the representative sufferer Israel has gone beyond itself and become the light of salvation to mankind."[91] In the concluding sentences of his classic *Israel and Revelation*, cryptically, but revealingly, Voegelin reflected on the story told in Acts 8:

> The Ethiopian eunuch of the queen, sitting on his cart and reading Isaiah, ponders on the passage: "Like a sheep he was led away to the slaughter." He inquires of Philip: "Tell me, of whom is the prophet speaking? of himself? or of someone else?" Then Philip began, reports the historian of

the Apostles, and starting from this passage he told him the good news about Jesus.[92]

Voegelin's comparison of the Hellenic and Christian heritages is arresting and instructive. The metaphysical center, he observed, "is the same in both Classic Philosophy and the Gospel movement. There is the same field of pull and counterpull, the same sense of life through following the pull of the golden cord, the same consciousness of existence in an In-Between of human-divine participation, and the same experience of divine reality as the center of action in the movement from question to answer."[93] In fact, on some crucial points of measurement the Christian view is inferior to classic philosophy: Christianity is "poorer by its neglect of noetic control"; "more restricted by its bias against the articulate wisdom of the wise"; and "more imbalanced through its apocalyptic ferocity."[94] Yet along other vital lines of measurement the Christian conception emerges as superior: It is "richer by the missionary fervor of its spiritual universalism"; "broader by its appeal to the inarticulate humanity of the common man"; "more imposing through its imperial tone of divine authority"; and "more differentiated through the intensely articulate experience of loving divine action in the illumination of existence with truth."[95]

Ultimately, in Voegelin's thinking Christianity emerges as a philosophical position superior to that of classical vintage. In the Hellenic mind, Vocgclin elaborated, "The individual never gained the personal status in his political unit which, under the influence of the Christian idea of man, characterized the political formations of Western civilization; it always remained in a status of mediation through the fictitious tribal and narrower blood-relationships within the polis."[96] With the Chosen People of Israel as with the classical polis, there was excessive emphasis upon compactness, upon the collectivity; there was too little emphasis upon individual and personal spiritual differentiation. Christianity was based upon this differentiation, and therein lay its philosophical superiority. Hellenic metaphysics was impressive in its "vision of the *agathon*" or "the divine paradigm." Its philosophical foundation was remarkably superior to the mythology of earliest antiquity, and its superseding "with its new authority the older authority of the myth" was an immeasurable metaphysical advancement. However, Voegelin noted, "the philosopher's authority, in its turn," was to be "superseded by the revelation of spiritual order through Christ."[97]

Even the great classical thinkers fell short of the philosophical heights attained by Christ. In Aristotle, there remained "the fundamental hesitation which distinguished the Hellenic from the Christian idea of man, that is, the hesitation to recognize the formation of the human soul through grace; there was missing the experience of faith...." Moreover, "the Aristotelian position does not allow for a...heightening of the immanent nature of man through the supernaturally forming love of God. It is true, the Aristotelian gods also love man ..., but their love does not reach into the soul and form it towards its destiny. The Aristotelian nature of man remains an immanent essence like the form of an organic being; its actualization is a problem within the world." As a result, "Transcendence does not transform the soul in such a manner that it will find fulfillment in transfiguration through Grace in death."[98]

In Voegelin's analysis Plato, too, yielded to Christ, for he "had at his disposition neither the idea of transcendental destiny of the soul, nor the idea of an intramundane, transfigured, ultimate history. His solution had to be found within the myth of nature and its cosmic rhythms."[99] With Plato and Aristotle, history tended to "move in cycles," while with Christianity it "acquired direction and destination."[100] Although Plato in his spiritual quest for the *summum bonum* had dramatically advanced the level of metaphysical understanding, his understanding was of a lower rank than Christ's. The Platonic metaphysic is fulfilled in Christ, but it is not equal to that of Christ's: The "Platonic evocation finds its fulfillment in the increasing spiritual ordering of a disordered world, through the figure of Alexander, through the soteriological kingship of the age, the Roman imperial order, and through

Christ."[101] In other words:

> Plato articulates his own position. . . by claiming the author-
> itative statesmanship of Athens against the renowned lead-
> ers who only in appearance are representative of the polis,
> until in the fullness of time this formula becomes the vessel
> for the assertion of the authority of Christ against the Old
> Law in the powerful repetitions: You have heard it said by
> those of old. . . . But I say unto you. . . [102]

Voegelin's position on the relative merits of Plato and Christ is
highly suggestive of that taken by Saint Augustine, who instructed that Plato is "a master rightly esteemed above all other
pagan philosophers," and he added that "none of the other philosophers has come so close to us as the Platonists have."[103] The
lesson is clear: Plato is philosophically "close to" Christ, but he
does not equal, let alone surpass, him.

It was the unmatched clarity, depth, intensity, and authority of
Christ's message that raised him to the preferred position in the
Western experience. "Something about Jesus," Voegelin mused,
"must have impressed his contemporaries as an existence. . . of
such intensity that his bodily presence. . . appeared to be fully
permeated by divine presence."[104] As a consequence, "when Jesus
answers the question of the apostle with his 'I am the way, the
truth, and the life' (John 14:6), he firmly [asserts his authority
over] the philosophers. From then onward the redemption of the
soul goes through Christ. . . ."[105] Jesus spoke not to the regional
empire, nor to the parochial polis, nor to the particularized Chosen People; instead, he spoke to the lone individual, and he made
a universal appeal—all persons were called, regardless of status
or rank. Rather than elaborating on the ancient and familiar concepts of the fascinations of earthly power and the achievements
of human knowledge, he spoke of man's finitude and dependence
and, accordingly, of the need for faith, grace, and love. While
Moses and Plato had offered considerable cause for hope, Christ
became the ultimate "leap in being," for the assurances he ten-
dered were not merely considerable, they appeared inexhaustible.

## V

Probably the key theoretical contribution of Eric Voegelin is his having delineated the nature and causes of what he called "the crisis" of Western civilization. The crisis resulted from the growth of what he called "gnosticism," and the cause of this development was the Western intellectual derailment from the Hellenic and biblical philosophical foundations. Voegelin spoke of "the radical incompatibility of the new attitude with the values of classical and Christian civilization."[106] "Out go the philosophers of Greece, the prophets of Israel, Christ, not to mention the Patres and Scholastics," Voegelin explained, "for man has 'come of Age,' and that means from now on man is the only possible creator of his own laws and the only possible maker of his own history.'" Henceforth, "man is the new lawmaker; and on the tablets wiped clean of the past he will inscribe the 'new discoveries in morality' which Burke had still considered impossible." Voegelin observed, "It sounds like a nihilistic nightmare. And a nightmare it is rather than a well considered theory."[107] As with nightmares, the result was not pleasant to contemplate: "The world is no longer the well-ordered [one]...in which Hellenic man felt at home; nor is it the Judeo-Christian world that God created and found good. Gnostic man no longer wishes to perceive in admiration the intrinsic order of the cosmos. For him the world has become a prison from which he wants to escape."[108] In sum, there is in the West an acute problem of "spiritual disorder" arising out of the emergence of the gnostic mind and the eclipse of the classical and Christian philosophical perspectives.

In the gnostic mind, Voegelin wrote, "The life of the spirit and the *bios theoretikos* are not merely pushed into the background..., they are definitely eliminated," for, in the gnostic view, "Man will be free when he has achieved perfect knowledge of the external world."[109] Gnosis in Greek literally means "knowledge," and to the gnostic, Voegelin noted, "The instrument of salvation is gnosis itself—knowledge."[110] "Knowledge—gnosis—of the method of altering being," Voegelin added, "is the central concern of the gnostic."[111]

In Voegelin's view, the fatal error of gnostic theorizing is in the turning away from the transcendent spiritual sustenance offered in the Hellenic and biblical conceptions and placing confidence in the perverse notion that man has it within his earthly capacity to achieve self-salvation and self-redemption. "[T]he dream of achieving the perfect society through organizing men according to a blueprint instead of forming them in an educational process, is a serious affair," Voegelin contended, for "it is something like the black-magic of politics. Most appropriately, therefore, the dream of Atlantis rises in luciferic splendor."[112] Voegelin continued, "The fallacy of gnosis consists in the immanentization of transcendental truth." [113] Stated simply: "Christ the Redeemer is replaced by the steam engine as the promise of the realm to come."[114] "The climax of this," Voegelin concluded, "is the magic dream of creating the Superman, the man-made Being that will succeed the sorry creature of God's making."[115] In short, gnosticism "is the dream of escape from the mystery of iniquity that has been expressed by T. S. Eliot in the verses"

They constantly try to escape
From the darkness outside and within
By dreaming of systems so perfect that no one will need to
be good.[116]

The result is Man "emptied of moral substance, and the forces of good and evil are transferred in their entirety to the analyst-legislator."[117] In the modern age, gnosticism has been manifest, in its most genteel form, as "progressivism," and in its most extreme and malignant forms as National Socialism and Communism—in a word, as totalitarianism. Voegelin wrote "And the totalitarianism of our time must be understood as journey's end of the Gnostic search for a civil theology."[118] Finally, then, gnosticism "blossoms out into the vision of the totalitarian workshop without escape."[119]

The components of gnosticism are diverse, but when congealed they produce intense ideologies. Invariably, gnosticism is ardently secularist. As Voegelin explained, "The *corpus mysticum Christi* has given way to the *corpus mysticum humanitatis.*"[120] Accompanying secularism is the most ancient of sins: human pride. "Not the spirit of God," Voegelin elaborated, "but the spirit of man...will bring salvation in immanent historical action."[121] Thus Voegelin noted, "The intramundane hubris of self-salvation culminates logically...in the improvement on God through the creation of a man who does not need salvation "[122] Out of secularism and pride springs the notion that unaided human intelligence and reason, through science, will redeem mankind by fully perfecting the earthly human condition. Accordingly, the emphasis is always upon progress: "It is," Voegelin wrote, "this dream of mankind marching towards wisdom and immortality like gods, this picture of mankind liberated from all its chains, beyond the reach of accident and chance, beyond the reach of the enemies of progress, that consoles the philosopher...."[123]

In its obsession with progress and perfection, the gnostic mind frequently lapses into fanaticism—there is considerable impatience to erect instanter the secular new Jerusalem. Fanaticism, Voegelin reflected, is seen most shockingly in "the massacres by the later humanitarians whose hearts are filled with compassion to the point that they are willing to slaughter one half of mankind in order to make the other half happy."[124] When the gnostic spirit abounds, Voegelin warned "[T]he social scene fills up with little emperors who each claim to be the possessor of the one and only truth; and it becomes lethal when some of them take themselves seriously enough to engage in mass murder of everyone who dares to disagree."[125] "With every turn of history," Voegelin concluded, "the self-made creators screw Eden deeper into its Hell."[126]

Finally, elitism is invariably a distinguishing element of the gnostic spirit. Voegelin observed, "Progress will no longer be a line of meaning to be discovered by the historian, it will be a direction in the process of mankind, intelligently accelerated by the enlightened elite."[127] As the masses are ignorant, it is the self-appointed elites who become "the executors of the historical will," for they alone can discern on behalf of the masses "what the historical process is all about."[128] The elites divine the meaning of history and grasp the levers of power in order to bend the historical process to their notions of the perfected earthly society.

Who are the founders and teachers of gnosticism? Their ranks are legion. Coming out of the Enlightenment, among others, there are Helvetius, D'Alembert, Turgot, Condorcet, and Voltaire. With the mind of the Enlightenment, and its unlimited confidence in the redemptive power of unassisted human reason, "an ethics of the Aristotelian type (with a scale of values oriented toward the *bios theoretikos*), or a spiritual morality of the Christian type (determined by the experience of the common ground in a transcendental reality), are beyond...reach."[129] To the enlightened mind, "Jesus appears as a 'sort of philosopher' who counsels mutual love and support without any intelligible authority or foundation for such counsels."[130] There emerged the "idea of an autonomous ethics, without religious or metaphysical foundation...."[131] The enlightened mind, Voegelin explained, "[C]ould sincerely believe that [it] need not bother about some 1500 years of Christian history and several centuries of Hellenism."[132]

Concerning the key role of Voltaire, Voegelin maintained that in spite of certain positive contributions as a literary figure Voltaire "has done more than anybody else to make the darkness of enlightened reason descend on the Western World."[133] "And with Voltaire," continued Voegelin, "begins...the concerted attack on Christian symbols and the attempt at evoking an image of man in the cosmos under the guidance of intraworldly reason."[134] "Voltaire was not a systematic thinker"; on the contrary, "his attack took the form of pamphlets...malicious witticisms...sarcasms and satires."[135] The result: "He inaugurates the type of man who is at the height of an age that conceives of itself as being at the height of human civilization."[136] Voltaire launched a "fierce attack on the life of the spirit":

[F]aced with the mysteries of religion he will frankly admit that he does not understand them and that, therefore, they have to be eliminated from the public scene. The light of reason should fall into every corner of the human mind, and if it falls on a substance that is solid enough not to be dissolved by its rays, the obstacle should be destroyed because it is a scandal to enlightened man.[137]

"The massive blow against the Augustinian construction," Voegelin noted, "was delivered by Voltaire."[138] With Voltaire, "there exists no Augustinian *anima animi* from which man reaches out in the *intentio* into the transcendent"; consequently, "The saint is neither good nor bad; he is nothing to us."[139] The theoretical system erected by Voltaire is spiritually barren: "The spiritual orientation and integration of personality is ignored as a problem, the principles of ethics are severed from their spiritual roots, and the rules of conduct are determined by the standard of social utility."[140]

Another key founder and teacher of gnosticism is Auguste Comte, the apostle of positivism. Voegelin declared, "Auguste Comte...is the first figure of the Western crisis."[141] Comte, the founder of the Religion of Humanity, looms large as one of the high priests of gnosticism in this self-appointed role as "spiritual dictator of mankind."[142] Comte personifies the overweening pride of the gnostic mind which conceives of itself as not only capable of divining in full the meaning of the human experience, but in addition visualizes itself as supremely capable of extricating man from all imperfections through the intense application of unaided human reason. It is a heady vision, and the wreckage from it lies all around—witness the death camps of modern totalitarianism.

With the positivist creed of Comte, "the *bios theoretikos* as a standard is abandoned," for "there can be no doubt that technical inventions are more useful to mankind than the expressions of the contemplative intellect."[143] Not only was the classical view rejected by Comte: "This is the first time in Western history that a man has arrogated to himself personally the place of Christ as the epochal figure which divides the ages."[144] "Comte," Voegelin charged, "was never shy in fixing his true importance in the history of mankind," for "he saw himself in the role of the Aristotle of the new age, as the...new Saint Paul, organizing the Church."[145] Conclusively proving that the pride of Comte knew no limits is his well-known Proclamation:

> In the name of the past and the future, the theoretical servants and the practical servants of Humanity assume befittingly the general leadership of the affairs of the earth in order to construct, at last, the true providence, moral, intellectual and material; they irrevocably exclude from political supremacy all the various slaves of God, Catholics, Protestants, or Deists, since they are retrogrades as well as perturbators.[146]

Voegelin is unrelenting in his critical assessment of Comte:

> Whatever the answer of the future will be, there can be no doubt even now that Comte belongs, with Marx, Lenin, and Hitler, to the series of men who would save mankind and themselves by divinizing their particular existence and imposing its law as the new order of society. The satanic Apocalypse of Man begins with Comte and has become the signature of the Western crisis.[147]

Concluded Voegelin: "[T]he positivistic dogma...could be accepted only by thinkers who did not master the classic and Christian science of man."[148]

## VI

Less strikingly than Voltaire and Comte, Machiavelli also contributed to the legacy of gnosticism. Plato had not believed in "the collective salvation of a people through a mediator-king," for "the problem of regeneration had become personal." Machiavelli offered "the other alternative." Machiavelli "also knew that a true order was impossible without a spiritual reform," and "[s]ince he found the spiritual resources neither in himself nor in anybody else, he confined himself to the evocation of the Prince who would achieve [national] unification through tactical means in power politics." The result was "the renunciation of the spirit and the fall into demonism."[149] Ultimately, in the unfolding of the age of nationalism, this meant that the "mystical bodies of the nations...could begin to substitute with increasing effectiveness for the mystical body of Christ."[150] With rejection of the universally unifying themes of the Hellenic *summum bonum* and the Christian *beatitude*, virulent nationalism resulted as a form of "fragmentation" and "particularism." There emerged limitless confidence in the redeeming power of nationhood; this was a strain of gnosticism; and for this a small debt was owed to Machiavelli.

Locke, the alleged theoretical patron saint of the American political tradition, had also contributed to the evolution of gnosticism. As Voegelin viewed the matter, it was not to Voltaire's credit that he "was profoundly impressed by the philosophy of Locke."[151] "[W]ith his inconclusive drifting in the surviving tradition of Christianity," Locke advised his readers: "All knowledge starts with sensation; all ideas are derived reflectively from sensation."[152] "From Locke directly stems the aversion against innate moral ideas," Voegelin noted, "and consequently the necessity to search for a new basis of morals."[153] Voegelin contended, "Locke's demolition of the assumption of innate ideas may be quite meritorious in itself, but it becomes a somewhat dubious achievement if we consider that he has nothing to offer in its place." He concluded, "The net result of Locke's speculation, thus, is not a new philosophy of morals but a thorough devastation on which nobody could build anything."[154] Locke, then, assisted in creating the intellectual vacuum into which the demonic powers of gnosticism moved.

More than Machiavelli and Locke, Hegel approached the levels of Voltaire and Comte as a contributor to the modern gnostic mind: "Hegel's philosophy of law and history marked the first major earthquake of the Western crisis."[155] Voegelin wrote, "For Hegel betrays in so many words that being a man is not enough for him; and as he cannot be the divine Lord of history himself,

198

he is going to achieve *Herrschaft* as the sorcerer who will conjure up an image of history—a shape, a ghost—that is meant to eclipse the history of God's making."[156] Yet this is only the beginning:

> Hegel, however, wanted to become, not a man, but a Great Man: The Great Man whose name marks an epoch in history was his obsession. Moreover, he did not want to become just any Great Man in history, preceded and followed by others, but the greatest of them all; and his position he could secure only by becoming the Great Man who abolishes history, ages, and epochs through his evocation of the Last Age that will forever after bear his imprint. The Great-Great Man in history is the Great Man beyond history.[157]

"Hegel's obsession was power."[158] After the fall of Jena to Napoleon in 1806, Hegel wrote, "I have seen the Emperor—this World-Soul—riding through town, and out of it, for a reconnaissance;—it is a wondrous feeling indeed to see such an individual who, concentrated in one point, sitting on a horse, reaches over the world and dominates it"[159] Concluded Voegelin "The passages give a fairly good picture of Hegel's state of mind in the critical years."[160] "To Hegel," Voegelin observed, "God is dead because man-god at last has come to life and will create a new realm in his image. To sum it up: The Hegelian man-god has eclipsed the reality of God and history and thereby gained both the freedom and authority to project Second Realities and impose them on the world."[161] Thus Hegel is a "thinker who believes that man can transform the world, which exists in tension toward God, into the very Realm of God itself."[162] For Hegel, "God and Man are eliminated from the universe of discourse," and "their place is taken by the imaginary" *Geist,* by the spirit of the times. The result is devastating: A "revolutionary destructiveness is engendered by . . . which arises Hegel's own deformation of the Holy Ghost into an absolute *Geist* that is meant to achieve the fulness of Revelation here and now in Hegel's system."[163]

While the classical and biblical "symbolisms express reality as experienced by a man whose soul is open toward the divine ground of the cosmos and his own existence," Hegelian "man deforms his existence by closing it toward the divine ground" and by conjuring up visions of world-immanent utopias.[164] It is an intoxicating and exceedingly destructive view: "The sorcerer has drawn into himself the power of both God and Christ." As Voegelin warned, "All mankind must join the sorcerer in the hell of his damnation."[165]

One of Hegel's "great successors in sorcery" was Nietzsche.[166] Nietzsche was the great practitioner of "the black magic of the isolated will."[167] Specifically, Voegelin noted, "Nietzsche... raised the question why anyone should live in the embarrassing condition of a being in need of the love and grace of God."[168] Nietzsche's solution was disarmingly simple: "In this dream of self-salvation, man assumes the role of God and redeems himself by his own grace."[169] The "will to power" was the instrument Nietzsche offered to accomplish the task of self-salvation. The Hellenic and biblical views had stressed man's dependence on transcendent being or authority and hence the need for reverence and awe—in a word, piety. In contrast, Nietzsche declared the total autonomy of the person, and he invited this wholly independent figure to achieve omnipotence through a sheer act of will. While the classical and biblical conceptions stressed reflection, contemplation, and attunement to the world of God's making, Nietzsche issued a call to action in pursuit of power in a world of man's making. Although perverse, Nietzsche's vision was tantalizing, and in time it produced madness: first, alienation, then despair, and finally nihilism—destruction for its own sake to relieve the intolerable pain of existence.

The quintessential gnostic is Karl Marx. Voegelin wrote, "At the root of the Marxian idea we find the spiritual disease, the gnostic revolt."[170] Indeed, "His spiritual impotence leaves no way open but derailment into gnostic activism."[171] With unbridled pride, Marx announced to the troubled world that through the singular process of his mind and reasoning faculties he had divined the meaning of history and of the human condition. There is "eschatological excitement" in Marx, and he sets forth the blueprint for the elitists—the Leninists—to grab the levers of power and to bludgeon a skeptical world into compliance with the Marxist vision. Reflective of the gnostic spirit in Marx is the pernicious "stop-history" dogma. Practitioners of this theoretical witchcraft preach the notion that previous history was an illusion and that "real" history will commence when their mind's-eye view of the earthly paradise has been imposed upon humankind.[172]

As a corollary theorem, there is the "Marxian suppression of questions."[173] That is, the Marxian mind is anti-philosophical; therefore, it is blatantly and grossly anti-Socratic. With his patently simplistic analysis of the human predicament, Marxian man senses that his system will not be able to endure serious philosophical scrutiny. Voegelin inquired, "Does this knowledge induce him to abandon his untenable construct?" Replied Voegelin, "Not in the least: it merely induces him to prohibit such questions."[174] Hence in "the clash between system and reality, reality must give way."[175] The inescapable conclusion: Marx perpetrates a monumental "intellectual swindle."[176] Certainly this is not surprising, for it was Marx who had proclaimed that "the philosophers have only interpreted the world, the point however is to change it." Marx had expressly and wantonly repudiated the classical intellectual heritage: Marx did not want dialogue; he wanted immediate and complete conformity to the simplicities of his analysis and his rabid call to action.

Similarly, Marx rejected the biblical legacy. "Our analysis," Voegelin continued, "has carried us closer to the deeper stratum of the Marxian disease, that is the revolt against God."[177] With Marx, "Faith and the life of the spirit are expressly excluded as an independent source of order in the soul."[178] Marx dismissed religion as no more than "the opium of the people." Moreover, he was not content with indifference toward religion; he found it imperative expressly to repudiate it. To Marx, the biblical God was his most powerful competitor. To eclipse the biblical God and to gain dominion over his creation, his existence and reality had to be explicitly denied. Indeed, God had to be depicted not merely as a fiction but as a symbolism created by the enemies of the masses to manipulate and exploit them. Marx instinctively understood the utility of hatred in the quest for earthly power and the erection of worldly utopias. He deliberately upended the biblical view: for the universal Gospel of love he substituted a doctrine of particularized class hatred. Briefly, Marxism-Leninism is gnosticism raised to the nth power, and in the process of accomplishing that end Marx led an "unambiguous attack on philosophy and Christianity."[179]

## VII

Voegelin maintained that a Christianity misconceived also had contributed to the gnostic movements. In fact, he observed, the gnostic impulses of the age of the Enlightenment were anticipated as early as the thirteenth century in the writings of Joachim of Flora. In Joachim is found "the idea of the Third Realm of the Spirit that would follow the Realms of the Father and the Son. This idea repudiated the Augustinian conception of the saeculum as a time of waiting for the second coming of Christ and envisaged a new era of meaning in sacred history."[180] Hence Joachim epitomized that sometimes muted but nonetheless pernicious strain in certain "Christian" thinkers to seek the realization of Christ's kingdom *on earth—now*. These thinkers are restless and impatient with the length of time it is taking to realize the ultimate fulfillment of Christ's promises. To placate their impatience, they yield to the temptation to offer present worldly utopias as substitutes for the ultimate Christian promise which, properly understood, will be realized only beyond history. Voegelin summarized: "When the Christian idea of supernatural perfection through Grace in death was immanentized to become the idea of perfection of mankind in history through individual and collective human action, the foundation was laid for the mass creeds of modern Gnosis."[181] Concerning the gnostic tendencies in some strains of supposedly Christian thought, Voegelin wrote,

"All of this has nothing to do with Christianity."[182] More than that, "[T]here is no passage in the New Testament from which advice for revolutionary political action could be extracted."[183]

In spite of his personal greatness and indispensability to Christianity, Voegelin contended, Saint Paul himself was partially responsible for the introduction of the gnostic strain into the Christian heritage. Commencing with Saint Paul, Voegelin explained, "The metastatic expectation of the Second Coming has begun its long history of disappointment."[184] In the thinking of Saint Paul, the promise of the Second Coming evolved into a doctrine of "fervent expectations" regarding the imminence of "the age of perfection."[185] In Pauline doctrine the end of history was at hand, and there was limited need for reflection or extended inquiry. Although Paul knew the age of perfection would come beyond history, his emphasis upon an imminent Second Coming, with the accompanying "eschatological excitement," subtly laid the theoretical foundation for those who would tire of waiting and in their impatience begin construction of earthly utopias. In Voegelin's view, Saint Augustine assumed a position on the Second Coming consistent with scripture and the inherent logic of the faith. Regarding the time of the Second Coming, Saint Augustine had written, "We know from the mouth of Truth that it is none of our business."[186] Quoting from Acts 1, Augustine explained, "Suffice it to say that the fingers of all such calculators were slackened by Him who imposed silence with the words: 'It is not for you to know the times or dates which the Father has fixed by his own authority.' "[187] In Augustinian theory there was no preoccupation with the timing of the Second Coming; instead, there was abiding concern with understanding the essence of the faith and the depth of the mystery.

In the tradition of Saint Augustine, Voegelin stressed essence and not literalism in interpreting the meaning of the Christian faith. Literalism produced "derailment" because "the symbols are torn out of their experiential context and treated as if they were concepts referring to a datum of sense experience."[188] As a result, literalism "converts the real truth...of a real experience

of real divine presence into the fictitious truth of human proposi-
tions about gods who are objects of cognition."[189] Literalism
leads to "doctrinal hardening" and "dogmatic incrustations"
that in turn lead away from the "essence" of the faith to its
"abuse"; therefore, literalism and resulting dogma are supporting
pillars of the gnostic tendencies in Christianity. Questions of
"faith," of "essence," and of "substance" are neglected; consequently, there is no need for the "inquiring mind" to explore the
perennial "mystery" of the meaning of the Gospel. "Christ is revealed," Voegelin reminded his readers, "not in the fulness of
doctrine, but in the fulness of Passion and Resurrection."[190] And
he summarized:

> [The hardened doctrine of gnosticism] is a far cry from the
> Matthean Jesus who calls to him the poor in the spirit, the
> gentle, the pure in heart, the peacemakers, those who hun-
> ger and thirst after righteousness and are persecuted for
> righteousness' sake. In Matthew 16, Jesus certainly does not
> intend to transform the Son of God into the Field-Marshal
> of the Pantocrator, but rather wants to transform the Mes-
> siah into the Son of God.[191]

Finally, the principal cause of the gnostic tendencies in Christianity lay with the very nature of Christianity itself. "Uncertainty is the very essence of Christianity," Voegelin wrote.[192]
Modern man hankers for security, and in the Christian message
"God is reduced to the tenuous bond of faith, in the sense of
Heb. 11:1, as the substance of things hoped for and the proof of
things unseen."[193] In perhaps his most eloquent lines, Voegelin
elaborated:

> The bond is tenuous, indeed, and it may snap easily. The life
> of the soul in openness toward God, the waiting, the periods
> of aridity and dullness, guilt and despondency, contrition
> and repentance, forsakenness and hope against hope, the si-
> lent stirrings of love and grace, trembling on the verge of a
> certainty which if gained is loss—the very lightness of this

fabric may prove too heavy a burden for men who lust for massively possessive experience.[194]

The opportunities for a "breakdown of faith" are extensive, for few persons are equipped with "the spiritual stamina for the heroic adventure of the soul that is Christianity."[195] The demands of the Gospel are heavy: "This thread of faith, on which hangs all certainty regarding divine, transcendent being, is indeed very thin. Man is given nothing tangible."[196] Once the bond of faith, fragile to begin with, is sufficiently weakened in a society the "spiritual strength of the soul which in Christianity was devoted to the sanctification of life could now be diverted into the more appealing, more tangible, and, above all, so much easier creation of the terrestrial paradise."[197] Concisely stated: As the presence of faith in society diminishes, the demonic spirits of gnosticism arise proportionately. Indeed, Voegelin reflected, "There are times, when the divinely willed order is humanly realized nowhere but in the faith of solitary sufferers."[198]

## VIII

In dealing with the crisis posed by modern gnosticism, Voegelin did not issue a nostalgic call for a blind return to some doctrinal fusion of classical Greek philosophy and Christianity. First, Voegelin rejected as puerile and unphilosophic the idea that one could turn back and restore in full the essence of an earlier Golden Age. One could benefit from studying the theoretical premises of earlier civilizations, but wisdom foreclosed the possibility of applying those premises uncritically and fully in the creation of some instant modern utopia—again, that was the error of the gnostic spirit. Rather, wisdom suggested the task was to learn of the theoretical essence of earlier civilizations and to discern if that learning had relevance to the specific circumstances of evolving contemporary societies. Secondly, Voegelin deplored the notion of "doctrine," for it evoked visions of the hardened and incrusted intellectual world of the gnostics themselves. In this regard Voegelin has adamantly resisted labeling himself:

On my religious 'position', I have been classified as a Protestant, Catholic, as anti-semitic and as a typical Jew; politically, as a Liberal, a Fascist, a National Socialist and a Conservative; and on my theoretical position, as a Platonist, a Neo-Augustinian, a Thomist, a disciple of Hegel, an existentialist, a historical relativist and an empirical sceptic; in recent years the suspicion has frequently been voiced that I am a Christian. All these classifications have been made by university professors and people with academic degrees. They give ample food for thought regarding the state of our universities.[199]

Clearly, Voegelin does not think of himself as "liberal," "conservative," "libertarian," "Platonist," "Christian," or otherwise: labeling leads to doctrinal hardening, which in turn is the basic theoretical error of gnosticism, the "ism" of anti-philosophy and the antithesis of the theoretical emphasis of Eric Voegelin. Gnosticism encompassed the intellectual world of the closed mind, the simplistic and intellectually primitive world of the ideologue. The ideologue envisioned himself as self-produced and capable of self-redemption through the theoretical construction in his closed mind's eye of an earthly new Jerusalem that would supersede the imperfect world of reality, the world of God's making. To Voegelin this was the crucial theoretical error of modern thought, and to overcome the perversities of gnosticism he found compelling relevance in the Hellenic and biblical views. He found relevance in these latter perspectives not because of any doctrinal purity they allegedly possessed, but because they represented philosophical postures that were anti-closed system and anti-doctrinaire. Both found their intellectual sustenance in the notion of "openness to transcendence," and both recognized that history is a "mystery in process of revelation."[200] In each case there was acknowledgement that man was a creature, not the creator, and that he was radically dependent on the creating force for his very being, including an understanding of that being. Hence in the classical and biblical views there was intense appreciation of the limitations of finiteness of the human predicament. History did continue, and the mystery did remain. There was pressing reason for piety, reverence, and awe; and the continually inquiring mind, open to transcendence, was the indispensable and ultimate instrument in the pursuit of understanding and Truth.

Voegelin is a teacher of hope. He counsels, "No one is obliged to take part in the spiritual crisis of a society; on the contrary, everyone is obliged to avoid this folly and live his life in order."[201] The crisis was not a matter of "inevitable fate"; the effort could be made to forge the intellectual tools to facilitate escape from the gnostic prisons. Should the effort be made? Quoting from Richard Hooker, Voegelin responded with a resounding "yes" in order that "posterity may know we have not loosely through silence permitted things to pass away as in a dream."[202] Although it was not specifically intended by Voegelin to abet any particular movement or "ism," in his thinking American conservatives have found considerable aid and comfort.

# Ludwig von Mises

Ludwig von Mises, and his former student, Friedrich A. von Hayek, have emerged as the key economic theorists of American conservative thought since World War II. Born in Lemberg, Galicia, in 1881, Mises received a doctor of jurisprudence degree from the University of Vienna in 1906. He held a professorship in the Graduate Institute of International Studies in Geneva, Switzerland, from 1934 to 1940. In 1938 he married Margit Sereny-Herzfeld, and in 1940, to escape the growing Nazi menace, the couple immigrated to the United States where Mises became a citizen. A co-founder of the Mont Pèlerin Society in 1947, Mises became well known as a frequent lecturer and prolific writer until his death in 1973 at the age of 92. Mises wrote 15 books or monographs and over 200 articles. Through his scholarly endeavors, he became known as the "dean" of the Austrian School of Economics. This school was founded by Carl Menger in 1871; Friedrich von Wieser and Eugen von Böhm-Bawerk were numbered among its preeminent figures. Although there was no "school" in the formal sense, in an age of increasing collectivism these men shared a commitment to the essentials of classical liberalism.

Mises's major works would include *The Theory of Money and Credit* (1912), *A Critique of Interventionism* (1929), *Socialism* (1936), *Bureaucracy* (1944), *Omnipotent Government* (1944), *The Anti-Capitalistic Mentality* (1956), *Theory and History* (1957), *Epistemological Problems of Capitalism* (1960), *The Free and Prosperous Commonwealth* (1962), *The Ultimate Foundation of Economic Science* (1962), *Planning for Freedom* (1974), *On the Manipulation of Money and Credit* (1978), *Notes and*

*Recollections* (1978), and his monumental work, *Human Action* (1949). Concerning this latter work, Henry Hazlitt wrote, "If any single book can turn the ideological tide that has been running in recent years so heavily toward statism, socialism, and totalitarianism, *Human Action* is that book."[1] On another occasion, Hazlitt said of Mises: "He was beyond question the foremost economist of his generation."[2] In his evaluation of *Human Action*, Henry Regnery wrote: "Few would deny that any more profound, complete or persuasive exposition and defense of the free market has been written than Ludwig von Mises's *Human Action*."[3]

Beyond Hazlitt and Regnery, there has been a continuing chorus of praise for Mises. For example, George Roche has maintained, "When the history of twentieth century thought is written, Ludwig von Mises will in all probability be recognized as the greatest economist of our age."[4] Israel Kirzner described Mises as "an inspiring teacher and towering scholar and thinker," while Friedrich von Hayek depicted him "as the leading interpreter and defender of the free enterprise system."[5] Murray Rothbard probably best summarized Mises's achievement as follows: "If we should truly be on the threshold of a resurrection of the spirit of freedom, then that rebirth will be the crowning monument to the life and the thought of a noble and magnifecant man."[6] In addition to these admirers, Mises inspired a host of intellectual followers, including Hans Sennholz, Wilhelm Röpke, Ludwig Lachmann, Fritz Machlup, Laurence Moss, Gottfried Haberler, William Peterson, Sylvester Petro, Edmund Opitz, and Leonard Read.

Mises described himself as a "liberal"; however, as he explained, "The term *Liberalism*... is to be understood in its classical nineteenth-century connotation, not in its present-day American sense, in which it signifies the opposite of everything that it used to signify in the nineteenth century."[7] "The word 'liberal'," Mises lamented, "means in American today socialist or interventionist."[8] In sum, contemporary American liberalism is "pseudo-liberal"; it is a perversion of true classical liberalism. Moreover, Mises viewed conservatism in its European context, and this gave it a negative connotation in his thinking. From this view, conservatism "advocated a return to monarchical absolutism" and "status privileges for the nobility."[9] "Stagnation" and "rigidity" were the fruits of conservatism, Mises concluded. "It is opposed to new ideas and to any spontaneity on the part of the subjects."[10] Of course, American conservative thought in the post-World War II era was not of that strain of conservatism; rather, it drew a portion of its intellectual sustenance, particularly on economic matters, from classical liberalism, and therein lay the appeal of Ludwig von Mises to American conservatives.

## II

From the vantage point of Mises's liberalism, "The key stone of Western civilization is the sphere of spontaneous action it secures to the individual."[11] Mises's concern for individualism goes decidedly beyond a general interest in the meanderings of the masses of individual men. He admires that rare figure emerging out of the mass of mankind and is fascinated by "the creative genius" or "the pioneer." What is the nature of "the pioneering genius?" "Leaders . . . are not pioneers. They guide people along the tracks pioneers have laid. The pioneer clears a road through land hitherto inaccessible and may not care whether or not anybody wants to go the new way. The leader directs people toward the goal they want to reach."[12]

Throughout his work Mises repeatedly maintained he was not proposing a theoretical position placing the individual in opposition to society. On the contrary, he asserted, "[T]he higher fulfillment of the individual's life is possible only in and through society."[13] Indeed, "In cooperating with their fellows, individuals do not divest themselves of their individuality."[14] Rather, they enhance it:

> There is in the long run no irreconcilable conflict between the rightly understood selfish interests of the individuals and those of society. Society is not a Moloch to whom man has to sacrifice his own personality. It is, on the contrary, for

every individual the foremost tool for the attainment of well-being and happiness. It is man's most appropriate weapon in his struggle for survival and improvement. It is not an end, but a means, the most eminent means for the attainment of all human desires.[15]

Thus, according to Mises, Hobbes erred in contending that the natural state of man in society was a dire condition of "the war of all against all."[16] As conceived by Mises, the individualism of liberalism does not lead to autarky, isolation, and perpetual hostility; instead, it points to "division of labor," "social cooperation," "harmony of interests," high levels of productivity, and ultimately to the building of superior civilizations. The creative individual working within society is the natural and preferred state of man. Mises's liberalism, which has distinctly political and economic dimensions, is constructed on that premise.

Above all an economist, Mises was primarily concerned in his writings with the essentials of economic freedom; however, he was not neglectful of political freedom, for in liberalism, he wrote, "Freedom is indivisible."[17] Significantly, the issue of freedom was the dividing line between the cultures of the East and the West. In Mises's words, "What separates East and West is first of all the fact that the peoples of the East never conceived the idea of liberty."[18] This distinction made an enormous difference in the respective developments of the West and East: "In Europe there was commotion; in the East there was stagnation, indolence and indifference." Mises explained, "The reason is obvious. The East lacked the primordial thing, the idea of freedom from the state. The East never raised the banner of freedom, it never tried to stress the rights of the individual against the power of the rulers."[19] Hence, Mises noted, "Western society was a community of individuals who could compete for the highest prizes."[20] In contrast, "Eastern society was an agglomeration of subjects entirely dependent on the good graces of the sovereigns." The result: "The alert youth of the West looks upon the world as a field of action in which he can win fame, eminence, honors and wealth; nothing appears too difficult for his ambition. The meek progeny of Eastern parents know of nothing else than to follow the routine of their environment."[21]

Mises staked out a position on individual political liberty that savors of the near absolutism of John Stuart Mill. "No one," Mises proclaimed, "has ever succeeded in advancing any tenable objections against the reasoning of the two classical books: John Milton's *Areopagitica*, 1644, and John Stuart Mills's *On Liberty*, 1859. Unlicensed printing is the life blood of literature."[22] Mises continued, "Freedom must be granted to all, even to base people, lest the few who can use it for the benefit of mankind be hindered."[23] "Liberalism demands tolerance," Mises explained, "as a matter of principle, not from opportunism. It demands toleration even of obviously nonsensical teachings, absurd forms of heterodoxy, and childishly silly superstitions. It demands toleration for doctrines and opinions that it deems detrimental and ruinous to society and even for movements that it indefatigably combats."[24] What justifies such an extreme doctrine of tolerance? "For what impels liberalism to demand and accord toleration is not consideration for the content of the doctrine to be tolerated, but the knowledge that only tolerance can create and preserve the condition of social peace without which humanity must relapse into the barbarism and penury of centuries long past."[25] Mises concluded, "A free man must be able to endure it when his fellow men act and live otherwise than he considers proper. He must free himself from the habit, just as soon as something does not please him, of calling for the police."[26]

In addition to this expansive position on individual political rights, Mises ardently defended the democratic ideal of representative government. Representative government was "the political corollary" of the free market. The latter allowed the consumer to be sovereign with each penny the equivalent of a vote, while the former allowed voter sovereignty through the ballot box. Hence, "Pareto, Georges Sorel, Lenin, Hitler, and Mussolini were right in denouncing democracy as a capitalist method."[27] Regarding representative government, Mises concisely explained, "Democracy means self-determination."[28] Government based upon the premise of self-determination was the only rational alternative:

> In the end the philosophy of the majority prevails. In the long run there cannot be any such thing as an unpopular system of government. The difference between democracy and despotism does not affect the final outcome. It refers only to the method by which the adjustment of the system of government to the ideology held by public opinion is brought about. Unpopular autocrats can only be dethroned by revolutionary upheavals, while unpopular democratic rulers are peacefully ousted in the next election.[29]

In Mises's view, peace was indispensable for the maintenance of social cooperation, which in turn led to a creative and productive civilization. "Without democracy the peaceful development of the state is impossible."[30]

Although a defender of the concept of political equality inherent in the democratic ideal of representative government, Mises was ardently opposed to the general egalitarian impulses of the modern age. He lamented, "This interpretation of history from the egalitarian point of view is the official philosophy of our age."[31] Egalitarianism was a grievous theoretical error, for it warred against the very nature of man. The notion that the coercive power of the state should be used to impose a leveling of opportunity and condition upon each citizen was both "absurd" and "pernicious":

> Nothing, however, is as ill-founded as the assertion of the alleged equality of all members of the human race. Men are altogether unequal. Even between brothers there exist the most marked differences in physical and mental attributes. Nature never repeats itself in its creations; it produces nothing by the dozen, nor are its products standardized. Each man who leaves her workshop bears the imprint of the individual, the unique, the never-to-recur.[32]

In summary, "All human power would be insufficient to make men really equal. Men are and will always remain unequal."[33] The political liberalism of Mises encompassed only equality before the law. Or as he wrote, "The equality Liberalism creates is equality before the law; it has never sought any other."[34] What is meant by equality before the law? "Nobody is hampered in his aspirations and ambitions by any legal obstacles. Everybody is free to compete for any social position or function for which his personal abilities qualify him."[35] Since equality before the law protects the uniqueness and ensures the opportunity for the development of the individual, it emerges as a vital element in Mises's liberalism.

Mises devoted a considerable portion of his writing to articulating the role of government in the liberal state. "With human nature as it is," Mises reasoned, "the state is a necessary and indispensable institution."[36] He asserted "Anarchism misunderstands the real nature of man. It would be practicable only in a world of angels and saints."[37] More particularly, "If men were perfect, there would not be any need for government."[38] Or even less demandingly, "If all men were pleasant and virtuous, if no one coveted what belongs to another, there would be no need for a government, for armies and navies, for policemen, for courts, and prisons."[39] However the real world of human nature involves persons who "are not faultless" and who possess "shortcomings of the human mind and character."[40] The social peace is not as fragile or vulnerable as Hobbes contended; however, because of some men's capacity for greed and violence, government is required in order to maintain the social tranquility necessary for the development and maintenance of a productive and humane civilization. A government capable of ensuring the internal and external social peace, and a government confining itself to those powers legitimately needed to ensure the social peace, was a government allowing for the maximum development of the individual and thereby became an integral component of Mises's thinking.

## III

The economic elements of liberalism were what most deeply concerned Mises. His analysis of their nature is found throughout his writings. "Economics," Mises explained, "is the philosophy of human life and action and concerns everybody and everything. It is the pith of civilization and of man's human existence." He continued, "As conditions are today, nothing can be more important to every intelligent man than economics. His own fate and that of his progeny is at stake."[41] With the stakes so high, Mises concluded, "[A]ll reasonable men are called upon to familiarize themselves with the teachings of economics. This is, in our age, the primary civic duty."[42] But he also lamented, "What is taught nowadays at most of the universities under the label of economics is practically a denial of it."[43] Regrettably, then, "Economics was no longer a matter of knowledge and ability, but of good intentions."[44]

In the pursuit of the "universally valid laws" controlling economic conduct, Mises stressed that the relevant laws could only be discerned with a theoretical approach. Economics is a "theoretical science."[45] More specifically, history and statistics were valueless in the study of economics, for they dealt solely with human conduct already concluded. The particular choices and actions of each person are totally unique due to individual subjective values and attending factors, which are so diverse as to defy any meaningful quantification for future projections by historians and statisticians. Because of the infinite diversity of individual choices, quantification was of antiquarian interest only; it could tell us nothing of ongoing and future human choice and action. History and statistics dealt with "the static," the "evenly rotating economy," and the conditions of "equilibrium," while the real world of economics had to deal with the unpredictable and interminable "flux" and change of present and future human conduct. As Mises expressed it, "[C]hange is the essence of life."[46] Ultimately, Mises concluded, "the basic notion of economics" is "the choosing and acting individual."[47] And equally significant, he added, "Economic knowledge necessarily leads to liberalism."[48]

Private property is the basic economic element in Mises's liberalism. Mises described this concept as "the essential teaching of liberalism." On another occasion he wrote, "In reality, the central notion of classical liberalism is private property, and not a certain misunderstood concept of free competition."[49] Furthermore, he observed, "If historical experience could teach us anything, it would be that private property is inextricably linked with civilization."[50] It was, then, an inescapable premise of the human predicament: "Only nations committed to the principle of private property have risen above penury and produced science, art and literature."[51] Private property is indispensable, Mises believed, for it facilitates and maximizes the opportunities for each person to participate as producer and consumer.

> Private property creates for the individual a sphere in which he is free of the state. It sets limits to the operation of the authoritarian will. It allows other forces to arise side by side with and in opposition to political power. It thus becomes the basis of all those activities that are free from violent interference on the part of the state. It is the soil in which the seeds of freedom are nurtured and in which the autonomy of the individual and ultimately all intellectual and material progress are rooted. In this sense, it has even been called the fundamental prerequisite for the development of the individual.[52]

To the enemies of individualism, "Private ownership in the means of production is the Red Sea which bars our path to this Promised Land of general well-being."[53] To Ludwig von Mises, "Every step that leads away from private ownership...is a step away from rational economic activity."[54]

Private property led to a productive and creative society, for it led to capital accumulation. Technology was no substitute for capital: "Mere technological knowledge is of no use if the capital needed is lacking. Indian businessmen are familiar with American ways of production. What prevents them from adopting the American methods is...lack of capital."[55] Nor, Mises argued, did such legislative edicts as minimum wage laws offer the easy path to increased material well-being: "Real wages can rise only to the extent that, other things being equal, capital becomes more plentiful."[56] The controlling economic premise was inescapable: "There is but one means to improve the material well-being of men, viz., to accelerate the increase in capital accumulated as against population. No psychological lucubrations, however sophisticated, can alter this fact."[57] Utopian speculations notwithstanding, Mises was adamant in maintaining that "it is additional capital accumulation alone that brings about technological improvement, rising wage rates, and a higher standard of living."[58]

In addition the source of capital that leads to genuine economic growth must itself be legitimate. Specifically, "expansion of credit cannot form a substitute for capital."[59] The facile expansion of credit through governmental manipulation is spurious and deceptive; there is the illusion of increased wealth rather than the reality. Genuine capital, and thereby genuine economic growth, must come from *bona fide* savings. Mises explained, "Capital is not a free gift of God or of nature. It is the outcome of a provident restriction of consumption on the part of man. It is created and increased by saving and maintained by the abstention from dissaving."[60] He concluded, "The Santa Claus fables of the welfare school are characterized by their complete failure to grasp the problems of capital."[61]

Capitalism had been enormously successful, Mises argued. Rooted in the notions of private property and capital accumulation, capitalism had produced the Industrial Revolution and thereby had dramatically and permanently transformed the quantity and the quality of life in the West: "What transformed the world of horse-drawn carriages, sailing ships, and windmills step by step into a world of airplanes and electronics was the laissez-faire principle of Manchesterism."[62] The great virtue of capitalism lay not only in its high level of material productivity; it lay in the fact that it "poured a horn of plenty upon the masses of wage earners."[63] Mises observed, "Modern capitalism is essentially mass production for the needs of the masses. The buyers of the products are by and large the same people who as wage earners cooperate in their manufacturing."[64] "The average American worker enjoys amenities," Mises wrote, "for which Croesus, Crassus, the Medici, and Louis XIV would have envied him."[65] He concluded, "The market economy needs no apologists and propagandists. It can apply to itself the words of Sir Christopher Wren's epitaph in St. Paul's: *Si monumentum requiris, circumspice* [If you seek his monument, look around]."[66] Beyond question, capitalism was the "essential feature of the advanced West."[67]

Proponents of capitalism understood that it "is precisely the scarcity of the nature-given conditions of his welfare that enjoins upon man the necessity to act." In short, "the nature-given means of removing human uneasiness are scarce."[68] In contrast, "The disciples of Jean Jacques Rousseau who raved about nature and the blissful condition of man in the state of nature did not take notice of the fact that the means of subsistence are scarce and that the natural state of man is extreme poverty and insecurity."[69] Mises mused, "There is no need to argue with the bucolic dreams of Virgil and of eighteenth-century poets and painters. There is no need to examine the kind of security which the real shepherds enjoyed. No one really wishes to change places with them."[70] Capitalism was based on an understanding that the natural condition of economic well-being is one of scarcity. In addition, there was the fact "that human wants are practically unlimited."[71] To attempt to close the gap between scarce supply and unlimited demand, it was imperative to encourage productivity. In these circumstances, the pertinent economic laws were the underlying principles of capitalism: the respecting of private property, the rewarding of capital accumulation, and the incentive to produce through profit.

"The market," Mises wrote, "is...the focal point of the capitalist order of society; it is the essence of Capitalism."[72] As Mises viewed it, the market was not something static, stationary, or fixed; rather, it was changing, evolving, and in a ceaseless state of flux. Mises explained, "The market is not a place, a thing, or a collective entity. The market is a process, actuated by the interplay of the actions of the various individuals cooperating under the division of labor." Moreover, he continued, "The forces determining the—continually changing—state of the market are the value judgments of these individuals and their actions as directed by these value judgments."[73] He concluded, "There is nothing inhuman or mystical with regard to the market. The market process is entirely a resultant of human actions. Every market phenomenon can be traced back to definite choices of the members of the market society."[74] The market is strikingly democratic, for at the center of its functioning is the "sovereignty" of the individual consumer. Finally, as a crucial feature of the market process, Mises noted, "In the unhampered market economy there are no privileges, no protection of vested interests, no barriers preventing anybody from striving after any prize."[75]

The acting individual working through a division of labor is the essence of the market process. "The core of liberal social theory," Mises believed, "is the theory of division of labour."[76] The need for division of labor arose out of the nature of things. Individuals were unique and varied greatly in their talents and interests, and the physical conditions for production were patently not consistent and uniform throughout a given society. As Mises explained, "Had the strength and abilities of all individuals and the external conditions of production been everywhere equal the idea of division of labour could never have arisen."[77] Division of labor was the antithesis of autarky. The latter stressed withdrawal, a fruitless effort for total self-sufficiency, hostility, and ultimately isolation and low productivity, while the former was based upon cooperation, dependence, peace, and ultimately a dynamic society of high productivity. Briefly, "in the society based on division of labour everyone is the servant of all and all the masters of each."[78] The notion of division of labor was one of "the greatest achievements" of Adam Smith, Mises contended, and it reflected "the social animal of which Aristotle spoke"[79] Clearly, the theoretical origins of the concept of division of labor were of noble pedigree.

220

"The market economy as such," Mises noted, "does not re-spect political frontiers. Its field is the world."[80] Mises was an ar-dent believer that the notions of the free market and division of labor should be global in scope. In brief, he was an unrelenting promoter of free trade. Mises posed this vision:

> Imagine a world in which the principle of private ownership of the means of production is fully realized, in which there are no institutions hindering the mobility of capital, labor, and commodities, in which the laws, the courts, and the ad-ministrative officers do not discriminate against any individ-ual or groups of individuals, whether native or alien.[81]

Mises's vision was at odds with protectionist ideology. Protection-ism invariably commenced with domestic governmental interven-tion, such as minimum-wage laws, which imposed  costs beyond those required by the free market. Because of these added costs, domestic industries found themselves greatly disadvantaged in the competition for international trade. As a counter move, a call for tariffs arose, and the labor unions, to protect their artificially high wages, clamored for immigration restrictions. Thus, the vi-cious cycle of protectionist ideology was set in motion. The result was the hapless quest for national economic self-sufficiency, for the isolated, hostile, and aggressive world of autarky: "The trend toward autarky is essentially a trend of domestic economic poli-cies; it is the outcome of the endeavor to make the state para-mount in economic matters."[82] In contrast to the "aggressive nationalism" and the "spirit of conquest" generated by autarky, the philosophy of free trade, grounded in the notions of mobility and "harmony of interests," resulted in peace and in maximum productivity and progress.

A final element of Mises's economic liberalism was the gold standard. "The gold standard," he observed, "was the world standard of the age of capitalism, increasing welfare, liberty, and democracy, both political and economic."[83] He continued, "sound money still means today what it meant in the nineteenth century: the gold standard."[84] Indeed, he argued, "[T]he idea of sound money...ideologically...belongs in the same class with political constitutions and bills of rights."[85] The worth of the gold standard lay in its freeing the value of money, the indispensable medium of exchange in any dynamic economy, from the machinations of fleeting politics: "The gold standard makes the determination of money's purchasing power independent of the changing ambitions and doctrines of political parties and pressure groups. This is not a defect of the gold standard; it is its main excellence."[86] In the modern age the enemies of the gold standard were legion. Their opposition was reflected in John Maynard Keynes, who termed it a "barbarous relic."[87] What motivated the enemies of the gold standard? As Mises explained, "The abhorrence of the gold standard is inspired by the superstition that omnipotent governments can create wealth out of little scraps of paper."[88] And then there were those enemies who had even less charitable goals in mind: "People fight the gold standard because they want to substitute national autarky for free trade, war for peace, totalitarian government omnipotence for liberty."[89] To Mises the matter of sound money was a profoundly serious issue. The gold standard went to the vital center of the "free and prosperous commonwealth," for it accommodated all of the economic elements of liberalism, which in turn allowed the highest expressions of individual human creativity and productivity.

## IV

In Mises's analysis the principal enemies of liberalism were positivism, socialism, and interventionism. Positivism found its origins in Auguste Comte, and it was, according to Mises, "the most conspicuous failure in the history of metaphysics."[90] Positivism was incompatible with liberalism. The essence of the latter was the conception of the free, reasoning, choosing, and acting individual. Positivism categorically denied that philosophical perspective. It began by denying the basic humanity of man. Man was not viewed as distinctive or unique by reason of his capacity for thought and choice; instead, "[m]an is just one of the elements in the universe."[91] As merely another element in the universe, man lost his dignity. One of the "main varieties of the neopositivistic assault" was behaviorism. Mises explained:

Behaviorism proposes to study human behavior according to the methods developed by animal and infant psychology. It seeks to investigate reflexes and instincts, automatisms and unconscious reactions. But it has told us nothing about reflexes that have built cathedrals, railroads, and fortresses, the instincts that have produced philosophies, poems, and legal systems, the automatisms that have resulted in the growth and decline of empires, the unconscious reactions that are splitting atoms.[92]

In addition to undermining the basic liberal notion of the freely choosing individual by denying his humanity and his capacity for choice, positivism was a corrosive agent on the key political institutions of Mises's liberalism. Representative government was disdained by the positivist, for self-determination required the idea of the thinking and freely choosing person. Positivism substituted a political elitism for representative government. The behaviorist, Mises explained, "proposes to operate the 'human Ford' the way the operator drives his car. He acts as if he owned humanity and were called upon to control and to shape it according to his own designs. For he himself is above the law, the godsent ruler of mankind."[93] Thus, positivism was proposing that human beings were to be arranged and ordered as any other form of matter might be manipulated. To the positivist elitists falls the readily accepted task of orchestrating the activities of the masses. Precisely how the elitists escape being of the same bovine character as the balance of mankind is never made clear. As Mises noted, the elitists are "above the law."

Similarly, positivism undercut anti-egalitarianism, one of the major political elements in Mises's liberalism. With its view of men as things to be ordered and arranged, the positivist mind was avowedly egalitarian. Men were innately equal; differences were intrusions produced by faulty education and institutions. Of course, these latter failings were to be corrected by the elites of positivism, which in turn would allow for the emergence of the perfected egalitarian mass man.

Nor did positivism spare equality before the law, one of the essential political ingredients in Mises's liberalism. To Mises equality before the law meant freeing man from arbitrary barriers so that the freely choosing person might maximize his individual development. In contrast, positivism, having rejected man's capacity for rationality and choice, was busy building obstacles to individual choice as it went grimly on its way erecting the collectivist promised land through egalitarian schemes.

Finally, positivism offered a conception of the state and government that contrasted sharply with Mises's. Mises advocated a limited state with the express responsibility of protecting the individual from threats to person and property, while otherwise leaving him free to order his own life. In contrast, positivism offered the omnicompetent and omnipotent state that zealously ferreted out and destroyed every vestige of individual choice. Mises offered the limited state of individual preference and growth; positivism proposed the total state of the elitist-collectivist model. Mises envisioned freedom; Comte lusted after control.

Likewise, socialism, and with particular virulence its Marxist form, warned against the essential components of Mises's liberalism. Under the impetus of the Marxist leaven, socialism subverted the central premise of Mises's liberalism because of "its subordination of the Individual to the Whole."[94] "In a socialist community," Mises explained, "the individual can have no more freedom than a soldier in the army or an inmate in an orphanage."[95] No less than positivism, socialism repudiated the idea of the reasoning and freely acting individual, except, of course, in the case of the socialist elites. Mises observed that Marx and Engels "never doubted...they were above the law."[96] Marxist doctrine viewed mankind not as thinking and choosing individuals; instead, men were assigned by historical fate or determination to mindless collectivities, such as classes, races, and nationalities. Ideas did not determine history; historical setting, or more particlularly class consciousness, determined ideas. Man was a cog, a mere entity, in the historical process. Man did not make history; rather, he was a product of it. From the liberal viewpoint, the nature of man had been wholly altered by this Marxist dogma.

In addition to denying the principal liberal tenet of individualism, socialism undermined the central political institutions of liberalism, for these institutions were expressly designed to implement the society of the independently thinking and choosing person. As had positivism, the socialist elitist-collectivist model excluded notions of representative and limited government and was overtly egalitarian in purpose. In brief, the socialist elites left no political barriers between themselves and the collectivist whole that might diminish their potential for total control.

More importantly, socialism was devastating in its theoretical and practical assault on the economic institutions of liberalism, which had been structured to shore up the sphere of autonomy for the individual. Where capitalism had been premised upon the idea of private property, and the accompanying right of capital accumulation to protect the individual as producer and consumer, the major tenet of socialism, as the antithesis of capitalism, was to destroy all economic arrangements that to any degree impaired the elitist quest for complete control. Hence, public rather than private ownership was decreed. Nor was socialism any gentler in its treatment of the free market. The granting of all economic power to the socialist elite, Mises wrote, "signifies elimination of the market, which indeed is the fundamental aim of Socialism, for the guidance of economic activity by the market implies organization of production and a distribution of the product according to that disposition of the spending power of individual members of society which makes itself felt on the market; that is to say, it implies precisely that which it is the goal of Socialism to eliminate."[97] Socialist theorists strongly attacked the free market, for it is a mechanism developed by its liberal proponents precisely for the purpose of allowing maximum individual involvement and choice as producer or consumer. The free market facilitated the very thing socialism sought to destroy: the thinking and freely choosing person.

Furthermore, socialist theorists intensely opposed the division of labor, a key element in Mises's liberalism. Division of labor is based on the idea that men varied greatly in their individual talents, in their interests, and in their independently exercised choices. In the economic market place, division of labor allowed each person to maximize talents, interests, and options. Specifically on those points the socialist theorists fervently denounced division of labor. From their viewpoint of the egalitarian mass man, a person was a thing, a cog, which suggested total interchangeability in all vocational slots. Rather than innate individual talents, diverse interests, and free choices, education and environmental manipulation determined job assignment; therefore, division of labor was a threat to socialist theory, for it reflected a view of man and human nature alien to the socialist vision of egalitarian mass man molded by socialist elites.

In addition, socialism was hostile to the liberal notion of free trade. To liberalism, free trade was the logical extension of the idea of the individual division of labor to the international level. Socialist theorists opposed free trade precisely because it facilitated the free movement among nations of capital, services, and products; in sum, it threatened to curtail severely the socialist potential for full economic control within a particular nation. Similarly, socialist theorists were instinctively hostile to the gold standard, for it was the function of the gold standard to protect the purchasing power of money from the political pressures of the state. By insulating purchasing power from political manipulation, the gold standard impeded the socialist grasp for complete economic power.

After destroying the economic components of liberalism, Mises contended that "the essential vice" of socialism emerged. This cardinal weakness was the inability of socialism to "permit monetary calculation and thus rational economic action."[98] Mises acknowledged that socialism in given countries could still calculate and temporarily avoid economic chaos by imitating the market prices of the capitalist societies; however, once the world economy had been reduced to the socialist model, economic chaos and collapse would inevitably ensue, for there would be no rational method to determine value and price. Elitist edicts on production and prices could never anticipate or reflect the wide diversity of values and preferences that are accommodated and reconciled in that flexible and supple mechanism called the free market. "In abolishing economic calculation," Mises concluded, "the general adoption of socialism would result in complete chaos and the distintegration of social cooperation under the division of labor."[99] In this state of distintegration and chaos, individualism, the keystone of liberalism, would perish, because in order to flourish the individual needs order and liberty, not the arch foes of chaos and despotism. To Mises the issue was clear: "[S]ocialism and liberalism are mutually exclusive ."[100]

Finally, "interventionism" was also a mortal enemy of Mises's liberalism. Interventionism was offered by its proponents as a "third way" or alternative to capitalism and socialism. The "prophet" of interventionism was John Maynard Keynes; among its chief practitioners was Franklin D. Roosevelt. As Mises observed, "In the terminology of American politics it is often referred to as the middle-of-the-road policy."[101] Compared with the harsh methods and brittle dogmas of socialism, interventionism was subtle and genteel; however, Mises argued, the result was the same, for interventionism was merely a "method for the realization of socialism by installments."[102] The "antagonism" between socialism and interventionism, Mises wrote, "is a controversy about the means to be resorted to for the attainment of a goal common to both of these factions, namely the establishment of all-round central planning and the entire elimination of the market economy."[103] The interventionists also sought to dismantle those political and economic institutions supporting individualism and to move "gradually," but inexorably, toward the elitist-collectivist model where the individualism of classical liberalism is blurred and then obliterated:

> The advocates of interventionism pretend to substitute for the—as they assert, "socially" detrimental—effects of private property and vested interests the unlimited discretion of the perfectly wise and the disinterested legislator and his conscientious and indefatigable servants, the bureaucrats. In their eyes the common man is a helpless infant, badly in need of a paternal guardian to protect him against the sly tricks of a band of rogues. They reject all traditional notions of law and legality in the name of a "higher and nobler" idea of justice.[104]

Intervention moved along the road to socialism in well-defined form. It commenced with "progressive" taxation to support its statist programs, which in time turned out to be confiscatory taxation resulting in lowered savings and diminished capital accumulation. As vitally needed capital was depleted, interventionists attempted to increase its availability through government-imposed lower interest rates, not by the realities of the free market where with capital scarce interest rates would be high. In addition to the folly of these artificial lower interest rates, interventionists sought to make capital available through money substitutes, such as banknotes and checkbook money, rather than through the proper avenue of increased savings encouraged through reduced taxation and higher interest rates paid on savings.

The result of these policies, Mises contended, was "unbridled credit expansion" leading to high inflation, for the money supply was dramatically increased without any corresponding increase in economic productivity. This government-induced credit expansion produced what Mises called an "artificial boom," which could not indefinitely sustain itself. Once the period of credit expansion reached its outer limits the processes of economic retrenchment invariably followed, meaning that "malinvestments" made during the heady days of the induced boom became apparent and commenced to falter and fail. The result was a decline into recession and possible depression where the painful corrections for the initial errors had to be made. Unfortunately, interventionists responded to the challenges of recession and depression not by acknowledging and recanting on earlier errors, commencing with progressive taxation, but by intensifying their calls for government involvement and thereby moving inexorably in the direction of the total socialist state where the thinking and freely choosing individual of Mises's liberalism became an increasingly muted and ultimately extinct voice.

V

In response to an age of accelerating collectivism and emerging totalitarianism, American conservative thinkers sought to identify and conserve the sustaining elements of the Western intellectual and spiritual tradition. Among those elements was the concept of the individual achieving fulfilment and dignity through choice. The origins of this concept in the Western experience were ancient and venerated, and in the twentieth century Mises added to this heritage an eloquent and moving voice. Not surprisingly, then, Mises's thinking was embraced by American conservatives. Furthermore, they concurred with him in his chilling assessment of the threat to individual freedom in the modern age. Mises had written, "We stand on the brink of a precipice which threatens to engulf our civilization," and he concluded, "Whether he chooses or not, every man is drawn into the great historical struggle, the decisive battle into which our epoch has plunged us."[105]

In addition, American conservatives admired the courageous streak they saw in Mises. He was compelled to give up a prestigious European professorship and become exiled to America because of his unyielding opposition to Nazism. In America he carried on the struggle against leftist collectivisms, including Communism, and he was penalized for his efforts by never being offered a permanent academic appointment at a major American university. Many American conservatives were understandably moved when Mises wrote, "The prevailing trend toward what

Hilaire Belloc called the servile state will certainly not be reversed if nobody has the courage to attack its underlying dogmas."[106]

Nor, as might have been the case with some exponents of classical liberalism, did Mises alienate the traditional sensitivities of American conservatives with an anti-religious posture. Mises did not write extensively on the subject of religion; however, he sufficiently clarified his position. First, Mises explained, "Liberalism has never pretended to be more than a philosophy of earthly life. . . . It has never claimed to exhaust the Last or Greatest Secret of Man."[107] This sentiment did not conceal an indifference or hostility to religious concerns; indeed, Mises wrote, "It is not to be denied that the loftiest theme that human thought can set for itself is reflection on ultimate questions."[108] More precisely, he instructed, "The liberals do not disdain the intellectual and spiritual aspirations of man."[109] Mises opposed religion only when it became dogmatic and imperialistic, when "religious orthodoxy enforced unswerving conformity and put an end to all intellectual activity and independent thinking."[110]

Beyond these strictures, Mises, who wrote principally as a student of the essential political and economic components of the free society, evinced no innate antagonism toward the historical faith of the West: "Might not the Church reconcile itself with the social principle of free cooperation by the division of labor? Might not the very principle of Christian love be interpreted to this end?"[111] Similarly, he pondered, "But it is not impossible that the Christian churches and sects will one day discover that religious freedom can be realized only in a market economy and will stop supporting anticapitalistic tendencies."[112] Thus, not only to libertarians, but to American conservatives of more traditional bent, Mises was highly appealing as a proponent of the free society.

Finally, and of first importance, Mises endeared himself to his conservative following by offering hope:

> Now our civilization is beginning to scent a whiff of death in the air. Dilettantes loudly proclaim that all civilizations, including our own, must perish: this is an inexorable law.

230

Europe's final hour has come, warn these prophets of doom, and they find credence. An autumnal mood is perceptibly beginning to set in everywhere.[113]

But he also counseled, "Yet, this outcome is not inevitable. It is the goal to which the prevailing trends in our contemporary world are leading. But trends can change and hitherto they always have changed.... To accomplish such a change is the task of the rising generation."[114] Mises was offering hope through a familiar and enduring American conservative theme, namely, "ideas have consequences." That is, the effects of positivism, socialism, and interventionism could be offset by understanding the philosophical essentials of individual freedom. On that premise Ludwig von Mises rested his case.

# Conclusion

As the only self-defined "classical liberal" among these seven theorists, Ludwig von Mises requires separate comment. The other six thinkers share common theoretical precepts that underlie their thinking. Although these thinkers differ considerably in approach and emphasis, the unifying and controlling theme is that of "the great tradition" of Western thought versus the weaknesses of modernism.

Modernism is rooted in a secular, naturalistic, and materialistic ethic concerning the human predicament. At its theoretical core, modernism is wholly man-centered. Mankind is self-produced and self-defining. Pride, ego, and an emphasis upon unlimited rights are corollaries to the theoretical core of man-centeredness. This self-centeredness of modernism is two-pronged in its thrust: one prong is ideological in character and the other hedonistic. The ideological prong is centrist, elitist, collectivist, and utopian in outlook. It manifests itself in a variety of "isms": for example, in the positivism of Comte, in the scientism of Harold Lasswell, in the socialism of the Marxists and Fabians, in the communism of Lenin, in the fascism of Mussolini, in the utilitarianism of Bentham, in the pragmatism of William James, and in the twentieth-century liberalism of John Dewey. In short, the modern ideologue believes in the redemptive power of human knowledge; he seeks for, indeed, lusts after, a worldly New Jerusalem.

The hedonistic element in modern self-centeredness results from an excruciating boredom. It seeks distraction and solace in an endless array of amusements and entertainment. Unphilosophical, unreflecting, and obsessed with motion and change as

233

ends in themselves, its vision is not a moral one that seeks to elevate or ennoble mankind. Rather, its vision is either idyllic, pursuing fantasy and pleasure, or diabolic, fascinated with the violent and degenerate qualities of man. Our six theorists view modernism as a "fearful descent" from the great tradition of Western thought.

The great tradition of Western political thinking has two principal components: one is classical in origin, the other is biblical. With classical thought, as personified in such thinkers as Plato and Cicero, there is an insatiable quest for truth concerning the genuine nature of things. This quest for truth seeks to ferret out the controlling physical laws of man's natural and material existence. In addition, there is a quest for the higher moral law, for those premises in the ethical realm that are transcendent, enduring, and permanent. In brief, there is a desire to know, as far as is humanly possible, of the whole "constitution of being." Thus there is "openness to transcendence" and the desire to attune man to the given operative laws, physical and moral. The desired result is harmony. The classical approach is philosophical, not ideological, in character, for it seeks insight, understanding, knowledge, and wisdom. Unlike the ideological approach, the philosophical approach eschews mere opinion and the imposition of visions upon mankind authored by simplistic, closed, and fanatical minds. Finally, in the classical moral emphasis, the priority is not upon self, pleasure, and rights; instead, it is upon duty, service, obligation, and sacrifice to the truth.

With the biblical component of the great tradition manifested, for example, in one of its higher forms in the writings of Saint Augustine, there is a profound apprehension of the creatureliness of the human condition, that is, man as creature and not as Creator. The individual's life is frail and finite; man is a "sojourner." The human predicament is marred by evil, tragedy, and sorrow, which inhere in the nature of things. Life individually or collectively is imperfectible. Awe, reverence, and humility are the appropriate philosophical stances. As Saint Augustine notes, pride is the most insidious "canker." Again, there is the servant role:

duty, service, obligation, and sacrifice beckon. Is the biblical view wholly direful and pessimistic? The answer is categorically No, for there is the Incarnation and the Pauline trilogy of faith, hope, and love, and ultimately there is the promise of eternal life. Therein lies the joy and peace of believing.

Even with extensive variations in individual analysis and emphasis, Kirk, Meyer, Weaver, Kendall, Strauss, and Voegelin agree that an earlier and greater tradition of political thought, based on classical and biblical heritages, offers a deep and impressive reservoir of ideas for altering what they conceive to be the shallow and disturbing theoretical foundations of modern thinking, the roots of which are traceable principally to the incipient secularism and man-centeredness of the Renaissance and the Age of Reason of the French Enlightenment.

Ludwig von Mises shows no hostility to the general approaches of Kirk, Weaver, Meyer, Kendall, Strauss, and Voegelin. As a self-professed classical liberal, he explains, "Liberalism has never pretended to be more than a philosophy of earthly life.... It has never claimed to exhaust the Last or Greatest Secret of man."[1] Moreover, he adds, "It is not to be denied that the loftiest theme that human thought can set for itself is reflection on ultimate questions."[2] And he finally advises, "The liberals do not disdain the intellectual and spiritual aspirations of man."[3]

The critical point is that von Mises wrote as an economist. He did not pretend to be doing more than that. His overwhelming concern was with the economic theoretical underpinnings of Western thought; however, he was not opposed to the kinds of theoretical endeavors that engrossed the other six thinkers. Indeed, concerning the biblical view, he reflects in passing, "But it is not impossible that the Christian churches and sects will one day discover that religious freedom can be realized only in a market economy and will stop supporting anticapitalistic tendencies."[4] He presses the point even further and inquires, "Might not the church reconcile itself with the social principle of free cooperation by the division of labor? Might not the very principle of Christian love be interpreted to this end?"[5]

There is one unifying theme underlying all seven of these writers. Perhaps this is the key theoretical premise undergirding the whole of the American conservative movement: the need to focus the attention of contemporary thought upon an ennobled conception of man and life. Modernism has degraded man. With the ideologues, man is merely an expendable material object to be ordered and arranged by visionary elitists, as one might order and arrange cinderblocks. The horrors of Buchenwald and the Gulag attest to this degraded, sorrowful, and tragic view of man. Nor is hedonism's record much more impressive: witness, for example, contemporary man's preoccupation with violence and pornography and his surrender to the drug culture. Clearly, these developments represent a gross degradation of human dignity and of the human prospect.

Russell Kirk, Richard Weaver, Frank Meyer, Willmoore Kendall, Leo Strauss, Eric Voegelin, and Ludwig von Mises possess a noble vision of man's predicament. They have labored heavily in the theoretical vineyard to elevate our sights. They have done so with much success, although the full harvest of their labors is not completed. The great tradition of Western thought, seeking to elevate and ennoble mankind, is continuing apace. There is, then, cause for gratitude for achievements to date, and there is hope for the future.

# Notes

## Russell Kirk

1. Charles Brown, *Russell Kirk: A Bibliography* (Mount Pleasant, Mich., 1981).
2. *Ibid.,* 130.
3. Edward J. Feulner, Jr., Preface in Russell Kirk, *Reclaiming a Patrimony* (Washington, 1982).
4. Russell Kirk, *Confessions of a Bohemian Tory* (New York, 1963), 29.
5. *Ibid.,* 304.
6. *Ibid.,* 308.
7. Russell Kirk, *The Intemperate Professor* (Baton Rouge, 1965), 131.
8. Russell Kirk, *Decadence and Renewal in the Higher Learning* (South Bend, Ind., 1978), 225.
9. Russell Kirk, *The Roots of American Order* (LaSalle, Ill., 1974), 225.
10. Russell Kirk, *The Conservative Mind* (6th ed., rev; Chicago, 1978), 370.
11. Kirk, *Roots,* 348.
12. *Ibid.,* 368, 349.
13. *Ibid.,* 412; Kirk, *Intemperate Professor,* 18.
14. Kirk, *Roots,* 398.
15. Russell Kirk, *Enemies of the Permanent Things* (New Rochelle, N.Y., 1969), 154.
16. *Ibid.*
17. *Ibid.,* 156.
18. *Ibid.,* 160.

19. *Ibid.,* 161.
20. Kirk, *Confessions,* 247.
21. Russell Kirk, *Edmund Burke* (New Rochelle, N.Y., 1967), 84.
22. Russell Kirk, *Beyond the Dreams of Avarice* (Chicago, 1956), 39.
23. Kirk, *Conservative Mind,* 169.
24. Russell Kirk, *Eliot and His Age* (New York, 1971), 234.
25. Kirk, *Conservative Mind,* 227, 230.
26. Russell Kirk, *A Program for Conservatives* (rev. ed.; Chicago, 1962), 173.
27. Kirk, *Confessions,* 52.
28. Kirk, *Eliot,* 323-24.
29. Kirk, *Intemperate Professor,* vi.
30. Kirk, *Eliot,* 332.
31. *Ibid.,* 334.
32. Kirk, *Confessions,* 222.
33. Kirk, *Program,* 130.
34. Kirk, *Roots,* 132; Kirk, *Eliot,* 218.
35. Kirk, *Avarice,* 190; Kirk, *Intemperate Professor,* 86; Kirk, *Avarice,* 223.
36. Kirk, *Program,* 284.
37. Russell Kirk, *John Randolph of Roanoke* (Indianapolis, Ind., 1978), 25; Kirk, *Program,* 206.
38. Kirk, *Program,* 63.
39. Kirk, *Enemies,* 105; Kirk, *Decadence and Renewal,* 252.
40. Kirk, *Confessions,* 306.
41. Kirk, *Edmund Burke,* 21.
42. *Ibid.,* 20.
43. *Ibid.,* 174.
44. Kirk, *Conservative Mind,* 425.
45. Kirk, *Edmund Burke,* 182.
46. Kirk, *Patrimony,* 48.
47. *Ibid.,* 67.
48. Kirk, *Intemperate Professor,* 79.
49. Kirk, *Program,* 75.

50. *Ibid.,* 112.
51. Kirk, *Patrimony,* 32.
52. Kirk, *Confessions,* 247.
53. Kirk, *Decadence and Renewal,* 275.
54. Kirk, *Enemies,* 216, 268.
55. Kirk, *Program,* 56, 50.
56. Kirk, *Roots,* 84.
57. *Ibid.,* 82.
58. Kirk, *Avarice,* 135.
59. Kirk, *Roots,* 84.
60. *Ibid.,* 77.
61. Kirk, *Enemies,* 209.
62. Kirk, *Roots,* 5.
63. Kirk, *Conservative Mind,* 406.
64. Kirk, *Enemies,* 259.
65. Kirk, *Patrimony,* 47.
66. *Ibid.*
67. Kirk, *Enemies,* 119.
68. Kirk, *Roots,* 30.
69. Kirk, *Conservative Mind,* 249.
70. Kirk, *Eliot,* 44; Kirk, *Enemies,* 302.
71. Kirk, *Enemies,* 303.
72. Kirk, *Conservative Mind,* 3, 6.
73. Kirk, *Edmund Burke,* 21, 17.
74. *Ibid.,* 153-54.
75. Kirk, *Eliot,* 7.
76. Kirk, *Patrimony,* 14.
77. Kirk, *Edmund Burke,* 152; Kirk, *Conservative Mind,* 25.
78. Kirk, *Conservative Mind,* 43.
79. Kirk, *Edmund Burke,* 84, 20; Kirk, *Program,* 26.
80. Kirk, *Edmund Burke,* 83; Kirk, *Eliot,* 27.
81. Kirk, *Eliot,* 373.
82. Kirk, *Enemies,* 61.
83. *Ibid.*
84. Kirk, *Conservative Mind,* 429.
85. *Ibid.*

86. Kirk, *Eliot,* 259.
87. *Ibid.,* 279.
88. Kirk, *Eliot,* 98-99.
89. *Ibid.,* 7.
90. *Ibid.,* 207.
91. *Ibid.,* 417.
92. Kirk, *Conservative Mind,* 431.
93. Kirk, *Eliot,* 140.
94. Kirk, *Conservative Mind,* 433.
95. Kirk, *Confessions,* 230.
96. *Ibid.,* 299.
97. Kirk, *Eliot,* 139.
98. *Ibid.,* 66.
99. *Ibid.,* 190.
100. Kirk, *Enemies,* 61.
101. Kirk, *Eliot,* 282.
102. *Ibid.,* 313.
103. *Ibid.,* 301.
104. *Ibid.,* 276, 142.
105. *Ibid.,* 204.
106. Kirk, *Avarice,* 137.
107. Kirk, *Conservative Mind,* 7.
108. Kirk, *Program,* 99.
109. Kirk, *Patrimony,* 97.
110. Russell Kirk, "The Living Edmund Burke," *Modern Age,* XXVI (Summer-Fall, 1982), 324.
111. Kirk, *Eliot,* 304.
112. Kirk, *Roots,* 155.
113. Kirk, *Eliot,* 291.
114. Kirk, *Roots,* 146.
115. Kirk, *Program,* 100.
116. Kirk, *Patrimony,* 32.
117. Kirk, *Eliot,* 154.
118. Kirk, *Conservative Mind,* 270.
119. Kirk, *Roots,* 475.
120. 1 Corinthians, 13:13.

121. Kirk, *Program,* 18.
122. *Ibid.*
123. Kirk, *Confessions,* 182.
124. Kirk, *Eliot,* 197.
125. Kirk, *Decadence and Renewal,* 75.
126. *Ibid.,* 224.
127. Kirk, *Patrimony,* 32.
128. Colossians 2:2; 3:14.
129. Kirk, *Program,* 140.
130. *Ibid.,* 148.
131. Kirk, *Patrimony,* 25.
132. Kirk, *Edmund Burke,* 84.
133. Kirk, *Patrimony,* 9, 25.
134. *Ibid.,* 31.
135. Kirk, *Program,* 47.
136. Kirk, *Patrimony,* 34; Kirk, *Program,* 49.
137. Kirk, *Program,* 49.
138. *Ibid.,* 23.

## Richard Weaver

1. Richard Weaver, *Life without Prejudice and Other Essays* (Chicago, 1965), 132.
2. Richard M. Weaver, "Agrarianism in Exile," *Sewanee Review,* LVIII (Autumn, 1950), 592.
3. Wilma R. Ebbitt, "Richard M. Weaver, Teacher of Rhetoric," *Georgia Review,* XVII (Winter, 1963), 416.
4. Frank S. Meyer, "Richard M. Weaver: An Appreciation," *Modern Age,* XIV (Summer-Fall, 1970), 243-44.
5. Willmoore Kendall, "How to Read Richard Weaver: Philosopher of 'We the (Virtuous) People'," in Nellie D. Kendall, ed., *Willmoore Kendall Contra Mundum* (New Rochelle, N.Y., 1971), 393.
6. Russell Kirk, Foreword, in Richard M. Weaver, *Visions of Order: The Cultural Crisis of Our Time* (Baton Rouge, 1964), ix.

7. Weaver, *Life without Prejudice,* 157.
8. Richard M. Weaver, Letter to the Editor, *New York Times Book Review,* March 21, 1948, 29.
9. Richard M. Weaver, *The Ethics of Rhetoric* (Chicago, 1953), 4.
10. Richard M. Weaver, *Academic Freedom: The Principle and the Problems* (Bryn Mawr, Penn., 1963), 3.
11. Weaver, *Life without Prejudice,* 158-59.
12. Richard M. Weaver, "Liberalism with a Ballast," *Sewanee Review,* LXII (April-June, 1954), 341.
13. Richard M. Weaver, *Ideas Have Consequences* (Chicago, 1948), 130-31.
14. *Ibid.,* 59
15. *Ibid.,* 23.
16. Weaver, *Ethics of Rhetoric,* 112.
17. Richard M. Weaver, "Illusions of Illusion," *Modern Age,* IV (Summer, 1960), 319.
18. Richard M. Weaver, *Relativism and the Crisis of Our Times* (Bryn Mawr, Penn., 1961), 3.
19. Richard M. Weaver, "Humanism in an Age of Science," *Intercollegiate Review,* VII (Fall, 1970), 16.
20. Weaver, *Life without Prejudice,* 17.
21. Weaver, *Visions of Order,* 13.
22. *Ibid.*
23. Weaver, "Illusions of Illusion," 317, 320.
24. Weaver, *Ideas Have Consequences,* 19.
25. *Ibid.,* 17.
26. Weaver, "Illusions of Illusion," 318.
27. *Ibid.*
28. Richard M. Weaver, *The Southern Tradition at Bay: A History of Postbellum Thought,* ed. George Core and M.E. Bradford (New Rochelle, N.Y., 1968), 36.
29. Weaver, *Ideas Have Consequences,* 40.
30. Weaver, *Visions of Order,* 16.
31. Richard M. Weaver, "The Humanities in the Century of the

Common Man," *New Individualist Review,* III, 3 (1964), 21.

32. Weaver, *Life without Prejudice,* 45, 15.
33. Weaver, *Visions of Order,* 140; Weaver, *Life without Prejudice,* 141.
34. Weaver, *Visions of Order,* 143.
35. Weaver, *Life without Prejudice,* 155.
36. Weaver, *Visions of Order,* 91.
37. Weaver, *Southern Tradition,* 43.
38. Weaver, *Visions of Order,* 99.
39. *Ibid.,* 88.
40. Richard M. Weaver, "Christian Letters," *Modern Age,* III (Fall, 1959), 420.
41. Richard M. Weaver, "Lord Acton: The Historian as Thinker," *Modern Age,* V (Winter, 1960-61), 15.
42. Richard M. Weaver, "Impact of Society on Mr. Russell," *Commonweal,* February 20, 1953, 504.
43. Weaver, *Visions of Order,* 67.
44. Weaver, *Life without Prejudice,* 146.
45. Richard M. Weaver, "Contemporary Southern Literature," *Texas Quarterly Review,* II (Summer, 1959), 139-40.
46. *Ibid.,* 127.
47. Weaver, *Ideas Have Consequences,* 11.
48. Weaver, "Humanities," 22.
49. Weaver, "Contemporary Southern Literature," 137.
50. Weaver, "Humanities," 11-12.
51. *Ibid.,* 12.
52. *Ibid.,* 21.
53. Weaver, *Ideas Have Consequences,* 187.
54. Weaver, *Life without Prejudice,* 143.
55. Richard M. Weaver, "Aspects of the Southern Philosophy," in Louis D. Rubin, Jr. and Robert D. Jacobs, eds., *Southern Renascence: The Literature of the Modern South* (Baltimore, Md., 1953), 20.
56. Weaver, *Southern Tradition,* 32.
57. Weaver, *Life without Prejudice,* 141.

58. Weaver, *Ideas Have Consequences,* 184.
59. *Ibid.,* 170.
60. *Ibid.,* 170-71 (italics added).
61. *Ibid.,* 185; Weaver, *Southern Tradition,* 33.
62. Weaver, *Life without Prejudice,* 144.
63. Weaver, *Ideas Have Consequences,* 3,2.
64. *Ibid.,* 21.
65. *Ibid.,* 52-53.
66. Weaver, *Visions of Order,* 38.
67. Weaver, "Illusions of Illusion," 320.
68. Weaver, *Ideas Have Consequences,* 57.
69. *Ibid.,* 65.
70. Weaver, *Relativism and the Crisis of Our Times,* 4.
71. *Ibid.,* 5-7.
72. *Ibid.,* 7.
73. Weaver, *Ideas Have Consequences,* 130.
74. Weaver, *Life without Prejudice,* 153.
75. Weaver, *Visions of Order,* 125; Weaver, *Relativism and the Crisis of Our Times,* 12.
76. Weaver, *Visions of Order,* 126.
77. Richard M. Weaver, "From Poetry to Bitter Fruit," *National Review,* January 25, 1956, 27; Weaver, *Life without Prejudice,* 63.
78. Weaver, *Visions of Order,* 115.
79. *Ibid.,* 128.
80. Weaver, "Humanities," 20.
81. Weaver, *Ideas Have Consequences,* 48; Weaver, *Visions of Order,* 115.
82. Weaver, *Ideas Have Consequences,* 104.
83. *Ibid.,* 108.
84. *Ibid.,* Chap. V.
85. *Ibid.,* 93.
86. *Ibid.,* 28.
87. *Ibid.,* 98; Weaver, *Visions of Order,* 53.
88. Weaver, *Ideas Have Consequences,* 112.

89. Richard M. Weaver, "Realism and the Local Color Interlude," *Georgia Review,* XXII (Fall, 1968), 302.

90. Weaver, *Ideas Have Consequences,* 88.

91. *Ibid.,* 89.

92. *Ibid.,* 83.

93. *Ibid.*

94. *Ibid.,* 84.

95. *Ibid.,* 85.

96. *Ibid.*

97. *Ibid.,* 86.

98. *Ibid.,* 87.

99. *Ibid.*

100. *Ibid.,* 185.

101. Richard M. Weaver, *Language Is Sermonic: Richard M. Weaver on the Nature of Rhetoric,* ed. Richard L. Johannessen, Rennard Strickland, and Ralph T. Eubanks (Baton Rouge, 1970), 140.

102. *Ibid.,* 221.

103. *Ibid.,* 220.

104. Weaver, *Ethics of Rhetoric,* 25.

105. Weaver, *Ideas Have Consequences,* 152.

106. Weaver, "Contemporary Southern Literature," 144.

107. Weaver, *Southern Tradition,* 389.

108. *Ibid.,* 396.

109. Richard M. Weaver, "The South and the American Union," in Louis D. Rubin, Jr. and James Jackson Kilpatrick, eds., *The Lasting South: Fourteen Southerners Look at Their Home* (Chicago, 1957), 50.

110. Richard M. Weaver, "An Altered Stand," *National Review,* June 17, 1961, 389; Weaver, "Humanities," 8.

111. Weaver, *Southern Tradition,* 330.

112. Weaver, "Contemporary Southern Literature," 126.

113. *Ibid.,* 133.

114. Weaver, *Southern Tradition,* 391.

115. Weaver, "The South and the American Union," in Rubin

and Kilpatrick, eds., *The Lasting South,* 126.

116. R.M. Weaver, "The South and the Revolution of Nihilism," *South Atlantic Quarterly,* XLIII (April, 1944), 196.

117. Weaver, "Aspects of the Southern Philosophy," in Rubin and Jacobs, eds., *Southern Renascence,* 19, 15.

118. Weaver, *Southern Tradition,* 376.

119. *Ibid.,* 48.

120. *Ibid.,* 143.

121. *Ibid.*

122. *Ibid.,* 147.

123. *Ibid.,* 209.

124. Richard M. Weaver, "Lee the Philosopher," *Georgia Review,* II (Fall, 1948), 303; also quoted in Weaver, *Southern Tradition,* 209-210.

125. Weaver, "Lee the Philosopher," 303.

126. Weaver, *Ideas Have Consequences,* 170.

127. Weaver, *Life without Prejudice,* 164.

128. *Ibid.,* 163.

129. *Ibid.,* 159.

130. Weaver, *Ideas Have Consequences,* 104.

131. Weaver, "Lee the Philosopher," 302.

## Frank S. Meyer

*I acknowledge my thanks to Mrs. Elsie Meyer for her kindness in making available to me materials for this study which were unobtainable elsewhere.*

1. Frank S. Meyer, *In Defense of Freedom: A Conservative Credo* (Chicago, 1962), 10.

2. Frank S. Meyer, *The Conservative Mainstream* (New Rochelle, N.Y., 1969), 423.

3. *Ibid.,* 14.

4. *Ibid.,* 417-18.

5. Frank S. Meyer, "In Re Professor Zoll: I - Order and Freedom," *National Review,* March 24, 1970, 311.
6. Meyer, *In Defense of Freedom,* 71.
7. *Ibid.,* 87-88.
8. *Ibid.,* 128.
9. *Ibid.,* 165.
10. *Ibid.,* 136-37.
11. *Ibid.,* 49.
12. Meyer, *The Conservative Mainstream,* 34.
13. *Ibid.,* 44, 38.
14. *Ibid.,* 463; see also Meyer, *In Defense of Freedom,* 97-98.
15. Meyer, *The Conservative Mainstream,* 430, 15.
16. *Ibid.,* 15.
17. *Ibid.,* 150.
18. *Ibid.,* 149.
19. *Ibid.,* 150.
20. *Ibid.,* 149.
21. Eph. 2:20-21; see also I Cor. 15:14.
22. Peter P. Witonski, "The Political Philosopher," *National Review,* April 28, 1972, 468. Witonski's piece is a brief eulogy of Meyer.
23. L. Brent Bozell, "Freedom or Virtue?" *National Review,* September 11, 1962, 181-87, 206. For Meyer's response, see *The Conservative Mainstream,* 43-51.
24. Meyer, *The Conservative Mainstream,* 41.
25. Frank S. Meyer, "Conservatism," in Robert A. Goldwin, ed., *Left, Right and Center: Essays in Liberalism and Conservatism in the United States* (Chicago, 1965), 15-16.
26. Meyer, *The Conservative Mainstream,* 37.
27. Frank S. Meyer, "Freedom, Tradition, Conservatism," in Frank S. Meyer (ed.), *What Is Conservatism?* (Chicago, 1964), 15-16.
28. Meyer, *The Conservative Mainstream,* 362.
29. *Ibid.,* 437.
30. *Ibid.,* 145-46.

31. *Ibid.,* 31.
32. Frank S. Meyer, "Libertarianism or Libertinism?" *National Review,* September 9, 1969, 910.
33. Meyer, *The Conservative Mainstream,* 76-77.
34. Meyer, "Freedom, Tradition, Conservatism," 14, 16.
35. Meyer, *The Conservative Mainstream,* 37, 50.
36. *Ibid.,* 51.
37. Frank S. Meyer, "What Kind of Order?" *National Review,* December 30, 1969, 1327.
38. Meyer, "Freedom, Tradition, Conservatism," 18-19. Also see Meyer, *The Conservative Mainstream,* 42-45, 55, 64-65; and Meyer, "Conservatism," 10-13.
39. Meyer, "Conservatism," 12; "In Re Professor Zoll: I - Order and Freedom," 311.
40. Frank S. Meyer, "Richard M. Weaver: An Appreciation," *Modern Age,* XIV (Summer-Fall, 1970), 243-44.
41. Meyer, *The Conservative Mainstream,* 60.
42. Meyer, "In Re Professor Zoll: I - Order and Freedom," 311.
43. Frank S. Meyer, review of Frederick D. Wilhelmsen and Jane Brett, *The War in Man: Media and Machine,* in *National Review,* February 23, 1971, 208.
44. Meyer, "Libertarianism or Libertinism?" 910.
45. Meyer, *In Defense of Freedom,* 90-92.
46. Meyer, "Conservatism," 6; see also Meyer, *The Conservative Mainstream,* 15.
47. Meyer, *In Defense of Freedom,* 79-80.
48. Meyer, *The Conservative Mainstream,* 397; Meyer, *In Defense of Freedom,* 120-21.
49. Meyer, *In Defense of Freedom,* 122.
50. Meyer, *The Conservative Mainstream,* 430. For Meyer's analysis of Rousseau's crucial role in the development of collectivist thought, see *In Defense of Freedom,* 119-27; *The Conservative Mainstream,* 442-43.
51. Meyer, *The Conservative Mainstream,* 470.
52. *Ibid.,* 474.
53. *Ibid.,* 471.
54. *Ibid.,* 472.

55. *Ibid.*
56. *Ibid.*
57. *Ibid.,* 470-72. For Meyer's analysis of Lincoln's role in the American political tradition in its entirety, see *ibid.,* 470-75.
58. Frank S. Meyer, "Collectivism Rebaptized," *The Freeman,* V (July, 1955), 560; Meyer, *In Defense of Freedom,* 33.
59. Meyer, *In Defense of Freedom,* 169.
60. *Ibid.,* 35.
61. *Ibid.,* 37. Richard M. Weaver called this "a brilliant paragraph." See his review of *In Defense of Freedom* in *National Review,* December 4, 1962, 443.
62. Meyer, *In Defense of Freedom,* 92.
63. Frank S. Meyer, *The Moulding of Communists: The Training of the Communist Cadre* (New York, 1961), 130.
64. *Ibid.,* 17.
65. *Ibid.,* p. 197, n.1.
66. *Ibid.,* 85.
67. *Ibid.,* p. 180, n.9.
68. Meyer, *The Conservative Mainstream,* 335.
69. *Ibid.,* 367.
70. Meyer, *The Moulding of Communists,* 40.
71. Meyer, *The Conservative Mainstream,* 336; Meyer, *The Moulding of Communists,* 133.
72. Meyer, *The Moulding of Communists,* 137.
73. For Meyer's position, see *ibid.,* 156; for Chambers's position, see *ibid.,* pp. 205-206, n. 8.
74. *Ibid.,* 66.
75. *Ibid.,* 71.
76. *Ibid.,* 156.
77. *Ibid.,* 157.
78. *Ibid.,* 156.
79. *Ibid.,* 157.
80. *Ibid.,* 107.
81. Meyer, *The Conservative Mainstream,* 378.
82. *Ibid.*
83. *Ibid.*
84. Frank S. Meyer, "Let a Hundred Flowers Bloom," *National*

*Review,* May 4, 1971, 482. Meyer reiterates this position throughout his writings.

85. Frank S. Meyer, "Peace In Our Time," *National Review,* August 10, 1971, 873. Italics added.

86. James Burnham, "The Anti-Communist," *National Review,* April 28, 1972, 471.

87. Frank S. Meyer, "Down the Primrose Path," *National Review,* September 10, 1971, 994.

88. Frank S. Meyer, "Isolationism?" *National Review,* December 3, 1971, 1356.

89. Meyer, *In Defense of Freedom,* 38.

90. *Ibid.,* 129, 131-32.

91. Meyer, "Collectivism Rebaptized," 561. For his insights into Burke, Meyer acknowledged his indebtedness to Richard M. Weaver. See *ibid;* Meyer, *In Defense of Freedom,* 45-46. For Weaver's position, see *The Ethics of Rhetoric* (Chicago, 1953), ch. III, "Edmund Burke and the Argument from Circumstance," 55-84.

92. Meyer, *The Conservative Mainstream,* 33.

93. Meyer, "Collectivism Rebaptized," 561.

94. Meyer, *In Defense of Freedom,* 142.

95. *Ibid.,* 47, 50, 52-53, 77.

96. *Ibid.,* 141.

97. Meyer, "Collectivism Rebaptized," 562.

98. Meyer, *In Defense of Freedom,* 145.

99. *Ibid.,* 26-28, 130.

100. *Ibid.,* 137.

101. Meyer, "Collectivism Rebaptized," 562.

102. Meyer, "Freedom, Tradition, Conservatism," 11-13; Meyer, *In Defense of Freedom,* 45-46.

103. Meyer, "Freedom, Tradition, Conservatism," 12-13.

104. *Ibid.,* 13.

105. Meyer, *In Defense of Freedom,* 145.

106. Whittaker Chambers to William F. Buckley, Jr., November 23 (?), 1958, in William F. Buckley, Jr., ed., *Odyssey of a Friend: Whittaker Chambers' Letters to William F. Buckley, Jr., 1954-1961* (New York, 1961), 216.

## Willmoore Kendall

1. Jeffrey Hart, "Willmoore Kendall: American," in Nellie D. Kendall, ed., *Willmoore Kendall Contra Mundum* (New Rochelle, N.Y., 1971), 9 (hereinafter cited as *Contra Mundum*).
2. Willmoore Kendall, *John Locke and the Doctrine of Majority-Rule* (1941; rpr. Urbana, Ill., 1965), 132.
3. *Ibid.,* 58.
4. *Contra Mundum,* 422-23.
5. *Ibid.,* 423.
6. Kendall, *Majority-Rule,* 75.
7. *Ibid.*
8. *Ibid.,* 77.
9. John Locke, *The Second Treatise of Government,* ed. Thomas P. Peardon (Indianapolis, Ind., 1952), sec. 243.
10. *Ibid.,* secs. 95-96 (italics added)
11. Kendall, *Majority-Rule,* 135.
12. Locke, *Second Treatise,* secs. 8, 135, 171, 199.
13. *Ibid.,* sec. 135.
14. *Ibid.,* chapter XIII.
15. *Ibid.,* 240.
16. *Ibid.,* sec. 243 (italics added).
17. *Ibid.,* sec. 225 (italics added).
18. *Ibid.,* sec. 168. (italics added).
19. Kendall, *Majority-Rule,* 134.
20. *Contra Mundum,* 418-48.
21. *Ibid.,* p. 430, n. 19.
22. *Ibid.,* p. 426, n. 12.
23. *Ibid.,* 446.
24. *Ibid.,* 433, 439.
25. Locke, *Second Treatise,* secs. 123, 124.
26. George Sabine, *A History of Political Theory* (3rd ed.; New York, 1961), 529, 538.
27. William Ebenstein, *Great Political Thinkers: Plato to the Present* (4th ed.; New York, 1969), 400.
28. *Contra Mundum,* 447.

29. *Ibid.,* 448.
30. *Ibid.*
31. Kendall, *Majority-Rule,* 118. (italics added).
32. Frederick D. Wilhelmsen and Willmoore Kendall, "Cicero and the Politics of the Public Orthodoxy," *Intercollegiate Review,* V (Winter, 1968-69), 85.
33. *Ibid.,* 85-86.
34. *Ibid.,* 86.
35. *Ibid.,* 88.
36. Willmoore Kendall, "The 'Open Society' and Its Fallacies," *American Political Science Review,* LIV (1960), 972-79.
37. John Stuart Mill, *On Liberty,* ed. Currin V. Shields (Indianapolis, Ind., 1956), 7, 16 (italics added).
38. *Ibid.,* 18.
39. *Ibid.,* 21.
40. Kendall, "The 'Open Society' and Its Fallacies," 976.
41. *Ibid.,* 977.
42. *Ibid.,* 979.
43. Mill, *On Liberty,* 81-82.
44. Kendall "The 'Open Society' and Its Fallacies," 978.
45. *Ibid.,* 976.
46. *Ibid.,* 977.
47. *Ibid.,* 978 and n. 31.
48. *Ibid.,* 977.
49. Karl Popper, *The Open Society and Its Enemies,* (5th ed., rev.; 2 vols; Princeton, N.J., 1966), I, 201. (italics added).
50. Kendall, "The 'Open Society' and Its Fallacies," 976.
51. *Contra Mundum,* 149-67.
52. Mill, *On Liberty,* 29-30.
53. Popper, *The Open Society and Its Enemies,* I, 189.
54. *Contra Mundum,* 150.
55. *Ibid.,* 164.
56. *Ibid.,* 165-66.
57. Alexander Hamilton, James Madison, and John Jay, *The Federalist,* ed. Benjamin Fletcher Wright (Cambridge, Mass., 1961), No. 55, p. 376.

58. Wilhelmsen and Kendall, "Cicero," 98.

59. Willmoore Kendall and George W. Carey, *The Basic Symbols of the American Political Tradition* (Baton Rouge, La., 1970), 94-95.

60. Kendall and Carey, eds., *Liberalism versus Conservatism: The Continuing Debate in American Government* (Princeton, N.J., 1966), 66-74.

61. Kendall and Carey, *Basic Symbols,* 94; Kendall and Carey, eds., *Liberalism versus Conservatism,* 68.

62. Kendall and Carey, *Basic Symbols,* 155.

63. *Ibid.,* 156.

64. Willmoore Kendall, *The Conservative Affirmation* (Chicago, 1963), 159-64.

65. Kendall and Carey (eds.), *Liberalism versus Conservatism,* 69.

66. *Contra Mundum,* 426.

67. Kendall and Carey, *Basic Symbols,* 99; See also *Contra Mundum,* 311.

68. *Contra Mundum,* 370-71.

69. *The Federalist,* No. 84, p. 534.

70. *Ibid.,* No. 22, p. 199.

71. *Contra Mundum,* 468.

72. Kendall and Carey, *Basic Symbols,* 105.

73. *The Federalist,* No. 63, p. 415; No. 1, p. 89; No. 37, p. 269.

74. *Ibid.,* No. 43, p. 316.

75. *Ibid.,* No. 6, pp. 112-13.

76. *Contra Mundum,* 408-11.

77. Willmoore Kendall and Mulford Q. Sibley, *War and the Use of Force* (Cambridge, Mass., 1959), 5.

78. *Ibid.*

79. *The Federalist,* No. 43, p. 316.

80. *Ibid.,* No. 75, p. 479.

81. *Contra Mundum,* pp. 369; 374; 388, n.7; and p. 502.

82. *Ibid.,* 469-506.

83. *Ibid.,* 468, 379.

84. *Ibid.,* 579.

85. *Ibid.,* 580.
86. Kendall and Carey, *Basic Symbols,* 136; see also *The Federalist,* No. 25. (in particular the concluding two paragraphs), No. 26, and No. 84.
87. *Contra Mundum,* 297, 323.
88. *Ibid.,* 374.
89. *Ibid.,* 202-27.
90. Kendall and Carey, *Basic Symbols,* 139.
91. *Contra Mundum,* 465; Kendall and Carey, *Basic Symbols,* 140-42.
92. Austin Ranney and Willmoore Kendall, *Democracy and the American Party System* (New York, 1956), 514-33.
93. Kendall and Carey, eds., *Liberalism versus Conservatism,* 400.
94. *Contra Mundum,* 108n.
95. Ranney and Kendall, *Democracy and the American Party System, passim.*
96. *The Federalist,* No. 78, p. 491 (italics added).
97. *Ibid.,* 490 and 493.
98. *Ibid.,* 492.
99. Kendall and Carey, *Basic Symbols,* 105.
100. *Ibid.*
101. Kendall, *Majority-Rule,* 135.
102. *Contra Mundum,* 399-400.
103. Richard M. Weaver, *Visions of Order: The Cultural Crisis of Our Time* (Baton Rouge, La., 1964). For Kendall's discussion of Weaver, see *Contra Mundum,* 366-402.
104. *Contra Mundum,* 393.
105. *Ibid.,* 400-401.
106. Weaver, *Visions of Order,* 14-15.
107. *Ibid.,* 14, 12.
108. *Ibid.,* 105, 130.
109. *Ibid.,* 131.
110. *Ibid,* 115.
111. *Ibid.,* 88, 91.
112. Kendall and Carey, *Basic Symbols,* 154.

113. *Ibid.,* 58.
114. *Ibid.,* 144-45.
115. *Ibid.,* 145.
116. Wilhelmsen and Kendall, "Cicero," 100.


Leo Strauss

1. Jacob Klein and Leo Strauss, "A Giving of Accounts," *The College* XXII (April, 1970), 2.
2. Milton Himmelfarb, "On Leo Strauss," *Commentary,* LVIII (August, 1974), 64.
3. Emma Brossard, "Leo Strauss: Philosopher and Teacher, Par Excellence," *Academic Reviewer,* (Fall-Winter, 1974), 5.
4. Walter Berns, "The Achievement of Leo Strauss: I," *National Review,* December 7, 1973, 1347.
5. Dante Germino, *Beyond Ideology: The Revival of Political Theory* (New York, 1967), 149.
6. Harry V. Jaffa, "The Achievement of Leo Strauss: III," *National Review,* December 7, 1973, 1355.
7. William F. Buckley, Jr., *Did You Ever See A Dream Walking? American Conservative Thought in the Twentieth Century* (Indianapolis, Ind. 1970), 398; Willmoore Kendall, "Who Killed Political Philosophy?" *National Review,* March 12, 1960, 175.
8. Kendall, "Who Killed Political Philosophy?" 175.
9. Leo Strauss, *The City and Man* (1964; rpr. Chicago, 1977), 3.
10. Leo Strauss, "On a New Interpretation of Plato's Political Philosophy," *Social Research,* XIII (September, 1946), 331.
11. Strauss, *The City and Man,* 1.
12. *Ibid.,* 2, 11.
13. Leo Strauss, *What Is Political Philosophy? and Other Studies* (1959; rpr. Westport, Conn., 1973), 101.
14. Leo Strauss, *Natural Right and History* (Chicago, 1953), 156.

15. Strauss, *The City and Man,* 21 (italics added).
16. Leo Strauss, *Xenophon's Socratic Discourse: An Interpretation of the Oeconomicus* (Ithaca, 1970), 83.
17. Leo Strauss, review of Alfred Verdross-Rossberg's *Grundlinien der antiken Rechts- und Staatsphilosphie,* in *Social Research,* XIV (March, 1947), 129.
18. Leo Strauss, *On Tyranny* (rev. ed; Ithaca, 1963), 108; Leo Strauss and Joseph Cropsey, eds., *History of Political Philosophy* (2nd ed.; Chicago, 1972), 45.
19. Leo Strauss, *Jerusalem and Athens: Some Preliminary Reflections* (New York, 1967), 22.
20. Strauss, *Natural Right and History,* 146-47.
21. Leo Strauss, *The Political Philosophy of Hobbes: Its Basis and Its Genesis,* trans. Elsa M. Sinclair (Chicago, 1952), 161.
22. Strauss, *What Is Political Philosophy?,* 85-86.
23. Strauss, *The City and Man,* 31.
24. Strauss, *Political Philosophy of Hobbes,* 146.
25. Strauss and Cropsey, eds., *History of Political Philosophy,* 17.
26. Strauss, *Natural Right and History,* 193.
27. Strauss, *What Is Political Philosophy?,* 87.
28. *Ibid.*
29. Leo Strauss, "On the Intention of Rousseau," *Social Research,* XIV (December, 1947), 485.
30. Strauss, *The City and Man,* 113.
31. Strauss, *What is Politiical Philosophy?,* 131-32.
32. *Ibid.,* 120.
33. Leo Strauss, *Thoughts on Machiavelli* (1958; rpr. Seattle, 1969), 243.
34. Strauss, *The City and Man,* 59.
35. Strauss, *What Is Political Philosophy?,* 28.
36. Leo Strauss, *Liberalism Ancient and Modern* (New York, 1968), 29.
37. Strauss, *Thoughts on Machiavelli,* 298.
38. Leo Strauss, *Persecution and the Art of Writing* (Glencoe, Ill., 1952), 9.

39. Leo Strauss, *Spinoza's Critique of Religion* (New York, 1965), 163.
40. Moses Maimonides, *The Guide for the Perplexed,* trans. M. Friedlander (2nd ed., rev.; New York, 1956), 5.
41. Strauss, *Liberalism Ancient and Modern,* 142.
42. Strauss, *Spinoza's Critique of Religion,* 165.
43. Leo Strauss, "On Abravenel's Philosophical Tendency and Political Teaching," in J.B. Trend and H. Loewe, eds., *Isaac Abravenel: Six Lectures* (Cambridge, England, 1937), 96.
44. *Ibid.,* 99, 104.
45. Strauss, *Liberalism Ancient and Modern,* 170.
46. Strauss, *Spinoza's Critique of Religion,* 190.
47. *Ibid.,* 158.
48. *Ibid.,* 148.
49. Maimonides, *Guide,* 6,8 (italics added).
50. *Ibid.,* 8 (italics added).
51. *Ibid.,* 9.
52. Strauss, *Spinoza's Critique of Religion,* 18.
53. *Ibid.,* 201.
54. *Ibid.,* 225.
55. *Ibid.,* 171-72.
56. *Ibid.,* 203.
57. *Ibid.,* 225.
58. *Ibid.,* 222.
59. *Ibid.,* 160, 164.
60. *Ibid.,* 172, 209.
61. *Ibid.,* 21.
62. Strauss, *What Is Political Philosophy?,* 226; Strauss, *Spinoza's Critique of Religion,* 170.
63. Strauss, *Natural Right and History,* 36.
64. Strauss, *Spinoza's Critique of Religion,* 11; the story of Martha and Mary is found in Luke 10:41.
65. *Ibid.,* 9.
66. Leo Strauss, "Philosophy as Rigorous Science and Political Philosophy," *Interpretation,* II (Summer, 1971), 7; Leo Strauss, "Social Science and Humanism," in Leonard D.

White (ed.), *The State of the Social Sciences* (Chicago, 1956), 420.

67. Strauss, *Spinoza's Critique of Religion,* 8-9.
68. *Ibid.,* 9.
69. Strauss, *Thoughts on Machiavelli,* 133, 32.
70. Strauss, *Liberalism Ancient and Modern,* 261.
71. *Ibid.*
72. Strauss, *Thoughts on Machiavelli,* 150.
73. Strauss, *Spinoza's Critique of Religion,* 29.
74. Strauss, *Liberalism Ancient and Modern,* 266.
75. *Ibid.,* 265-66.
76. *Ibid.,* 267.
77. *Ibid.,* 270.
78. Strauss, *What Is Political Philosophy?,* 281.
79. Strauss, *Jerusalem and Athens,* 3.
80. *Ibid.,* 5.
81. Strauss, *What Is Political Philosophy?,* 111.
82. *Ibid.*
83. Strauss, *Jerusalem and Athens,* 20.
84. Hilail Gildin, ed., *Political Philosophy: Six Essays by Leo Strauss* (Indianapolis, Ind., 1975), 86.
85. Strauss, *Jerusalem and Athens,* 21.
86. *Ibid.,* 27.
87. Leo Strauss, "Comment on the Weber Thesis Reexamined," *Church History,* XXX (March, 1961), 101.
88. Strauss, *What Is Political Philosophy?,* 40.
89. Strauss, *Thoughts on Machiavelli,* 224.
90. *Ibid.,* 175.
91. *Ibid.,* 295.
92. Strauss, *What Is Political Philosophy?,* 180; Strauss, *Natural Right and History,* 178.
93. Strauss, *Thoughts on Machiavelli,* 176.
94. *Ibid.,* 194.
95. Strauss and Cropsey, eds., *History of Political Philosophy,* 278.
96. Strauss, *Thoughts on Machiavelli,* 294.
97. *Ibid.,* 142.

98. *Ibid.*, 170.

99. *Ibid.*, 190.

100. *Ibid.*, 199.

101. *Ibid.*, 178-79.

102. *Ibid.*, 191.

103. *Ibid.*, 13.

104. *Ibid.*, 94.

105. *Ibid.*, 132, 136.

106. *Ibid.*, 167.

107. *Ibid.*, 207-208.

108. Strauss, *Natural Right and History,* 178.

109. Strauss, *Thoughts on Machiavelli,* 296-97.

110. *Ibid.*, 13-14.

111. *Ibid.*, 295.

112. Strauss, *What Is Political Philosophy?,* 289.

113. Niccolo Machiavelli, *The Prince,* trans. Luigi Ricci, rev. E.R.P. Vincent (New York, 1952), chap. 15.

114. *Ibid.*, chap. 18.

115. Strauss, *Thoughts on Machiavelli,* 67-68.

116. *Ibid.*, 80.

117. *Ibid.*, 209.

118. *Ibid.*, 214-15.

119. *Ibid.*, 215.

120. *Ibid.*, 221.

121. Machiavelli, *The Discourses,* trans. Leslie J. Walker, rev. Brian Richardson, ed. Bernard Crick (Harmondsworth, England, 1970), Bk. III, chap. 31.

122. Strauss, *What Is Political Philosophy?,* 42.

123. Strauss, *Thoughts on Machiavelli,* 279; Strauss, *What Is Political Philosophy?,* 43.

124. Machiavelli, *The Prince,* chap. 25.

125. Strauss, *Thoughts on Machiavelli,* 82.

126. *Ibid.*, 127.

127. Machiavelli, *The Prince,* chap. 24.

128. Strauss and Cropsey, eds., *History of Political Philosophy,* 287.

129. Strauss, *Thoughts on Machiavelli,* 282.

130. *Ibid.,* 9.
131. Machiavelli, *The Discourses,* Bk. I, chap. 27.
132. Strauss, *Thoughts on Machiavelli,* 9, 107.
133. Strauss, *Political Philosophy of Hobbes,* xv.
134. Strauss, *Natural Right and History,* 177.
135. Strauss, *Political Philosophy of Hobbes,* 5.
136. *Ibid.,* 100.
137. *Ibid.,* 163-64.
138. Strauss, *Natural Right and History,* 170.
139. Strauss, *Political Philosophy of Hobbes,* 23.
140. Strauss, *What Is Political Philosophy?,* 185.
141. *Ibid.,* 189-90.
142. Strauss, *Political Philosophy of Hobbes,* 23.
143. Strauss, *Natural Right and History,* 194.
144. Strauss, *What Is Political Philosophy?,* 48-49.
145. Gildin, ed., *Political Philosophy,* 89.
146. Leo Strauss, "The Spirit of Sparta or the Taste of Xenophon," *Social Research,* VI (November, 1939), 536.
147. Friedrich Nietzsche, *Genealogy of Morals,* in Walter Kaufmann, ed. and trans., *Basic Writings of Nietzsche* (New York, 1968), 476-77.
148. Nietzsche, *Beyond Good and Evil,* in Kaufmann, ed. and trans., *Basic Writings of Nietzsche,* 211.
149. Gildin, ed., *Political Philosophy,* 97-98, 94.
150. Leo Strauss, "Note on the Plan of Nietzsche's *Beyond Good and Evil,*" *Interpretation,* III (Winter, 1973), 112.
151. *Ibid.*
152. Leo Strauss, "The Crisis of Political Philosophy," in Harold J. Spaeth, ed., *The Predicament of Modern Politics* (Detroit, 1964), 91.
153. Strauss, *Thoughts on Machiavelli,* 203.
154. Strauss, "The Crisis of Political Philosophy," in Spaeth, ed., *Predicament of Modern Politics,* 91.
155. Strauss, *What Is Political Philosophy?,* 25.
156. Strauss, *Natural Right and History,* 17.
157. *Ibid.,* 59.

158. Gildin, ed., *Political Philosophy,* 82.
159. Leo Strauss, " 'Relativism'," in Helmut Schoeck and James W. Wiggins, eds., *Relativism and the Study of Man* (Princeton, 1961), 151.
160. Strauss, "Social Science and Humanism," in White, ed., *State of the Social Sciences,* 422.
161. Strauss, *Natural Right and History,* 292, 221, 184, 271; Strauss, "Note on the Plan of Nietzsche's *Beyond Good and Evil*," 112.
162. Strauss, *Spinoza's Critique of Religion,* 2.
163. *Ibid.,* 15, 17.
164. Strauss, *Political Philosophy of Hobbes,* 147.
165. Strauss, *The City and Man,* 3.
166. Leo Strauss, "An Epilogue," in Herbert J. Storing, ed., *Essays on the Scientific Study of Politics* (New York, 1962), 317.
167. *Ibid.,* 327.
168. Strauss, *What Is Political Philosophy?,* 260: Strauss, *Jerusalem and Athens,* 25.
169. Strauss, *What Is Political Philosophy?,* 130.
170. *Ibid.,* 218; Strauss and Cropsey, eds., *History of Political Philosophy,* 273.
171. Strauss, *Natural Right and History,* 251.
172. *Ibid.,* 294.
173. Strauss, *Liberalism Ancient and Modern,* 56.
174. Strauss, *Natural Right and History,* 319.
175. *Ibid.,* 83.
176. *Ibid.,* 321.

Eric Voegelin

1. Peter Stanlis, "Plato and Aristotle," *Modern Age,* III (Spring, 1959), 192.
2. Frank S. Meyer, *The Conservative Mainstream* (New Rochelle, N.Y., 1969), 399.

3. *Ibid.,* 408.
4. Russell Kirk, *Enemies of the Permanent Things* (New Rochelle, N.Y., 1969), 259.
5. *Ibid.,* 264.
6. Eric Voegelin, *From Enlightenment to Revolution,* ed. John H. Hallowell (Durham, N.C., 1975), 85.
7. Eric Voegelin, *Science, Politics and Gnosticism: Two Essays* (Chicago, 1968), 15.
8. *Ibid.*
9. Eric Voegelin, *The New Science of Politics: An Introduction* (Chicago, 1953), 2.
10. Voegelin, *Enlightenment,* 79.
11. *Ibid.,* 277.
12. Eric Voegelin, *The World of the Polis* (Baton Rouge, 1957), 197. Vol. II of Voegelin, *Order and History,* 5 vols. projected.
13. *Ibid.,* 275.
14. *Ibid.,* 208.
15. Eric Voegelin, *Israel and Revelation* (Baton Rouge, 1956), 453. Vol. I of *Order and History,* 5 vols. projected.
16. Voegelin, *Science, Politics and Gnosticism,* 107.
17. Voegelin, *Israel and Revelation,* 3-4.
18. Voegelin, *World of the Polis,* 324.
19. *Ibid.,* 43.
20. Eric Voegelin, *Plato and Aristotle* (Baton Rouge, 1957), 108. Vol. III of Voegelin, *Order and History,* 5 vols. projected.
21. Voegelin, *Science, Politics and Gnosticism,* 63-64.
22. Voegelin, *World of the Polis,* 5.
23. Eric Voegelin, "Reason: The Classic Experience," *Southern Review,* X (April, 1974), 241.
24. Voegelin, *World of the Polis,* 115.
25. Voegelin, *Plato and Aristotle,* 324.
26. *Ibid.,* 250.
27. Voegelin, *World of the Polis,* 236; Voegelin, *Plato and Aristotle,* 225.

28. Eric Voegelin, "On Classical Studies," *Modern Age,* XVII (Winter, 1973), 3; Voegelin, *The Ecumenic Age* (Baton Rouge, 1974), 223. Vol. IV of Voegelin, *Order and History,* 5 vols. projected.
29. Voegelin, *Plato and Aristotle,* 126.
30. Voegelin, *World of the Polis,* 118.
31. Voegelin, *Science, Politics and Gnosticism,* 42.
32. Voegelin, "On Classical Studies, 3.
33. Voegelin, "Reason: The Classic Experience," 239.
34. Voegelin, *Plato and Aristotle,* 81.
35. *Ibid.,* 365.
36. Voegelin, *New Science of Politics,* 70.
37. Voegelin, *Plato and Aristotle,* 354.
38. *Ibid.,* 273.
39. *Ibid.,* 276.
40. *Ibid.*
41. *Ibid.*
42. *Ibid.,* 161.
43. *Ibid.,* 289.
44. *Ibid.*
45. *Ibid.,* 277.
46. *Ibid.*
47. Voegelin, *World of the Polis,* 365.
48. Voegelin, *Plato and Aristotle,* 69.
49. *Ibid.,* 193, 356.
50. Voegelin, *World of the Polis,* 274.
51. Voegelin, "Reason: The Classic Experience," 238.
52. Voegelin, *World of the Polis,* 252.
53 Eric Voegelin, "Nietzsche, the Crisis and the War," *Journal of Politics,* VI (May, 1944), 195.
54. Eric Voegelin, "World Empire and the Unity of Mankind," *International Affairs,* XXXVIII (April, 1962), 184.
55. Eric Voegelin, *"The Turn of the Screw," Southern Review,* n.s., VII (January, 1971), 45.
56. Voegelin, *World of the Polis,* 22.
57. Voegelin, *Israel and Revelation,* 123.

58. *Ibid.,* 116.
59. *Ibid.,* 355.
60. *Ibid.,* 112.
61. *Ibid.,* 440.
62. *Ibid.,* 485.
63. Voegelin, *Enlightenment,* 26.
64. *Ibid.,* 275.
65. *Ibid.,* 220.
66. *Ibid.,* 233.
67. Voegelin, *Israel and Revelation,* 239.
68. Voegelin, "Nietzsche, the Crisis and the War," 202.
69. Voegelin, *Israel and Revelation,* 131.
70. Voegelin, *Enlightenment,* 96.
71. Voegelin, *New Science of Politics,* 119-20.
72. *Ibid.,* 123.
73. Voegelin, *Science Politics and Gnosticism,* 12.
74. Eric Voegelin, "The Origins of Scientism," *Social Research,* XV (December, 1948), 489.
75. Eric Voegelin, "Liberalism and Its History," *Review of Politics,* XXXVI (October, 1974), 517.
76. Voegelin, *New Science of Politics,* 131.
77. Eric Voegelin, "Machiavelli's Prince: Background and Formation," *Review of Politics,* XII (April, 1951), 153.
78. Voegelin, *New Science of Politics,* 118.
79. Voegelin, *Enlightenment,* 6.
80. *Ibid.*
81. Eric Voegelin, "Configurations of History," in Paul G. Kuntz, ed., *The Concept of Order* (Seattle, 1968), 33-34.
82. Voegelin, *Enlightenment,* 26.
83. Voegelin, *Israel and Revelation,* 132.
84. Voegelin, *New Science of Politics,* 164.
85. Voegelin, *Israel and Revelation,* 398.
86. Voegelin, *World of the Polis,* 263.
87. *Ibid.*
88. Voegelin, *Israel and Revelation,* 310.
89. *Ibid.*

90. Voegelin, *World of the Polis,* 203.
91. Voegelin, *Israel and Revelation,* 515.
92. *Ibid.*
93. Eric Voegelin, "The Gospel and Culture," in Donald G. Miller and Dikran Y. Hadidian, eds., *Jesus and Man's Hope* (2 vols; Pittsburgh, Penn., 1970), II, 80.
94. *Ibid.,* 77.
95. *Ibid.*
96. Voegelin, *World of the Polis,* 115.
97. Voegelin, *Plato and Aristotle,* 96.
98. *Ibid.,* 364.
99. *Ibid.,* 174.
100. Voegelin, *New Science of Politics,* 118.
101. Voegelin, *Plato and Aristotle,* 157.
102. Voegelin, *World of the Polis,* 202.
103. Saint Augustine, *City of God,* trans. Gerald G. Walsh, Demetrius B. Zema, Grace Monahan, and Daniel J. Honan (Garden City, N.Y., 1958), Bk. VIII, Chaps. 4-5, pp. 149-50.
104. Voegelin, "The Gospel and Culture," in Miller and Hadidian, eds., *Jesus and Man's Hope,* 81.
105. Voegelin, *World of the Polis,* 204.
106. Voegelin, *Enlightenment,* 79.
107. Eric Voegelin, "The Origins of Totalitarianism," *Review of Politics,* XV (January, 1953), 75-76.
108. Voegelin, *Science, Politics and Gnosticism,* 9.
109. Voegelin, *Enlightenment,* 268.
110. Voegelin, *Science Politics and Gnosticism,* 11.
111. *Ibid.,* 87.
112. Voegelin, *Plato and Aristotle,* 209.
113. Voegelin, *Enlightenment,* 265.
114. *Ibid.,* 267.
115. *Ibid.,* 302.
116. *Ibid.,* 51.
117. *Ibid.*
118. Voegelin, *New Science of Politics,* 163.
119. Voegelin, *Enlightenment,* 193.

120. *Ibid.,* 10.
121. *Ibid.,* 200.
122. *Ibid.,* 134.
123. *Ibid.*
124. *Ibid.,* 28.
125. Voegelin, "Reason: The Classic Experience," 36.
126. Voegelin, *"The Turn of the Screw,"* 36.
127. Voegelin, *Enlightenment,* 129-30.
128. *Ibid.,* 215, 294.
129. *Ibid.,* 81.
130. *Ibid.*
131. *Ibid.*
132. *Ibid.,* 85.
133. *Ibid.,* 32.
134. *Ibid.,* 23.
135. *Ibid.*
136. *Ibid.*
137. *Ibid.,* 95, 24.
138. Voegelin, *World of the Polis,* 15.
139. Voegelin, *Enlightenment,* 26-27.
140. *Ibid.,* 29.
141. *Ibid.,* 74.
142. *Ibid.,* 136.
143. *Ibid.,* 87.
144. *Ibid.,* 161.
145. *Ibid.,* 16.
146. *Ibid.,* 141.
147. *Ibid.,* 159.
148. Voegelin, *New Science of Politics,* 11.
149. Voegelin, *Plato and Aristotle,* 225.
150. Voegelin, *Enlightenment,* 3.
151. *Ibid.,* 24.
152. *Ibid.,* 89.
153. *Ibid.,* 42.
154. *Ibid.,* 37.
155. Voegelin, *New Science of Politics,* 2.

156. Eric Voegelin, "On Hegel—A Study in Sorcery," in J.T. Fraser, F.C. Haber, and G. H. Muller, eds., *The Study of Time: Proceedings of the First Conference of the International Society for the Study of Time, Oberwolfach (Black Forest)—West German* (Berlin, 1972), 424.

157. *Ibid.,* 432.

158. *Ibid.,* 435.

159. *Ibid.,* 436.

160. *Ibid.*

161. Eric Voegelin "The Eclipse of Reality," in Maurice Natanson, ed., *Phenomenology and Social Reality: Essays in Memory of Alfred Schultz* (The Hague, 1970), 192.

162. *Ibid.*

163. Voegelin, *The Turn of the Screw,"* 35.

164. Voegelin, "Hegel—A Study in Sorcery," in Fraser, Haber, and Muller, eds., *The Study of Time,* 437.

165. *Ibid.,* 445.

166. *Ibid.,* 433.

167. Voegelin, *Enlightenment,* 166.

168. Voegelin, *New Science of Politics,* 129.

169. Eric Voegelin, "Immortality: Experience and Symbol," *Harvard Theological Review,* LX (July, 1967), 260.

170. Voegelin, *Enlightenment,* 298.

171. *Ibid.*

172. *Ibid.,* 73.

173. Voegelin, *Science, Politics and Gnosticism,* 27.

174. *Ibid.*

175. *Ibid.,* 45.

176. *Ibid.*

177. Voegelin, *Enlightenment,* 261.

178. *Ibid.,* 273.

179. Voegelin, *World of the Polis,* 19.

180. Voegelin, *Enlightenment,* 3.

181. Voegelin, *Plato and Aristotle,* 278.

182. Voegelin, *New Science of Politics,* 147.

183. *Ibid.,* 145.

184. Voegelin, *Ecumenic Age,* 241.
185. *Ibid.,* 268.
186. Augustine, *City of God,* Bk. XVIII, Chap. 53, p. 421.
187. *Ibid.*
188. Voegelin, *Plato and Aristotle,* 276.
189. Voegelin, *Ecumenic Age,* 37.
190. Voegelin, "The Gospel and Culture," in Miller and Hadi- dian, eds., *Jesus and Man's Hope,* 93.
191. *Ibid.,* 95.
192. Voegelin, *New Science of Politics,* 122.
193. *Ibid.*
194. *Ibid.*
195. *Ibid.,* 123.
196. Voegelin, *Science Politics and Gnosticism,* 108.
197. Voegelin, *New Science of Politics,* 129.
198. Voegelin, *Israel and Revelation,* 465.
199. Eric Voegelin, "On Readiness to Rational Discussion," in Albert Hunold, ed., *Freedom and Serfdom: An Anthology of Western Thought* (Dordrecht, 1961), 280.
200. Voegelin, *Ecumenic Age,* 6.
201. Voegelin, *Science, Politics and Gnosticism,* 22-23.
202. Voegelin, *New Science of Politics,* ii.

*Ludwig von Mises*

1. Henry Hazlitt, "Two of Ludwig von Mises' Most Important Books," in Mary Sennholz, ed., *On Freedom and Free Enterprise: Essays in Honor of Ludwig von Mises, Presented on the Occasion of the Fiftieth Anniversary of His Doctorate, February 20, 1956* (Princeton, N.J., 1956), 38.
2. Henry Hazlitt, "Three New Books by Ludwig von Mises," *Freeman,* XXVIII (April, 1978), 248.
3. Henry Regnery, "The Book in the Market Place," in F.A. von Hayek *et al.,* eds., *Toward Liberty: Essays in Honor of Ludwig von Mises on the Occasion of His 90th Birthday,*

*September 29, 1971* (2 vols.; Menlo Park, Cal., 1971), II, 303.

4. George Roche, "Introduction," in Hazlitt *et al.,* eds., *Champions of Freedom: The Ludwig von Mises Lecture Series* (Hillsdale, Mich., 1974), 1.

5. Israel Kirzner, "Tribute to von Mises: IV. On the Market," *National Review,* November 9, 1973, 1246, and F.A. Hayek, "Tribute to von Mises: II. Vienna Years," *ibid.,* 1245.

6. Murray N. Rothbard, *The Essential von Mises* (Lansing, Mich., 1973), 60.

7. Ludwig von Mises, *The Ultimate Foundation of Economic Science: An Essay on Method* (Princeton, N.J., 1962), 138.

8. Ludwig von Mises, "Economic Freedom in the Present-Day World," *U.S.A.,* January 17, 1958, 5.

9. Ludwig von Mises, *Theory and History: An Interpretation of Social and Economic Evolution* (New Rochelle, N.Y., 1969), 348.

10. *Ibid.,* 376, 372.

11. *Ibid.,* 374.

12. Ludwig von Mises, *Human Action: A Treatise on Economics* (3rd rev. ed.; Chicago, 1966), 139.

13. Ludwig von Mises, *Socialism: An Economic and Sociological Analysis,* trans. J. Kahane (2nd ed.; London, 1951), 402.

14. Mises, *Theory and History,* 253.

15. Ludwig von Mises, "The Treatment of 'Irrationality' in the Social Sciences," *Philosophy and Phenomenological Research,* IV (June, 1944), 543.

16. Mises, *Socialism,* 66.

17. Mises, *Human Action,* 322.

18. Ludwig von Mises, *The Anti-Capitalistic Mentality* (Princeton, N.J., 1956), 90.

19. *Ibid.,* 103.

20. *Ibid.,* 104.

21. *Ibid.*

22. *Ibid.,* 55.

23. *Ibid.,* 108.

24. Ludwig von Mises, *The Free and Prosperous Common-wealth: An Exposition of the Ideas of Classical Liberalism,* trans. Ralph Raico, ed. Arthur Goddard (Princeton, N.J., 1962), 56.
25. *Ibid.,* 57.
26. *Ibid.,* 55.
27. Ludwig von Mises, *Omnipotent Government: The Rise of the Total State and Total War* (New Rochelle, N.Y., 1969), 53.
28. Ludwig von Mises, *Bureaucracy* (New Rochelle, N.Y., 1969), 120.
29. Mises, *Human Action,* 863.
30. Mises, *Socialism,* 83.
31. Mises, *Theory and History,* 330.
32. Mises, *Free and Prosperous Commonwealth,* 28.
33. *Ibid.*
34. Mises, *Socialism,* 78.
35. Mises, *Theory and History,* 115.
36. Mises, *Omnipotent Government,* 47.
37. Mises, *Free and Prosperous Commonwealth,* 36-37.
38. Mises, *Ultimate Foundation of Economic Science,* 99.
39. Mises, *Bureaucracy,* 24.
40. Mises, *Ultimate Foundation of Economic Science,* 101, 98.
41. Mises, *Human Action,* 878.
42. *Ibid.,* 879.
43. *Ibid.,* 234.
44. Ludwig von Mises, *A Critique of Interventionism* (New Rochelle, N.Y., 1977), 39-40.
45. Mises, *Human Action,* 10.
46. *Ibid.,* 852.
47. *Ibid.,* 647.
48. Mises, *Critique of Interventionism,* 86.
49. Mises, *Omnipotent Government,* 48; Mises, *Critique of Interventionism,* 18.
50. Mises, *Human Action,* 264.
51. Mises, *Socialism,* 583.

52. Mises, *Free and Prosperous Commonwealth,* 67-68.
53. Mises, *Socialism,* 345-46.
54. *Ibid.,* 119.
55. Mises, *Human Action,* 774.
56. *Ibid.,* 775.
57. Ludwig von Mises, *Planning for Freedom and Twelve Other Essays and Addresses* (3rd ed.; South Holland, Ill., 1974), 143.
58. Mises, *Human Action,* 851.
59. Ludwig von Mises, *The Theory of Money and Credit,* trans. H.E. Batson (2nd ed.; Irvington-on-Hudson, N.Y., 1971), 22.
60. Mises, *Anti-Capitalistic Mentality,* 84.
61. Mises, *Human Action,* 848.
62. Mises, *Ultimate Foundation of Economic Science,* 127.
63. Mises, *Human Action,* 616.
64. *Ibid.,* 590.
65. *Ibid.,* 265.
66. *Ibid.,* 854.
67. Mises, *Omnipotent Government,* 101.
68. Mises, *Human Action,* 648.
69. Mises, *Theory and History,* 173.
70. Mises, *Human Action,* 852.
71. *Ibid,* 853.
72. Mises, *Socialism,* 138.
73. Mises, *Human Action,* 257-58.
74. *Ibid.,* 258.
75. Mises, *Theory and History,* 114.
76. Mises, *Socialism,* 316.
77. *Ibid.,* 293.
78. *Ibid.,* 276.
79. Mises, *Theory and History,* 235; Mises, *Free and Prosperous Commonwealth,* 25.
80. Mises, *Human Action,* 323.
81. *Ibid.,* 685.
82. Mises, *Omnipotent Government,* 3.

83. Mises, *Human Action,* 472.
84. Mises, *Theory of Money and Credit,* 438.
85. *Ibid.,* 414.
86. Mises, *Human Action,* 474.
87. *Ibid.,* 471.
88. *Ibid.,* 474.
89. *Ibid.,* 475.
90. Mises, "Treatment of 'Irrationality,' " 536.
91. Mises, *Theory and History,* 244.
92. *Ibid.,* 245-46.
93. *Ibid.,* 249.
94. Mises, *Socialism,* 395.
95. Mises, *Omnipotent Government,* 52.
96. Mises, *Human Action,* 74.
97. Mises, *Socialism,* 141.
98. Mises, *Critique of Interventionism,* 87.
99. Mises, *Human Action,* 861.
100. Mises, *Critique of Interventionism,* 79.
101. Mises, *Planning for Freedom,* 50-71, 19; Von Mises, *Human Action,* 315.
102. Mises, *Planning for Freedom,* 33.
103. *Ibid.,* 98-99.
104. Mises, *Human Action,* 734-35.
105. Mises, *Socialism,* 24, 515.
106. Mises, *Planning for Freedom,* 179.
107. Mises, *Socialism,* 48.
108. Ludwig von Mises, *Epistemological Problems of Economics,* trans. George Reisman (Princeton, N.J., 1960), 49.
109. Mises, *Human Action,* 154.
110. Mises, *Theory and History,* 375.
111. Mises, *Socialism,* 422.
112. Mises, *Theory and History,* 169.
113. Mises, *Free and Prosperous Commonwealth,* 188.
114. Ludwig von Mises, "On Equality and Inequality," *Modern Age,* V (Spring, 1961), 147.

## Conclusion

1. Ludwig von Mises, *Socialism: An Economic and Sociological Analysis,* trans. J. Kahane (2nd ed.; New Haven, Conn., 1951), 48.
2. Ludwig von Mises, *Epistemological Problems of Economics* trans. George Reisman (Princeton, N.J., 1960), 49.
3. Ludwig von Mises, *Human Action: A Treative on Economics* (3rd rev. ed.; Chicago, 1966), 169.
4. Ludwig von Mises, *Theory and History: An Interpretation of Social and Economic Evolution* (New Rochelle, N.Y., 1969), 169.
5. Mises, *Socialism,* 422.

# Index